NAPOLEON'S
CAVALRY
and its Leaders

NAPOLEON'S CAVALRY
and its Leaders

DAVID JOHNSON

Que de souvenirs! Que de regrets!
Lucien Bonaparte

Holmes & Meier Publishers, Inc.
New York

For Bryan Drury Markwell
late 10th Baluch Regiment attached 2nd North Staffords
old companion of Egypt and Palestine

and in memory of Lieutenant George C.B. Harrison
King's Shropshire Light Infantry

UA
704
.A6
J63

First published in the United States of America 1978 by
Holmes & Meier Publishers, Inc.
30 Irving Place
New York, New York 10003

Copyright © 1978 by David Johnson

Library of Congress Cataloging in Publication Data
Johnson, David, 1927–
  Napoleon's cavalry and its leaders.

  Bibliography: p.
  Includes index.
  1. France. Armée. Cavalerie—History—18th
century.   2. France. Armée. Cavalerie—History—
19th century.   I. Title.
UA704.A6J63   357'.1'0944   78-5596
ISBN 0-8419-0390-5

Printed in Great Britain

Contents

List of Illustrations

Acknowledgments

The author is indebted to Captain J.M. Carew, M.C., for permission to quote from Sir John Fortescue's A HISTORY OF THE BRITISH ARMY, and to Doctor F.G. Hourtoulle, author of LE GENERAL COMTE CHARLES LASALLE, for permission to quote from the correspondence reproduced in that book.

The author and publisher would like to thank the following for permission to use illustrations from their collections: The British Library 3, 4, 5, 8, 9; Bibliothèque Nationale, Paris 2; Musée de Versailles 1; Radio Times Hulton Picture Library 13, 15, 16, 17; The Mansell Collection 11, 12; Musée de l'Armée, Paris 14; Photo Ellebé/Musée des Beaux Arts, Rouen 10; illustrations 6 and 7 are from the author's collection.

Author's Note

The accepted practice has been followed of using 'sabres' as a generic term for bodies of cavalry, even for those which included regiments equipped with thrusting-type swords as opposed to sabres. The word 'sabring' is used to describe slashing sword motions even when carried out by dragoon or heavy cavalry swords.

In referring to heavy cavalry, the term *cuirassiers* is used for French regiments, and *kurassiers* for Austrian and Russian ones.

Introduction

The outbreak of the French Revolution, and the period of upheaval that followed it, had a profound effect on the French army. The aristocrats who fled abroad for fear of the guillotine included large numbers of career soldiers, and the French cavalry, which had always attracted a high proportion of young noblemen, lost many of its officers. Nor were its losses confined to the officer class; two entire regiments of cavalry deserted *en masse* to join the enemies of the Republic.

The flight of these émigrés coincided with a great expansion of the French army, since the Republic was forced to introduce military conscription to defend itself against the armies of Europe's monarchies. Partly due to the shortage of officers, and partly due to Republican doctrine, men who had been troopers or NCOs when the Bastille fell found themselves commanding squadrons and even regiments soon after war broke out in 1792. The system of promoting men because of their Republican zeal produced such bizarre characters as General Macard, who rode yelling into battle stripped naked from the waist up, looking more like a hairy wild beast than a leader of cavalry.

In spite of all this, the French cavalry of the Revolutionary Wars was certainly not without good leaders. Many aristocrats continued to serve in the Revolutionary army, including some extremely able cavalry officers, and some of the leaders who had risen from the ranks proved almost as skilful. Too often, however, they were frustrated by over-cautious superiors and an over-worked Ministry of War.

'If the French triumph,' a member of the National Convention* had declared, 'it will be the guillotine that has worked the miracle'; but in regard to cavalry tactics the guillotine was more of a hindrance than an incentive. Because they were afraid of suffering defeats that might cost them their heads, French generals were reluctant to commit their cavalry, preferring to use it only as a last resort. Instead of maintaining a

---

* P. Delbrel.

11

powerful reserve of massed horse, the War Ministry allowed Generals-in-Chief commanding in the field to attach their mounted regiments to the infantry divisions.

Forty years earlier, Frederick the Great's grasp of the essential difference between light and heavy cavalry had been mainly responsible for the ascendancy of the Prussian hussars and kurassiers on European battlefields. The Prussian method of using light horsemen to scout, and heavy ones to charge in solid masses, had been generally adopted; but under the new French system of dispersal the lessons of Rossbach and Zorndorf could not be applied. In the divisions to which they were now attached, French mounted regiments were apt to be regarded simply as all-purpose units of the *cavalerie de bataille,* no matter whether they were heavy cavalry, dragoons, hussars or chasseurs. As a result, regiments were frequently given tasks for which they had been neither trained nor intended; if they succeeded in carrying them out, it was largely due to the patriotic zeal and lust for victory which inspired the fighting-men of the Republican armies.

The administrative chaos caused by the Revolution added to the cavalry's problems. In one month alone 6,000 horses of the Rhine armies died for want of forage. Troopers fighting the Austrians in the Low Countries were short of boots and firearms, sabres and spurs, and their harness was literally falling apart; yet compared with those fighting the Spanish in Catalonia they were well provided for.

Ill-equipped and badly mounted, lacking in almost everything except courage, French cavalrymen were nevertheless formidable opponents, especially when they were led by generals like André de Labarre. Tall and resolute, a good-looking man with exceptionally attractive manners, Labarre had begun his career in the old Royalist army, serving as a dragoon officer under Lafayette during the American Revolution. Early in 1794 he was posted as cavalry commander to the Army of the Eastern Pyrenees, which had just been taken over by the Creole General Dugommier.

Unlike most other French Generals-in-Chief, Dugommier was prepared to gamble. Although two of his predecessors had been guillotined for incompetence, he was not afraid to give a thrusting subordinate like Labarre his head, even at the risk of compromising his cavalry. The results were electrifying.

Dugommier's was probably the most destitute force of cavalry in Europe: seven under-manned regiments,* mounted on half-starved

---

* 1st Hussars; 14th, 19th and 22nd Chasseurs; 14th and 15th Dragoons; 27th Heavy Cavalry of the line. The total strength was under 2,000 sabres.

horses, and a battery of flying artillery. 'It depresses me to have to command cavalry which is so bad in every respect,' Labarre informed Dugommier soon after his arrival, 'and I foresee nothing but dishonour for the man who commands it.'

Events proved otherwise. Over the next three months Labarre created havoc wherever he went, always using his handful of guns to give his cavalry close and highly effective support. In one action on the River Tech, thanks to his faultless combination of controlled artillery fire and full-blooded sabre charges, he turned an orderly Spanish retirement into a terror-stricken rout, and captured the whole of the enemy baggage train.

Labarre's successes were striking proof of what French troopers might achieve when they were properly used and skilfully led; but since few people in France either knew or cared about what was happening in the far-off gorges and desolate hill country of the Eastern Pyrenees, his example was as wasted as his talents.

In the summer of 1794 he met his death while charging a body of Spanish horse more than four times stronger than his own, and Dugommier was killed in action at the end of the same year.

Fortunately the Republic possessed other leaders who, like Labarre were capable of exploiting to the full the extraordinary latent power of the French cavalry. All they needed was a General-in-Chief like Dugommier who would allow them to do it.

★   ★   ★

At the time of General de Labarre's death there was only one unwritten law for the French cavalry; 'Never manoeuvre in the presence of the enemy.' Cavalry officers who had seen Labarre in action at Le Boulou and elsewhere might have been tempted to add another one; 'Never attack without artillery support.'

There was one more aspect, however, of the vital relationship between artillery and a successful cavalry charge which might not have been apparent to observers in the Eastern Pyrenees. Since trotting cavalry covered approximately 600 paces in two minutes, and 6-pounder guns worked point-blank at between 800 and 900 paces, a line of charging cavalry did not suffer over-much from enemy cannon fire; the greatest damage that enemy artillery could inflict was on cavalry that was kept halted within range of its guns.

For 20 years after Labarre's death Europe's monarchies struggled to break the military power of France, and for 15 of those years the French

Introduction

Notes on these diagrams
can be found on pages 162–3

Col Colonel
MJ Major joint
   (Staff officer, attached)
AM Adjutant Major
A Adjutant
CD Chef d'Escadron
BT Brigadier Trompette
   (Trumpet Major)
C Captain

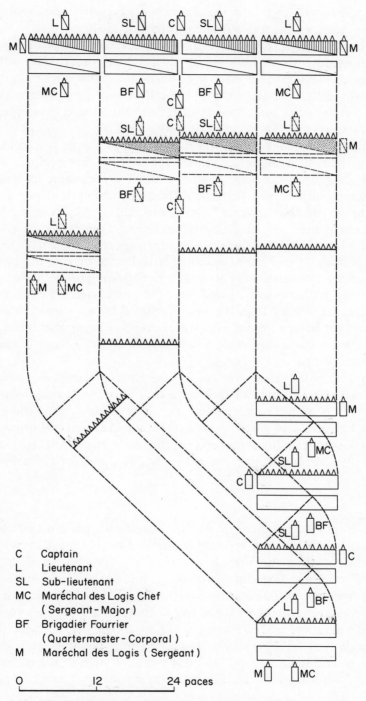

C   Captain
L   Lieutenant
SL Sub-lieutenant
MC Maréchal des Logis Chef
    (Sergeant - Major)
BF Brigadier Fourrier
    (Quartermaster - Corporal)
M   Maréchal des Logis (Sergeant)

0   12   24 paces

Note : The brigadiers (corporals) and most of the sergeants were posted
in the ranks, in positions which varied from one squadron to the next.

nation was governed, and the French army was commanded, by a military genius who was a former officer of artillery.

As may be imagined, Napoleon fully understood the power of cavalry charges made with artillery support. 'Support your cavalry with light infantry and artillery,' he once admonished Marshal Victor, 'and it will fear nothing.' Under the Empire the tallest recruits in every conscription were posted to the Line cavalry (since the Guard cavalry accepted only veterans) and the next tallest to the artillery.

Partly because they contained men whose physique would have earmarked them in most other armies for the infantry regiments of the Guard, Napoleon's heavy cavalry units were capable of making a tremendous impact on a battlefield. Napoleon himself always expected them to do so. 'No sabring!' he would call sternly to his cuirassier regiments, as they rode past him to the charge. 'Give point!'

In the opinion of the German cavalry expert von Bismark, if Napoleon's cuirassiers had been equipped with lances they would have been the deadliest horsemen ever seen on a European battlefield. Penetrating by velocity rather than by pressure, a properly handled lance caused a much deeper wound than the one produced by a sword thrust; and a sword thrust from a French cuirassier, even assuming that it did not kill or cripple a man, would almost certainly keep him *hors de combat* for a considerable time.

Fortunately for their opponents, Napoleon's cuirassiers were never issued with lances; instead they were sent into action armed with long, cumbersome swords that were virtually useless in hand-to-hand cavalry fighting, and whose power of penetration was not improved by having the point on the upper edge of the blade. Most cuirassier colonels had them re-ground until the point was in the centre (see Plate 7).

★   ★   ★

As the Napoleonic system of warfare developed, the laws affecting the handling of cavalry *vis-à-vis* artillery applied with ever growing force. At Austerlitz in 1805 the French cavalry numbered barely 20,000 in an army of 70,000; at Borodino, in 1812, 30,000 out of Napoleon's 130,000 soldiers were mounted men. And as the size of Napoleon's cavalry grew, so did the strengths of its basic units. In 1806 a cuirassier regiment's establishment was altered from 550 to 820, and in 1807 to 1,040. In 1805 the regimental strengths laid down for the dragoons and the light cavalry were 880 and 1,075. 'If I did not need men in the infantry and artillery,' Napoleon declared in 1807, 'and could put as many men as I desired into the mounted arm, I would not hesitate to increase the dragoon regiments to 1,000 men and the chasseurs and hussars to 1,200.'

When massed regiments of this size charged full out over suitable ground, against an enemy already demoralized by cannon fire, they were well-nigh irresistible. On the other hand, since they offered so huge a target, to launch them over difficult ground was an act of considerable folly, and to keep them halted under enemy artillery fire was sheer madness.

The fact that both these errors were committed on more than one battlefield helps to explain, along with the romantic uniforms and the charisma of its generals, why Napoleon's cavalry retains so powerful a hold on the imagination.

No other cavalry force in history was led so brilliantly and handled so badly.

I

Bonaparte and Bessières

In the early spring of 1796 a horde of starving beggars lay camped in and around Nice. Dressed in rags and infested with lice, many of them had no shelter except for holes dug out of the earth, covered over with branches and thyme. Repulsive to look at, with their matted beards and dirty flesh, they had survived the winter by begging for bread, stealing livestock, and making marauding expeditions into the surrounding countryside. The local citizens told each other hopefully that these terrifying parasites would soon be gone: for they were soldiers of the French army, and the campaigning season was about to start.

That spring, Austria's long struggle against the Revolution was entering its fourth year; half a million men were under arms in a vast theatre of war stretching from Belgium to the Mediterranean. Although the French armies were slightly outnumbered in the field, orders had gone out for a bold offensive stroke, a two-pronged advance towards the Austrian capital, Vienna. The main effort would be a thrust through Southern Germany, for which France could call on nearly 200,000 veterans formed in three armies; but the only troops available for the second thrust, which must be made via the Riviera and Northern Italy, were the 30,000 tatterdemalions at Nice.

All told they mustered four weak divisions. When they crawled out of their dug-outs and formed up in ranks they were a grotesque sight. Three out of every ten men wore plaited straw on their feet; the cavalrymen covered their heads with handkerchieves, which they also used for sword-knots; the officers carried haversacks on their backs. Because they had fought the previous year against the Austrians and Sardinians in Piedmont and Lombardy, they bore the ludicrous title of the Army of Italy.

In March the elderly general in charge of this rabble was replaced by Napoleon Bonaparte, a 26-year-old Corsican, who arrived at Nice on the 27th to take up his command. Two weeks later he opened his campaign.

Bonaparte launched his men into battle because they would otherwise have starved. Once he had begun to fight he could not stop, for at the first order to retreat the Army of Italy would have dissolved; hence the amazing activity of his First Italian Campaign, which in less than a year produced fourteen pitched battles and seventy combats.

After four weeks of forced marches and hard fighting the French had driven across Piedmont, a province of Austria's ally Sardinia, and carried the war into Austria's Italian territory. On 15 May Bonaparte entered the Milanese capital, riding a white charger at the head of 500 cavalry, and looking more like a king, as some observers thought, than a general of the Republic. Milan was not exactly Paris. The public buildings were dirty, the water supply was tainted, and the bite of a Milanese gnat was like that of a French horse-fly; but at least there was a theatre and a large female population.

As a compliment to the army that had liberated them from the Austrians, the better-class prostitutes wore gowns *à la guillotine,* with scooped neck-lines and starched collars, and tied tricolour ribbons in their hair. In the evenings they could be found at the Casino and the Casa Tanzi, or in the carriages that drove slowly along the Corso. The carriages were specially built with a very low clearance, so that the occupants could converse with a man standing on the pavement. They did not give much away. 'They are lovely and elegant,' wrote one disillusioned French officer. 'But when one of them gives you a present, you remember it for a long time.'[1]

The next objective was Mantua. At the end of May the French headquarters were in a house on the outskirts of Valeggio, a village ten miles north of the city. On the 30th, which was a very hot day, Bonaparte was sitting with both feet in a basin full of hot water, believing this would cure the headache that afflicted him. It was late afternoon, and no-one was expecting trouble. Half-dressed and drowsy in the heat, the men of Masséna's infantry division were preparing their evening meal; outside the village, a party of French gunners were collecting up cannon left behind by the retreating Austrians.

Fortunately these gunners had their wits about them; seeing two strange-looking infantry battalions advancing towards the village, they brought the captured guns promptly into action.

At the sound of the cannon Bonaparte assumed that the Austrians were attacking Valeggio, and so did his men. Running past his own unbridled charger, the barefoot General-in-Chief managed to stop a flying French dragoon and requisitioned his mount. By that time, however, the enemy had retired; moreover they were not even Austrians, but Neapolitans who did not know that the village was occupied. Had they succeeded in entering it, as Marshal Marmont put it, the French Commander-in-Chief would probably have been captured by 'a very small part of the very bad army of a very minor sovereign.'[2]

For his future protection, Bonaparte provided himself with a body-guard of infantry veterans; he also formed a small cavalry escort, which he named the General-in-Chief's Company of Mounted Guides. The command of this mounted company was given to Jean-Baptiste Bessières, a young captain of the 22nd Chasseurs.

Son of a Prayssac barber-surgeon, Bessières had joined the army in 1792. He had fought in Spain in the ill-equipped Army of the Eastern Pyrenees, in which any cavalryman who owned a pair of spurs had been an object of envy; even in the Army of Italy, veterans of the Eastern Pyrenees were conspicuous by their lean bodies and gaunt features.

Unlike most other French cavalry officers of the period, Bessières was reserved and dignified, and there was nothing of the dashing sabreur about him; but he was a tough soldier, hardened by constant riding and short rations, and a tireless worker.

His new post was no sinecure. '*Im Italien, sieg nicht der Kavallerie*' was a well-known saying in the Austrian army, for the broken ground of Northern Italy made mounted operations difficult; the unorthodox General Bonaparte, however, worked his modest cavalry force exceedingly hard. Whenever he beat the Austrians, he flung every available cavalry unit into a vigorous pursuit; and as the General-in-Chief's mounted bodyguard, Bessières and his Guides were available wherever Bonaparte happened to be. Since they were hand-picked troopers, Bonaparte also expected them to make exemplary charges on the battlefield; consequently Bessières had every opportunity to display courage and leadership. For taking an Austrian gun at Roveredo he was promoted *chef d'escadron,* or squadron commander; at the end of the campaign he was made *chef de brigade,* the Revolutionary equivalent of colonel. His company of Guides had grown to two squadrons of élite troopers, smartly dressed in light green uniforms and cocked hats, which would soon be replaced by elegant busbies.

★   ★   ★

In 11 months Bonaparte had taken all Northern Italy for the Republic, and when he closed his astonishing campaign he was only 65 miles from

Vienna. The Directors of the French Government were thoroughly alarmed. Here was a general of 27, clearly a military genius, who had audaciously signed an armistice with the Austrians on his own initiative, and who was rapidly becoming a national hero. The further such a man could be removed from the seat of power, the better.

Fortunately Talleyrand had given the Directors the perfect excuse, by suggesting that a French military expedition to Egypt might disrupt England's communications with India. The suggestion was approved. The expedition sailed from France in the spring of 1798, with General Bonaparte in command.

II

Compared to Italy, with her abundant wines and pleasant climate, Egypt was the average French soldier's idea of hell on earth. On the long desert marches, glaring sunshine and blown grains of sand irritated a man's eyes until pus oozed from the pupils. Stragglers captured by the natives were tortured, maimed and finally decapitated. Bread and wine were almost unobtainable, and for days on end there was nothing to eat but roasted pigeon meat, which tasted almost as nauseating as it looked. The enemy scimitars inflicted terrible injuries, and even small bullet wounds festered into hideous sores, in which blueflies laid their eggs. To make matters worse the ship carrying the army's medical supplies had been sunk by an English man-o'-war; after one action, the only comfort available for the wounded was a small barrel of spirits that Colonel Bessières had been saving for his Mounted Guides.

A number of men shot themselves during the advance to Cairo, which was occupied on 24 July.

The cavalry was used mainly for reconnaissance. Although Egypt was a Turkish fief, its defence had been left in the hands of the local beys, whose forces included thousands of Mamelukes. French troopers were no match for these superb horsemen. At every engagement where Mamelukes were present in strength, Bonaparte wisely kept his mounted regiments inside the infantry squares.

For a French cavalry commander, Egypt's only redeeming feature was the unique training ground provided by vast stretches of sand, on which mounted formations could manoeuvre full out without risk either to men or horses. Bessières kept his Guides in the saddle for hours on end, practising deployment and changes of front at the gallop. Because of his devotion to duty he was appointed tutor to Eugène de Beauharnais, Bonaparte's 17-year-old stepson. Despite the difference in their ages, the two men became close friends.

Apart from Eugène, Bessières' favourite companion in Egypt was the cavalry commander, General Joachim Murat, who had entered the army as a trooper two years before the Revolution. The son of an inn-keeper, Murat was arrogant and unprincipled, a boaster and a womaniser To all outward appearances, the swaggering general and the reserved colonel of the Guides had nothing in common, but they were both homesick for the same *'petit pays'*,[3] the fertile hills of Quercy and the picturesque valley of the Lot. They often talked together in the Cahorsin patois, which to their colleagues sounded almost as incomprehensible as Arabic.

In Cairo, Bessières was a frequent visitor to Murat's fine house by the Nile, where dinner was always followed by a game of cards, usually by torch-light in the extensive garden. At one of these *soirées* a quarrel developed between Andoche Junot of the cavalry and the infantry general Lanusse, who agreed to fight a duel. Lanusse suggested using pistols, but Junot prided himself on his marksmanship and refused to take advantage of it. 'I'm not fighting you with pistols, you couldn't hit a barn door,' he told his opponent. 'We're both wearing sabres, and that's what we'll use.'

As aide de camp to Bonaparte in Italy, Junot had led several pursuits at the head of the Mounted Guides, and Bessières knew that he had once sabred six Austrian Uhlans in a single mêlée: but he also knew something about François Lanusse. 'You're being very unwise,' he warned Junot. 'Lanusse is an expert swordsman.'

Junot refused to listen and the party moved into the garden, Bessières still trying to dissuade his friend from fighting the man who had won a sabre of honour at Castiglione and been first across the famous bridge of Lodi. In the subsequent duel, at which Murat and Bessières acted as seconds, Junot received a painful wound in the stomach.

When the news reached Bonaparte he was naturally furious, and warned everyone concerned in the affair that he would not have his officers fighting each other like crocodiles. Since he had done his best to prevent the meeting, Bessières was not pleased by the rebuke. He was even less pleased to learn that Bonaparte had decided to add 300 dis-mounted Guides to his command. Unwilling to command anything but mounted troops, he asked Bonaparte to reconsider his decision, and on being refused reported sick.

Resorting to flattery, Bonaparte sent him the most singular letter ever written by a General-in-Chief to a colonel under his orders. 'My trust in you,' he assured Bessières, 'is as great as my appreciation of your military talents, your courage, and your love of order and discipline.'

★   ★   ★

By the summer of 1799 Bonaparte's cavalry officers had given up any
ideas of winning fresh laurels in Egypt; but their hopes revived in July,
when a Turkish army landed at Aboukir to thrown the French invaders
into the sea. When Bonaparte rode up on the 24th he found 18,000 Turks
defending three lines of trenches on a tongue of land running into the
Bay of Aboukir, in which supporting gun-boats lay at anchor. He
attacked next day.

Murat was on the French right, practically at the water's edge, with
three cavalry regiments.[4] Formed in column, they remained at the halt
while the French infantry opened the battle with a frontal assault on the
Turkish trenches. The attack failed. As the French infantry fell back the
Turks ran out to decapitate the wounded, the Sultan having promised to
reward any man who returned home with a Christian head. On his own
initiative Murat trotted his three regiments along the shore, halted,
formed into line, unlimbered his four guns, cannonaded the first trench
from the rear, and sabred the defenders as they came out. Then, through
a storm of shot from the gun-boats, he led his men on to charge the
remaining trenches, followed by Bessières and the Mounted Guides.

The Turks ran into the sea to escape the sabre blows, until the bay was
dotted with bobbing white turbans. 'Our cavalry charged into the sea
until the water reached our horses' bellies,' wrote Eugène de Beauharnais. 'The only prisoners we took were the Pasha and 150 men.'

It was a striking example of the panic and destruction that French
cavalrymen could create when they had the right kind of leadership and
their blood was up; Bessières had seen nothing like it since the reckless
charges led by André de Labarre, Dugommier's cavalry commander in
the Army of the Eastern Pyrenees. One of the finest horse generals of his
generation, the aristocratic Labarre had died untimely, his head split
open by a Spanish dragoon; but in the innkeeper's son, Joachim Murat,
he seemed to have a worthy successor.

Aboukir was Bonaparte's cue to return to France. His army had won
a splendid victory, and since Nelson's fleet was preventing it from
receiving reinforcements it had small chance of winning another.
Furthermore, things were going badly for the French armies in Europe
and the Directory was unpopular; there would never be a better time for
a successful general to enter politics.

On 22 August two frigates sailed from Egypt bearing the General-in-
Chief and a handful of his most trusted officers, including Murat and
Bessières.

III

On the morning of 9 November 1799, the clatter of hooves on pavé disturbed Monsieur Ouvrard, the financier and naval contractor, whose Paris home was at the corner of Rue de Provence and the Chaussée d'Antin. Going to the window, he was just in time to see Bonaparte ride by on a huge black horse, followed by a glittering cavalcade of officers. Realising what was afoot, Ouvrard sat down at his desk and began writing letters. To his agents at the Bourse he sent instructions to buy. To his friend Admiral Bruix he wrote, 'A change is coming in our political affairs.'

Before the letters were delivered, the change was well under way; within 48 hours it was accomplished. The month following the *coup d'état*, Bonaparte was appointed First Consul in the new Government.

Now that he was the virtual dictator of France, he was able to raise an impressive mounted bodyguard, and Bessières was given the agreeable task of forming an élite body of men from the best regiments of the French cavalry. Only half the Mounted Guides had returned from Egypt, and being mostly light cavalrymen they were not entirely the type of men that Bonaparte wanted. For his new bodyguard he required squadrons of heavy cavalry troopers: men who would look magnificent, not only on the battlefield, but on State occasions in Paris as well.

To raise them, Bessières selected men of good physique and character from the dragoon and heavy cavalry regiments, and merged them with a small mounted troop that had acted as escort to the Directors of the late Government. Dressed in tall black bearskins, blue coats, tight breeches and jack-boots, they were given the title of the Grenadiers à Cheval of the Consular Guard. The Mounted Guides were formed into a light cavalry company under Eugène de Beauharnais, and renamed the Chasseurs à Cheval of the Consular Guard. As Bessières was appointed overall chief of the Guard cavalry, he now commanded nearly 600 élite troopers,[5] whose handsome uniforms and splendid horses were the talk of Paris.

They did not stay in Paris for long. Bonaparte was already planning another campaign in Northern Italy, where everything that he had gained for France three years earlier had been taken back by the Austrians. Not content with that, the Austrian commander in Italy was preparing to invade the South of France with 100,000 men, and waited only for a beleaguered French garrison at Genoa to surrender.

In the spring of 1800 the army for Bonaparte's Second Italian Campaign assembled at Geneva, led by officers who had served under him in Italy or Egypt. The artillery was commanded by Marmont, the cavalry by Murat, the first two infantry corps by Victor and Lannes; Louis Desaix returned from Egypt just in time to lead the third. The advance began in May, over the Alps into Piedmont and Lombardy. On 2 June Bonaparte rode once more into Milan, while Lannes pushed onto Pavia and Murat's cavalry entered Piacenza.

Recently married to Bonaparte's sister Caroline, Murat had been promoted general of division for his conduct at Aboukir. He was delighted to be back in Italy. When Moncey's corps arrived there from the Army of the Rhine he learned that it included the 12th Chasseurs, the light cavalry regiment in which he had begun his service as a trooper, and arranged an inspection. The event was recorded in his journal by Sub-Lieutenant Montaglas, a cantankerous man who refused to share General Murat's pleasure at the reunion.

General Murat reviewed us at three in the afternoon, as he had begun his career as a chasseur in our regiment. He expressed his affection for us and said that because of it he would never forget us. Nevertheless, that is what he has done on numerous occasions.[6]

★　　★　　★

So long as Masséna held out at Genoa, the Austrian commander Melas was trapped, sandwiched between Masséna's garrison in the south and Bonaparte's army in the north. Unable to reach the sea at Genoa, the only way he could extricate his army was by breaking through the mass of bayonets that Bonaparte had thrown across his rear. A strong force under Ott was sent to make just such a break-through, but on 9 June it was beaten by Lannes at Montebello. Three days passed. By 12 June the French army was spread out on the vast plain east of Alessandria, and there was still no sign of Melas. On the 13th, following a violent thunderstorm, French cavalry patrols reported that several thousand Austrians were in Marengo, a hamlet on the western edge of the plain. They were attacked and driven out.

Masséna's garrison had surrendered on the 5th, and at some time on the 13th Bonaparte became convinced that Melas was now moving on Genoa, so as to occupy the port and evacuate his army by sea. To bar his passage, Bonaparte ordered General Desaix to take Boudet's division of his corps towards Rivalta. Since Moncey's corps had already been detached, the sending away of Boudet's division put Bonaparte in a most dangerous position. So far from marching on Genoa, Melas was actually in Alessandria with 30,000 men: only the River Bormida divided him from the weakened French army. On 14 June he moved out to give battle.

The French soldiers, many of whom were conscripts, watched in awe as the long columns of 'Kaiserliks' crossed the Bormida by two bridges – bridges that the French thought had been destroyed. The dense masses moved slowly into the plain, their wings protected by nearly 6,000 troopers of the Imperial Austrian cavalry, which at that time was regarded as the finest in Europe. Completely deceived by the enemy and his own judgment, Bonaparte was forced to make a fighting withdrawal. By 3 p.m. his position was desperate, and gallopers had been dispatched to find Desaix and bring him back.

On the French right, the infantry commanded by Lannes was supported by Bessières and the cavalry of the Consular Guard. It was an unhappy combination, for the two men disliked each other, and Lannes felt that Bessières was compromising him by making half-hearted charges. When Lannes ordered him to attack unbroken infantry over ground covered with vines, Bessières disobeyed; in Eugène de Beauharnais' opinion he was justified in doing so.

> We advanced to within a musket shot of the two Austrian battalions, who awaited us arms in hand and in good order. Having formed us, Colonel Bessières was just going to order the charge when he saw that some enemy cavalry was deploying on our left and about to out-flank us. So he ordered '*Demi-tour à gauche!*' and we crossed over the vines under the fire of grape-shot and musketry. Arrived on the far side we put on a brave face, enough to intimidate the enemy horse. Lannes was not satisfied with our movement: but it is certain that if we had carried out his orders very few of us would have come back.[7]

On the French left, Victor's retreating infantry was covered by a brigade of heavy cavalry under General François-Etienne de Kellermann, a 30-year-old veteran of the '96 campaign. Thanks to his father, who had beaten the Prussians at Valmy eight years earlier, Kellermann bore one of the most famous names in the army. He was about to make it still more famous.

For several hours he had conformed to the general retirement, withdrawing his regiments by alternate troops, and by three o'clock his brigade had been reduced to 150 men. Convinced that he had won the battle, the Austrian commander had already returned to Alessandria; but as Melas rode away to write his report, General Desaix arrived on the field with Boudet's division and eight guns. Bonaparte ordered him to attack on the French left, covered by his own guns and ten more that Marmont had managed to save from the enemy. Kellermann, reinforced by an extra 250 troopers,[8] would provide cavalry support.

As Desaix led his men into a storm of musketry he was shot dead, but the advance continued. Marmont's guns went forward, and as he followed them he came across three more pieces of the Consular Guard. He immediately ordered their gunners to limber up, but before the horses could be attached the sight of a French regiment falling back ahead of him made him change his mind. He told the gunners to hold their ground and load with case-shot.

Thanks to his discovery of those three guns, Marmont had set the stage for one of the most brilliant cavalry charges ever made. From a thick cloud of dust and smoke a mass of infantrymen presently emerged; at first Marmont thought that they were French. Then, realising that they were grenadiers leading an Austrian column, he ordered his guns to open fire. There was barely time to loose four rounds before Kellermann swept across Marmont's front with his 400 troopers.

A few moments earlier Kellermann's cavalry had been in line formation, but seeing the Austrian grenadiers to his left he knew that he been given a marvellous opportunity, and took it with both hands. Ordering 'Left by troops, forward!' he converted his line into column and charged the enemy's flank and rear.

The grenadiers forming the Austrian column had fought hard all day and suffered heavy losses. They were tired, their muskets were empty, and they had been following an apparently beaten foe. They failed to see Kellermann's approach, which was hidden by vines; above all they had been checked and dismayed by Marmont's unexpected case-shot. Before they could recover they were hit by heavy cavalry. Kellermann's leading troops traversed the column and then rode back along it, dealing savage sabre blows. Utterly demoralised, the Austrians began to throw down their arms.

Kellermann had not finished. His leading squadrons by now had split up into groups, but the rearmost ones were still intact, and he saw that the surrender of the grenadiers had apparently unnerved a flanking body of Austrian horse. Ordering '*Pelotons à droit!*' he wheeled his half-column right into line and charged again. The enemy cavalrymen panicked and streamed inwards across the field, just as Bessières was going forward with the cavalry of the Guard. Joseph Petit, who fought that day with the Grenadiers à Cheval, describes the charge:

The moment had come. Colonel Bessières, full of ardour and whom

we all loved, addressed us like a soldier who knows how to lead his
men to glory. We drew sabres, crossed our cloaks over our chests,[9]
adjusted our reins and drew up our horses, which alas were very tired.
The trumpeters sounded the Charge and we swept forward at a
gallop. The earth trembled . . . Austrian cavalry came at us in column
and we turned to the left. A distance of about thirty paces plus a ditch
two metres wide separated us from them. We jumped the ditch,
re-formed, enveloped the two leading troops and sabred them. All
this took less than five minutes.[10]

As a result of the French cavalry charges, 6,000 Austrian troopers were
now galloping back towards the Bormida, knocking down anything that
stood in their way. The French line went forward, and the Austrian
infantry finally broke. 'We pushed them back towards the river,' wrote
Eugène, 'sabring all the time.'

Next day Melas signed the Convention of Alessandria, giving
Northern Italy back to France.

★   ★   ★

For his faultless charge at Marengo, Bonaparte had good reason to be
grateful to General Kellermann, but he refused to concede that a few
squadrons of the line had outshone the cavalry of the Guard. 'You made
a pretty good charge,' he observed to Kellermann on the evening of the
battle. The little general was furious, especially when Bonaparte
gushingly told Bessières, 'The Guard cavalry covered itself with glory
to-day.'

The following month they were both promoted; Kellermann to
general of division, Bessières to general of brigade.

★   ★   ★

That autumn, accompanied by Murat, Bessières revisited his *petit pays*.
A reception for the two young Quercynois horse generals was held in the
province's ancient capital of Cahors; afterwards Bessières went home to
Prayssac, the little town where he had once helped his father to cut hair
and make wigs. People whom he had not seen for seven years came up to
him in the street and spoke to him in the Cahorsin patois: '*Eh, Tsann!
Coumén bas? Té soubénès?*'[11] He was pleased that so many people
remembered him, but somewhat disappointed to find that his six sisters
were still unmarried.

IV

The first phase of the great struggle between France and Austria was now drawing to a close, and for the next few years Bessières lived the pleasant life of a peace-time soldier, sharing an apartment in Paris with Eugène de Beauharnais. Resplendent in uniforms tailored by Sandoz, together they attended the Opera and the theatre, balls and firework displays. According to Junot's pretty fiancée Laure Permon they made a handsome pair, despite the fact that Eugène had awful teeth like his mother's. For Bessières she had nothing but admiration.

He was rather old-fashioned, like something out of Plutarch. His figure was elegant, especially in uniform, and he had eyes à la Montmorency,[12] which gave great charm to his appearance. In the Guard he was like every soldier's adopted brother; his door was never closed to them. 'I came from the ranks,' he used to say, 'and must never forget it.'[13]

Laure also approved of Bessières' gentle wife, whom he married in the autumn of 1801. As the eldest son, Bessières received a wedding present of 650 francs, the traditional one-ninth of his father's assets. He returned it to Prayssac, so that it could be added to his sisters' marriage dowries.

The following year he was appointed Colonel General of the Guard cavalry, which now numbered over 2,000 men in two full regiments.[14] Since his regiments drew their replacements from the cavalry regiments of the line, accepting only men who had fought in at least three campaigns,[15] Bessières was becoming increasingly unpopular with line cavalry colonels and with young Kellermann's father, the French cavalry's Inspector-General. Because the Guard was taking all the best troopers, Kellermann reported, young soldiers in the line regiments had no-one to set them a good example; consequently they did not know how to carry or present the sabre, their harness was badly kept, and the pavé in their stables was slippery.

His acid comments did not improve the tempers of line cavalry colonels or their feelings towards General Bessières.

★   ★   ★

When Bonaparte became Emperor of France in 1804, 18 French generals were appointed Marshals of the Empire. The fact that neither Junot nor Marmont had been included surprised many of their friends, but the last name on the list surprised them even more. Only nine years

earlier, Jean-Baptiste Bessières had been a captain in the tattered legion
of the Pyrenees; now he was Marshal Bessières, Colonel-General of the
Imperial Guard cavalry, entitled to 24 horses, 2,000 francs pay by the
month, and 66 francs lodging allowance per day.

Junot was bitterly disappointed. 'You think I've done you an in-
justice,' Napoleon told him, 'giving a bâton to Bessières and not to you. I
know Bessières is rather young, and that he has never commanded in the
field. But I wanted to make my four commandants of the Guard
Marshals of the Empire.'

Marmont consoled himself with the thought that whenever people
spoke of him they would ask, 'Why wasn't he made a Marshal?' When
they spoke of Bessières, they would ask, 'What was he made a Marshal
for?'

In spite of Marmont's criticism, Bessières discharged heavy responsi-
bilities in the Guard, which had grown into a miniature army consisting
of foot, horse, guns and ancillary services. Bessières was a key figure in
this élite body. The other three Colonel-Generals of the Guard did not
serve with it on campaign, since they had their own *corps d'armée* to look
after; consequently Bessières acted as chief administrator for the whole
of the Guard, in addition to commanding its cavalry arm.

A born organiser, he had a natural talent for staff work. At the start of
a campaign he knew exactly what time the leading cavalry troop or the
last infantry detachment would reach Strasbourg; but like all masters of
detail he was reluctant to delegate. 'Where are you off to this time?'
someone once asked General Dorsenne, who commanded the Foot
Grenadiers of the Guard. 'I'd be grateful if you'd tell me,' he answered
drily. ''All *I* know is that we're leaving Paris by the Porte Saint Martin.'

According to General Thiébault, Bessières was a cold and un-
attractive martinet, whose rigorous standards made him feared and
disliked even by his own staff. Alexandre de Bourjolly, who served for
three years as the Marshal's aide de camp, drew rather a different picture
of him.

He was cool, calm, dignified and proud, but underneath he was very
human. He saw much and spoke little, rarely writing anything down
and insisting on seeing everything for himself. On combat days he was
all eyes and ears and never dismounted, wearing out three or four
horses in a day. On the march, and while working, he'd exist on a
piece of bread rubbed with garlic, like the huntsmen back home in
Quercy.[16]

He never had any money because he gave it all away to wounded soldiers, and we often saw him refuse gifts of paintings and weapons that municipalities wanted to give him. All his baggage went in a little vehicle that wouldn't have satisfied a major. Although very courteous in manner he could be harsh and he could instil fear; but his men loved him like a father. Always elegantly dressed, he used to put on his full uniform for a battle.

Under fire he was superb. His *sang-froid* was without equal, but when the moment came to charge the enemy his face lit up and his eyes flashed; then his voice rose above the noise of battle as he took the lead and galloped at the head of his squadrons.

He didn't like loose talk or blasphemous jokes.[17]

In addition to the standard dress of a French Marshal, Bessières was entitled to wear a special uniform as Colonel-General of the Guard cavalry, consisting of a cut-away green coat, red breeches heavily laced with gold, and Hessian boots. With his long hair powdered and queued *à la brigadière*, and a cocked hat worn rakishly *en bataille*,[18] he brought a touch of the *ancien régime* to the battlefields of the First Empire.

2

The Road to Austerlitz

As dictator of an increasingly prosperous country, Napoleon was able to give the French cavalry the best of everything; more important, he had the authority he needed to remould it to his own design.[1]

Uppermost in his mind was the memory of the cavalry charges at Aboukir and Marengo; they had proved beyond all doubt that cavalry, if it was boldly led and aided by artillery, could produce a moral effect out of all proportion to its numbers. Of the two, Kellermann's charge was the more remarkable, since it had succeeded against well-trained European troops; but it had only a limited bearing on the future. Kellermann had enjoyed the rare advantage of surprise at Marengo, largely because he had charged with only 400 men; in the battles that Napoleon envisaged, cavalry would charge not in hundreds but in thousands.

In the *cavalerie de bataille* of the Revolutionary armies, which had never charged in huge masses, the essential difference between light and heavy regiments had often been over-looked or forgotten. Napoleon believed that this was a great mistake, and that the functions of the two branches ought never to be confused. Light cavalry should be used mainly for reconnaissance, heavy cavalry to deliver the final punch in battle.

The art of warfare, he declared, was the proper use of time, weight and force. In terms of a cavalry charge, the secret was impact. Impact was the ultimate aim, the absolutely vital element; and provided that he rode a sufficiently powerful horse, the cavalryman who produced the greatest impact on his target was the one who wore a cuirasse.

Napoleon saw great advantages in the cuirasse. Apart from giving a trooper added weight, the breast-plate protected him from musketry, and in the mêlée which always followed a charge, when even the bravest trooper turned his back to the enemy, the back-plate protected him from sword thrusts. In the Revolutionary armies, however, the cuirasse had been abolished in all heavy cavalry regiments except the 8th; troopers of the other regiments had no protective armour apart from the *calotte,* a small iron cap worn under the cocked hat.

During Napoleon's Consulate the cuirasse was gradually reintroduced into selected units of the *cavalerie de ligne,* as the heavy cavalry was then called, and in 1803 the 24 regiments that comprised the *cavalerie de ligne* were reorganized and merged to form 12 regiments of armoured cuirassiers. It only remained to replace their cocked hats with metal helmets, and the famous heavy cavalry uniform of the First Empire was complete.

Initially, the merging of two old regiments into one of cuirassiers had a bad effect on discipline. In every cuirassier regiment there were two cliques of officers, mutually antagonistic, always ready to assert the superiority of their former regiment over that of their colleagues. In the 6th Cuirassiers the rivalry amounted to a feud, which in the opinion of a newly-joined subaltern was aggravated by the attitude of the colonel, 'a blundering and partial man'. Since the officers lived in enmity and frequently fought each other the NCOs and troopers followed their example: 'in consequence there was no discipline, no smartness, no drill'.[2] Fortunately for this regiment, its blundering commander was presently replaced by Colonel d'Avenay, who quickly established a proper *esprit de corps.*

Esprit de corps was certainly not lacking in the 8th Cuirassiers, least of all in the colonel. In view of the fact that the 8th Cavalry had never ceased to wear the cuirasse, he suggested to the Minister of War that the 8th Cuirassiers ought to be renumbered as the 1st. This suggestion was not adopted, partly due to strong representations from the 1st Cuirassiers' colonel.

The heavy cavalry of the line now numbered 14 regiments, for in addition to the new-style cuirassiers there were two heavy regiments known as the Carabiniers, which had been inherited from the old Royalist army. The men in these regiments wore neither helmets nor cuirasses; their headdress continued to be a tall black bearskin, similar to that worn by the Grenadiers à Cheval of the Imperial Guard.

The Guard cavalry was still growing. In addition to the Grenadiers à Cheval and the Chasseurs, each 1,018 troopers strong, Bessières now commanded 632 gendarmes d'élite and 124 Mamelukes. A relic of the Egyptian campaign, the Mameluke company consisted of Syrians and Copts who had joined the French in Syria, plus deserters from the armies of Ibrahim and Murad Bey. Dressed in Eastern costume, they were armed with pistols and scimitars.[3]

★   ★   ★

On the eve of Napoleon's first great Imperial campaign, there were thousands of serving cavalry soldiers who remembered the campaigns against the Austrians on the Rhine. In those days many of them had been without cloaks and saddles ; others had even lacked boots and sabres, even after the victory of Jemappes. Things were very different now. In the five years that had elapsed since the Brumaire *coup d'état*, Napoleon had transformed the ramshackle cavalry of the Revolutionary armies into a well-equipped, highly organized force of 81 regiments.[4] It was not without faults. Unlike the well-trained professional bodies of Austria and Prussia, the French army was the product of a *levée en masse*, and in the cavalry both the sword drill and the equitation lacked refinements. Prussian troopers, for example, were taught how to cut leftwards using the back of the sword-blade, a movement ideally designed to protect the mounted man's left rear, which had always been his Achilles heel. In the French cavalry the movement was unknown.

Many of the regimental officers were former NCOs who owed their promotion to the Revolution, and who had never received a formal military education suitable to their rank, especially insofar as tactics were concerned. To assist them, a cavalry instruction manual three inches thick, adapted from the 1788 regulations, had been issued in 1801.

As this work explained, the ultimate aim of cavalry tactics was to produce a charge of mounted men in straight and compact lines. Ideally it would consist of not less than two successive shocks on the enemy, no matter whether the unit employed was a squadron of four troops or a division of four regiments.

In a good regimental charge the men should be halted 200 or 300 metres distant from the target. On the command '*Escadrons, en avant-marche!*' the advance would begin at walking pace; then the colonel would order '*Au trot!*' After trotting for half the distance towards the enemy, the colonel would order '*Au galop!*' Finally, at 60 metres distance from the enemy and on the command '*Chargez!*' the horses would be thrown into the Full or Triple Gallop. If this was properly carried out, the horses did not tire before the impact and the lines were kept straight. The first rank must split up on reaching the objective, allowing the second wave formed by the rear rank to deliver a further shock.

The classic method of attack for a regiment was by successive squadrons, each squadron formed of two long lines of troopers riding boot to boot; thus a regiment of four squadrons would charge in eight lines, one behind the other, each line having a frontage of 40 to 48 men.[5] However, if the ground was suitable and space allowed, a regiment might charge with all its squadrons in line abreast, making two lines with a frontage of nearly 200 men.

Sometimes it was necessary to charge in column – for example, when riding to attack through the gaps between friendly infantry squares; then again, as Kellermann had shown at Marengo, cavalry in line or column might need to change formation immediately before the charge.

Changing formation was the cavalry's peculiar problem. In an infantry column, a foot soldier could pivot on his heel to right or left without taking up any extra space or displacing the man next to him; but a cavalryman could not, mainly because he was riding a horse that was four times longer than its width. To form line from column, cavalry had to wheel at an angle of 45 degrees or less.

Theoretically, well-trained cavalry could change formation at the gallop without losing its alignment, but very few of Napoleon's cavalry regiments attained such perfection of drill and discipline; and since their troopers could not carry out complicated movements at speed, French cavalry colonels did not have to be brilliant tacticians. Generals of division, on the other hand, needed to have something approaching genius.

To handle massed cavalry required highly specialized skills and knowledge, including a deep understanding of what cavalry was and how much it could achieve, plus the ability rapidly to survey and evaluate the ground over which it would attack. This *coup d'oeil* was the rarest skill of all, exceedingly hard to acquire; furthermore it had to be combined with physical courage of the highest order and superb leadership. The outstanding horse generals of Napoleon's army had all these qualities, as the men whom they led well knew; and it was this utter confidence in his leaders, coupled in many cases with his affection for them, that enabled the average French trooper to rise above his far from brilliant horsemanship and his imperfect discipline.

★   ★   ★

In 1805 the Carabiniers and eight of the cuirassier regiments were grouped into two divisions. To command these splendid formations, Napoleon chose two highly experienced heavy cavalry generals, both of whom were aristocrats. Born at Bordeaux in 1768, Etienne de Nansouty was a product of the military academies at Brienne and Paris, and had been a captain of infantry before the Revolution. He had seen much service against the Austrians on the Rhine, both as a heavy cavalry colonel and as a brigade commander. A stern disciplinarian, on the battlefield he was prudent and calculating, sometimes to the point of caution; on more than one occasion he had been told to act with more spirit. As leader of the 1st Heavy Cavalry Division he commanded three brigades, formed by the two regiments of Carabiniers and four regiments of cuirassiers.

Jean Joseph d'Hautpoul[6] led the four cuirassier regiments of the 2nd Heavy Cavalry Division. At 51 he was 14 years older than Nansouty, and came from one of the oldest families in Languedoc, with a pedigree of soldier ancestors stretching back to the Crusades. Entering the army in 1771, he had taken 12 years to reach the rank of lieutenant; forced to resign during the Revolution because of his nobility, he had rejoined as a trooper. Within five years he had risen to general of brigade, and in two more to general of division.

Unlike the cultured Nansouty, who had once served under him, d'Hautpoul had had very little formal education. He liked to wear the cuirasse, and from his cocked hat to his *bottes fortes*[7] he was every inch the tough general of cuirassiers. Although his men loved him he took little interest in their welfare; once, when his division was stationed in Germany, he had requisitioned such modest supplies for his men and horses that the grateful local inhabitants had presented him with a sabre of honour. While the conscientious Nansouty inspected fetlocks and pasterns, harness straps and forage trusses, sword blades and boots, d'Hautpoul left everything to his brigade commanders; but what he lacked in application he made up for in *panache*. 'Soldiers,' he would announce after a successful charge, 'I kiss you all on the tu-tu!' In action he was bold and improvident, full of fire and energy, utterly reckless of his own safety and the lives of his men. His idea of cavalry tactics could have been summed up in two words – speed, and brutality.

II

England had declared war in 1803. Until the summer of 1805 the French army held a line stretching from the Channel ports to Hanover, ready to invade; but when Austria and Russia joined England and Sweden to form the Third Coalition, the French strategy changed. Instead of an attack on England, Napoleon's aim became the destruction of the Austrian and Russian armies in the field.

Without waiting for the Russians, an Austrian army of 80,000 had invaded France's ally Bavaria and occupied Munich. Officially this army was commanded by the young Archduke Ferdinand, but it was directed by its Chief of Staff, Karl Mack, who had risen from private to field-marshal-lieutenant in the most class-conscious army in Europe. Napoleon intended to destroy Mack first, then to mass against a Russian force under Kutusov that was marching to join him.

At the end of September 1805 the French army was spread out in a 250-mile crescent which began at Wurzburg in Bavaria and curved through Mannheim and Strasbourg to Basle. Light cavalry brigades having been attached to the infantry corps for reconnaissance and outpost duties, the two heavy cavalry divisions and four dragoon divisions were formed into a strategic Corps de Reserve commanded by Murat.[8] These groupings, however, were not inflexible. In case of need, a corps commander might apply for cavalry reinforcements from the Reserve: conversely, Murat might draw on the detached light cavalry brigades.

On 26 September Napoleon set his army in motion. If a balloonist had drifted east from Strasbourg over the next three weeks, he would have understood something that Austrian generals had yet to learn: the extraordinary mobility that Napoleon's army could achieve by brilliant staff-work and hard marching. Also, he would have seen an unforgettable sight: squadrons of blue- and green-clad cavalry pouring through the defiles of the Black Forest, columns of infantry converging on the Danube from Donauworth to Ratisbon, then curling south and closing in on Ulm, where Mack's headquarters were.

To distract Mack's attention from the storm that was gathering to the north and east of Ulm, Murat's cavalry was advancing on him from the west, making marches of up to 50 kilometres a day. This pace soon told on the horses, especially the ones who had been cooped up for weeks in the invasion barges. Their backs were rubbed into sores by saddles and crupper-loops, saddle-cloths and harness-straps. 'Our regiment was a walking infirmary,' wrote a trumpeter of the 8th Chasseurs.[9]

'The important thing,' Napoleon had declared, 'is not for the cavalry regiments to arrive on the field with the maximum number of horses, but with horses in the best possible condition.' Because of the distances they were made to cover, the condition of even the fittest horses gave cause for alarm. In the Reserve Cavalry, which had to be ready to mount up at a moment's notice, they were kept saddled all night; by early October the loss of horses had reduced squadrons which had started out with 120 sabres to 60.

The cavalry brigades attached to the *corps d'armées* were in a similar state. 'Sixth Corps cavalry is exhausted,' Marshal Ney informed the Emperor on 30 September. 'My three regiments consist of eight to nine hundred men, a force that will be totally inadequate when we meet the enemy.'

It was all, however, to good purpose. At the start of October Mack was still waiting in Ulm for Kutusov's Russians, confident that the French army was still miles away to the west behind its cavalry screen. By the 15th he was surrounded; on the 20th he surrendered with 33,000 men. With Mack in attendance, Napoleon watched the Austrians march out of Ulm to hand over their arms and equipment, 40 standards and 60 guns. With the panache that the Napoleonic army always brought to such occasions, the drums of Mack's crack infantry regiments were slashed and punctured by the sabres of French light cavalry trumpeters.

Refusing to share Mack's humiliation, the inexperienced young Archduke Ferdinand collected 2,000 cavalrymen and ordered them to follow him to Bohemia. This spirited action was witnessed by Lieutenant von Grueber of the Albrecht Kurassiers, one of three regiments commanded by General von Werneck. Meeting a French general at an inn near Wertheim, von Werneck prepared to surrender with his brigade, but his three colonels would not obey him. At that moment, von Grueber relates, Ferdinand came spurring up with his staff; before von Werneck realised what was happening, his regiments departed at the gallop to join Ferdinand's column. For three days and nights the Austrian horsemen stopped neither to eat nor drink, and despite Murat's efforts to stop him Ferdinand got clear away with 28 squadrons.

Murat then turned his attention to the survivors of Mack's army who were still at liberty in Bavaria. In five days he led his regiments well over 100 miles and fought eight separate actions, capturing 18 Austrian generals, 11 standards, 15,000 men, over 1,000 waggons and 128 guns. On 29 October his troopers crossed the River Inn and strung out their picket lines on Austrian soil.

During this extraordinary pursuit Murat enjoyed the unusual honour of commanding the Guard Chasseurs, who were in disgrace. Napoleon's favourite cavalry regiment was an élite one in every sense. Its troopers wore the richest uniform in the French army,[10] and in addition to being extremely elegant they were extremely tough, armed to the teeth with pistol, musketoon and sabre. Some of them had ten or more wound scars.

In such a regiment, many of whose NCOs became officers of the Legion of Honour,[11] arrogance was only to be expected, but it was not always condoned. At Ulm, following their habit of seizing the best available quarters, the Chasseurs took over a building reserved for the Imperial carriages, and when the grooms and drivers tried to enter the cavalrymen threw them out. To punish the Chasseurs Napoleon handed them over to Murat and told him to use them as his advance guard; meanwhile the Emperor's escort was furnished by Mamelukes and the Grenadiers à Cheval.

* * *

As winter approached the heavy cuirassier horses began to suffer from the cold. So did their riders, who passed the chilly nights huddled together for warmth. For General d'Hautpoul's nephew, who was serving with the horse artillery attached to Nansouty's division, this arrangement was far from ideal.

At any other time of year we would have bivouacked, but because of the cold in this season of rain and snow we had to find a better shelter, and we often bargained fiercely for the meanest of peasant hovels. We slept fully dressed on wooden benches, the only furniture to be found in such dwellings, or on straw spread out on the ground. In the latter case we slept in a mass side by side, but it was hard on those who didn't go to sleep quickly, for the deep snoring of all those tired men produced such a discordant volume of sound that sleep was impossible.[12]

III

On hearing of Mack's surrender at Ulm, the Russian commander Kutusov had retired into Moravia, halting at Olmutz to receive Austrian reinforcements. Having occupied Vienna, Napoleon moved north to meet him, and on 2 December fought the combined Austro-Russians near the village of Austerlitz.

The Allied dispositions were drawn up by the Austrian general Weyrother. Reading out his orders on 1 December to a council of senior officers, he assured them that he was well acquainted with the ground, having commanded manoeuvres in the area the previous year. 'Do not make the same mistakes this year,' murmured his aide de camp.

When the Russian corps commander Bagration studied Weyrother's orders next morning he said gloomily, 'We are going to lose this battle.'

For the Austrians, Bagration's pessimism was at least preferable to the attitude of the other Russian leaders. The Austrian army, after all, was an extremely tough fighting force, which had done the lion's share of the fighting against the armies of the Revolution. It was led by hard-bitten and highly experienced generals; many of those who fought at Austerlitz, such as Lichtenstein and the one-armed Kienmayer, were veterans not only of the Rhine campaigns but of terrible battles against the

Turks as well. They were angered and humiliated by Russian boasts that Napoleon, who had never fought real soldiers before, would soon learn the difference between lily-white Kaiserliks and the invincibles of the Tsar.

The Tsar and the Austrian Emperor were both present at the battle. When they arrived on the field, Alexander was displeased to find that the advance had not begun, and that the Russian muskets were still piled. General Kutusov explained that he was waiting for more columns to arrive.

'We are not on the Champ de Mars,' said Alexander coldly, 'where the parade only begins when all the regiments are present.'

'Sire,' Kutusov replied, 'it is precisely because we are not on the Champ de Mars that I am waiting. But if Your Majesty orders it?'

'I order it.'

As the armies took the ground, it became plain that the stage was being set for a tremendous cavalry combat. On the French left, where Murat supported the infantry corps of Marshal Lannes, 80 French squadrons faced 82 Allied ones under Prince Lichtenstein, plus a strong body of Russian horse forming part of Bagration's corps. In addition to his cuirassiers and dragoons, Murat also disposed of two light cavalry brigades and a light cavalry division led by the hero of Marengo, Kellermann.

Kellermann's luck was out that day. After leading his four regiments in several vigorous charges he was furiously attacked by Russian uhlans, dragoons and kurassiers. His division suffered heavy losses. Kellermann himself was badly wounded and carried off the field.

Having deployed his force of 5,000 cavalry, Lichtenstein prepared to attack the infantry of Lannes' corps, behind which stood the long lines of Nansouty's heavy cavalry division. Nansouty saw that he must charge the mass of Allied horse, but he did not like the look of the ground in front of him. Ordering right by troops, he moved his six regiments inwards in column; then reforming into line of battle he had his trumpeters sound the trot, and immediately afterwards the charge. The fighting which followed established the reputation of the French heavy cavalry for a decade to come. Lichtenstein's first line was broken by the Carabiniers, his second line by supporting waves of cuirassiers. Nansouty rallied his regiments on the bank of a stream, the colonels standing up in their stirrups and shouting at their men to close ranks. '*Serrez, cuirassiers, serrez! Casques en tête!*'[13]

Nansouty charged again, and the whole of the Reserve Cavalry flooded into movement. Led by Murat, d'Hautpoul's division rode to the attack followed by dragoons and light cavalry, sabring Bagration's infantry and over-running his artillery. As the French left wing went forward, d'Hautpoul's division was joined to Nansouty's, creating one of the most impressive sights ever seen on even a Napoleonic battlefield: ten regiments of heavy cavalry riding in line abreast. 'They resembled a wall of iron,' wrote d'Hautpoul's nephew, the horse artillery lieutenant. 'Advancing on the enemy ranks, they overthrew them at the first impact.'[14]

While these charges multiplied on the left of the battle, the Guard cavalry remained halted close to the centre, and for at least one of Bessières' officers the time seemed to be passing very slowly. That morning Lieutenant Michel Ordener was acting as aide de camp to his father, who commanded the Grenadiers à Cheval. It was the first time that young Ordener had faced artillery fire, and as the cannon shots began whistling over his head he could not help bending lower in the saddle.

'You salute the enemy,' General Ordener observed. 'It's your privilege, since you're seeing him for the first time. But don't forget, it's a polite gesture that a man of spirit doesn't make twice.'

Immediately in front of Ordener's squadrons were the massed ranks of Oudinot's grenadiers. Beyond them the ground rose gently, leading to the elevation known as the Pratzen heights. For Napoleon, the possession of this high ground was the key to victory, and when the infantry divisions of Soult's corps had succeeded in taking it the battle was half won. In a desperate effort to dislodge them, Russian Guard infantry attacked under the Grand Duke Constantine, younger brother to the Tsar. The attack having failed, Constantine collected the cavalry of the Russian Guard and led it to the charge; Hussars and Horse Guards in first line, Cossacks and the Chevalier Guards in support.

A mile away, Marshal Bessières waited for orders with his senior aide de camp, César de Laville. Presently they saw French infantrymen running back down the slopes ahead. Bessières noticed that they kept looking back over their shoulders, which could mean only one thing: they were running away from enemy horse. 'We shall have a cavalry action soon, Laville,' he predicted.[15]

To assist Soult's hard-pressed infantry, Napoleon sent forward half the Guard cavalry under his Alsatian aide de camp, Rapp. Riding at the head of the Guard Chasseurs and Mamelukes, Rapp arrived on the Pratzen to find the horsemen of Constantine's first wave hacking and slashing at the French infantry. One square had already been broken and cut to pieces. 'Avenge them!' Rapp shouted. 'Avenge our comrades!'

His charge forced the Russians back through the gaps in the French squares, but in the heat of action Rapp rode too far forward in pursuit; attacked by Constantine's second line, his men found themselves fighting for their lives against the best swordsmen in the Tsar's cavalry. The deputy colonel of the Guard Chasseurs[16] was killed; Rapp was wounded by a sword cut on the head and half-blinded by his own blood. As the Chasseurs fell back before the Chevalier Guards, Marshal Bessières advanced with the Grenadiers à Cheval.

It was a sight that Jean Coignet, watching from the ranks of Napoleon's Guard infantry, remembered all his life; Bessières in his brilliant Colonel-General's uniform: Ordener's Mounted Grenadiers in their tall bearskins, each man a veteran of 12 years' service: the long lines of superb black horses. As they rode to the attack they were swallowed up in a cloud of dust.

To Coignet, and his comrades in the infantry, the next few minutes seemed like a century; they knew that if Bessières and his *Chevaux Noirs*[17] were beaten, they would soon be facing the gigantic horsemen of the Russian Guard.

It was all over in a quarter of an hour. The Chevalier Guards were routed, leaving one squadron almost completely destroyed; when the smoke and dust cleared away the only Russian cavalrymen that Coignet could see were stretched out on the ground. As Bessières rode on to Austerlitz, Soult's corps was swung right to strike the Allied left; by 4 p.m. Napoleon had won a crushing victory.

'*Quelle bataille, Messieurs!*' an Austrian colonel exclaimed admiringly to a group of French officers. '*Vous avez tué trente mille Russes! Trente mille Russes!*'[18]

★   ★   ★

For the French cavalry the results of Austerlitz could hardly have been more brilliant. In a single charge the Grenadiers à Cheval had soundly defeated the finest mounted regiments of the Russian Guard; as to the Reserve Cavalry, its achievements were not unfairly described by General Belliard, Murat's Chief of Staff.

Two standards captured, 27 pieces of artillery taken with their caissons, squadrons entirely destroyed, battalion squares broken, regiments scattered, twelve or fifteen hundred dead left on the field, more than 3,000 wounded – such was the outcome of this splendid and brilliant day.

In brief, the Austerlitz campaign had been Napoleonic warfare at its best, both for the generals and the men who followed them. While their brothers back home toiled in the fields or at their benches, sweating out their lives in drudgery and ignorance, Napoleon's troopers had ridden from Strasbourg to Vienna, responsible only for their horses, arms and uniforms.

No-one had enjoyed it more than Sub-Lieutenant Thomas Aubry of the 12th Chasseurs, who had drunk the famous wine of Tokai in an Imperial castle at Pressburg and slept in the Empress of Austria's bed.[19] Twenty-five years old, proud of his regiment, trusted by his colonel and respected by his men, Aubry had no complaints about life in the French cavalry.

> What a fine country Austria is! The people are gentle and civilized and they received us kindly. We danced, we were well fed, and naturally we behaved ourselves, even helping the peasants working in the countryside . . . In short, the Austerlitz campaign had been for us one of the happiest and most pleasurable imaginable. To ride through such a fine land as Germany, as we had done, is one of the best things a man can experience in this life.[20]

IV

After Austerlitz the French cavalry entered cantonments in Bavaria, there to await replacements from the depôts in France. Men were more easily replaced than horses, which were impossible to buy in France except at inflated prices.[21] As late as September 1806 Napoleon was writing to Berthier:[22] 'Many regiments must be using inferior horses. Authorize them to buy all they can in Germany.'

Each regiment was given a special allowance of 10,000 francs, and the minimum regulation heights for cavalry mounts were relaxed, even in the cuirassier regiments. Some regimental commanders failed to use all the money for buying horses: others bought only very handsome animals for which they paid far too much. A few colonels even insisted on keeping up the peace-time practice of mounting their first squadron on black horses, the second squadron on bays, and the third on chestnuts.

By the end of September Napoleon's available cavalry forces totalled just under 17,000 sabres,[23] which was 5,000 less than at the start of the Austerlitz campaign. And time was pressing.

Austria had temporarily withdrawn from the struggle, but Russia and England were still at war with France. In September 1806 they were joined by Prussia.

On 8 October, in glorious autumn weather, the French army began its advance to Berlin.

3

Prussia and Poland

I

Prussia's military traditions and discipline were the finest in the world. Her oldest regiments, which had been in existence for centuries, carried battle honours that had been won during the Thirty Years' War; the infantry was still trained to attack in the parade-ground formations used by Frederick the Great. The aristocratic Prussian generals were openly contemptuous of Napoleon's conscript army, whose infantry could only attack in column, and in which a hairdresser's son was permitted to command the cavalry of the Guard. For 14 years they had been waiting to punish the French for Valmy, where the Prussian Army had been inexplicably made to look ridiculous, and they were quite sure of their ability to do it.

The King of Prussia did not share his generals' confidence, and the opening actions of the 1806 campaign did nothing to reassure him. 'You said that the French cavalry was worthless,' he told his advisers after Saalfeld.[1] 'Look what their light cavalry have done to us! Imagine what their cuirassiers will do!'

His fears were fully realized on 14 October, when the French won two simultaneous victories at Jena and Auerstaedt. The French cavalry arrived late on the field at Jena, but Murat was still in time to lead an electrifying charge of cuirassiers and dragoons.

> The cuirassiers fell upon the enemy cavalry and overthrew them at the first impact; then they turned on the infantry squares and sabred them; they took the gun parks and created havoc wherever they went. In short that avalanche of men and horses, under the leadership of Murat, won us an outright victory.[2]

Murat's astonishing role in the campaign was only just beginning. After the double defeat of 14 October 70,000 Prussians drew off northwards, hoping to join a Russian army that was slowly advancing west through Poland. To complete the Prussian army's destruction Napoleon ordered the infantry corps of Lannes and Bernadotte in pursuit; but before the Prussians could be destroyed they had to be found, which could only be done by cavalry. For the next 24 days Murat became the key figure in the drama.

His command consisted of two light cavalry brigades, three dragoon divisions and a brigade of d'Hautpoul's cuirassiers. With light cavalry in the lead, his regiments fanned out into the flat German countryside; eight days after Jena Lasalle's hussars were riding across the Elbe. Thirty-one years old, a former colonel of the 10th Hussars, Lasalle was the advance guard commander *par excellence*, utterly fearless yet highly intelligent, expert at obtaining information and analyzing its meaning. Addicted to soldiering and deeply in love with his wife, the handsome young cavalry general had everything to live for; yet soon after the pursuit began he was tempted to end his career by suicide.

A Prussian column commanded by Blucher was located by the dragoons of General Klein, who immediately alerted his nearest colleague, Lasalle: but when Blucher arranged a parley and claimed that Napoleon had agreed to a six-week truce, the two French generals accepted his word and let him pass. Napoleon expressed his anger with them in an Order of the Day. 'In allowing passage to two broken columns of the enemy,' the French army read, 'both of them had the extreme naiveté to believe everything the enemy General Blucher told them. Since when has His Majesty passed on his orders by means of the enemy?'

Murat had no desire to take the blame for his subordinates. 'I certainly would not try to excuse them,' he assured the Emperor.

★   ★   ★

Murat's first objective was to find the main Prussian body led by Prince Friedrich von Hohenlohe, which was not an easy task. In effect, the Reserve Cavalry was operating on a chessboard over 100 miles in length. The right hand edge of the board was formed by the frontier of Russian Poland, which Hohenlohe would have to cross in order to join up with the Russian army. Hohenlohe's force lay at the bottom left-hand corner of the board. His quickest route to the border lay due east, but this way was barred to him by the French army, which was advancing up the board on his right flank. He therefore decided to make a diagonal march to the top right-hand corner of the board, hoping to reach Russian

Poland via the fortress of Stettin.

By 25 October, having skirted Berlin well to the north, he was only 50 miles from Stettin, but his men were exhausted. Murat's regiments, too, were nearly spent. For ten days they had been making forced marches of up to 40 miles a day, and the horses' backs were covered in sores. The patrols were out at first light every morning, intercepting letters, questioning travellers and local inhabitants, searching for wheel-marks or trails of manure. On 26 October their efforts were rewarded. 'I am finally on the enemy's traces,' Murat informed the Emperor. 'General Lasalle has found him at Zehdenick.'

The enemy whom Lasalle had found were 15 squadrons of cavalry that Hohenlohe had left behind as a rearguard. Anxious to regain Napoleon's favour, Lasalle was burning to engage them, but he had only three squadrons under his hand.[3] Knowing that Grouchy's dragoons were close behind him he halted his men, ordered them to draw their sabres, and breathed his horses. As soon as Grouchy's leading squadron came into sight he led a furious charge, driving the Prussians for three miles down the road to Templin. Before he could rally he was attacked by a fresh regiment, but this was charged and routed by Grouchy's dragoons. Five hundred Prussian horsemen were taken prisoner and the remainder fled; but instead of rejoining their main body they rode straight for the safety of Stettin. Hohenlohe's rearguard, on which he was relying to break the bridges behind him, had ceased to exist.

The action was reported to Imperial Headquarters by both Murat and Grouchy, who characteristically tried to claim all the credit for his dragoons. To Murat the Emperor replied that, whilst greatly pleased by the brilliant victory over 15 squadrons of cavalry, he would have preferred him to have pursued the enemy's main body.

Two days later Murat found it halted at Prenzlau. Lasalle and Grouchy charged through the suburbs of the town and drove the Prussian outposts before them. Attended only by a trumpeter, General Belliard then rode to meet Hohenlohe and demanded his surrender, which was refused. Followed by a group of ardent young cavalry officers, Murat went to meet Hohenlohe himself, and repeated his surrender terms. Further resistance, Murat explained, was useless, since Hohenlohe's force was surrounded by 100,000 French soldiers, including the army corps of Lannes, Bernadotte and Soult. By a happy coincidence, somewhere in the distance an ammunition waggon exploded. 'That is Marshal Soult's signal,' observed a quick-witted French officer, consulting his watch, 'announcing that he has reached and cut your line of retreat.'

Apart from Murat, the only French Marshal in the vicinity was Lannes, who had recently arrived with a handful of his Fifth Corps infantry; between them they had barely 5,000 men against 10,000 Prussians. Fortunately for Murat, the Prussian commander had lost the will to fight, and the bluff succeeded.

'Will you allow me to pile arms?' Hohenlohe asked.

'Your Highness,' Murat replied, 'there is too much honour attached to Prussian arms for a French commander to have them thrown down.'

Counting enemy detachments brought in by the flanking squadrons, the total number of prisoners was about 12,000. To Napoleon, Murat reported that he had captured 16,000 infantry, six regiments of cavalry, 64 standards and 60 guns. 'I hope to have carried out the intentions of Your Majesty,' he ended, 'and to have convinced him of my love and zeal in his service.'

Lannes was furious to discover that Murat's report made no mention of the Fifth Corps infantry, especially since his own report had praised the cavalry's role at Prenzlau. 'I told His Majesty that Your Highness had made the finest charge I ever saw,' he informed Murat. 'No doubt Your Highness' great preoccupations made you forget that I was at your side.'

General Grouchy was also dissatisfied with the Reserve Cavalry report. 'The Division Grouchy,' he pointed out to Imperial Headquarters, 'is the only one that charged in this action, since General Beaumont had been sent to pursue the Prince Auguste and the hussars remained in rear of the Division Grouchy.'

By this time Lasalle's hussar brigade, which had started the campaign with 1,100 sabres, had been reduced to 785. Without further assistance from General Grouchy, Lasalle now led his two regiments the remaining 40 miles to Stettin, halted them outside the walls, and sent the 5th Hussars colonel inside to tell the Governor that Marshals Lannes and Murat were at his gates with 30,000 men. Seeing no reason to disbelieve it, the Governor marched out with his garrison of 5,000. As soon as French infantry arrived to occupy the place, Lasalle rode back west to join in the search for Blucher. At 7 p.m. on 30 October he reached Falkenwald, from where he wrote Murat:

I have arrived here to rest my horses which were bridled at three o'clock this morning. To-morrow at six I shall start for Uckermunde, which is five miles from here. From a postilion coming from Anklam, who left there at five o'clock yesterday evening, I learn that outside that place there are many infantrymen, cavalry and baggage, but no guns. This force consists of Garde du Corps, green Hussars,[4] kurassiers and dragoons. The name of the commander is not known.

Acting on this information, Murat sent a force of dragoons on Anklam, where the column that Lasalle had described surrendered. Lasalle himself rode on to Uckermunde, to find orders from Murat directing him to Stretense. These he ignored, except for informing Belliard that he was not obeying them. 'I cannot believe this order,' he wrote. 'It will put me in second line to the dragoons, where it seems to me that I shall be employed solely in capturing any prisoners who may escape.'

('You were wrong, my dear Lasalle, not to proceed to Stretense,' was Belliard's mild reaction.)

Meanwhile Murat was reporting to Napoleon that some of the Prussian horsemen captured at Zehdenick were Guard Hussars, who wore tiger-skin pelisses to commemorate their regiment's heroic actions in the Seven Years' War. 'Could not Your Majesty give these pelisses to his hussars?' Murat suggested. 'The Brigade Lasalle has covered itself with glory in this campaign.'

Apart from 15,000 men who had escaped with the King to Koenigsberg,[5] Blucher's Prussians were now the only ones left in the field. Determined to join the King, Blucher began to march due north towards the port of Stralsund, intending to take his force to Koenigsberg by sea; but as the French cavalry moved to head him off he was forced to turn due west, followed by Murat and the infantry of Lannes and Bernadotte. On 8 November he surrendered at Ratkau.

As Murat put it, there were no more enemies left to fight. Leaving Prussia garrisoned by French conscripts and convalescents, Napoleon swung the Grand Army east to meet the Russians.

II

Counting the 15,000 Prussians who had reached Koenigsberg, the Russian general Kamenski had 100,000 men at his disposal. Napoleon's plan was to isolate the Prussians from their allies, then work round Kamenski's flank to cut him off from Russia.

Once again Murat's regiments rode ahead to find the enemy, but in Poland and East Prussia they found the fog of war almost impossible to penetrate. The rain fell in torrents, turning the low-lying countryside into muddy swamps. In Poland the roads were mere banks of earth, rarely even revetted, and when cavalry columns tried to move across country they frequently had to skirt huge lakes that were not marked on any map.

Starved of intelligence, ignorant of the enemy's strength and movements, Napoleon decided to create a special cavalry reconnaissance corps under Bessières, and the necessary orders went out on 13 December. Unlike Murat, who led a charge or a reconnaissance with equal gusto, Bessières was no advance guard expert, nor was he used to the responsibility of an independent command; but the Emperor had picked him, and there was no way out. At midnight on 13 December he left Posen with his staff for Thorn, where his corps was beginning to assemble.

It was an impressive command. General Tilly was already at Thorn with three regiments of light cavalry. On the 15th came Grouchy and Sahuc with four dragoon regiments apiece. Two days later General d'Hautpoul rode in at the head of his steel-clad cuirassiers. Instead of the three regiments which he normally commanded, Bessières now found himself responsible for 15.[6]

Napoleon had given him three objectives.

The first task of Marshal Bessières is to clear the plain and join his right to the light cavalry of Marshal Soult. His second task is to throw the enemy beyond the Ukra and to assist the passage of the corps of Marshal Augereau, the corps of Marshal Davout, and the cavalry of the Grand Duke of Berg. His third task will be to reconnoitre the enemy between Pultusk and Willenberg, so as to discover their intentions.

The first two tasks were the kind that Bessières thoroughly understood, and they were duly carried out. The third task was much more difficult, especially for an officer of Bessières' background. Fortunately General Grouchy was an old hand at the business, and by the time that he had written his reports he had done most of the Marshal's work for him. On 20 December Grouchy wrote:

Squadron Leader Dejean tells me that when he relieved the outposts at the end of the day he saw infantrymen with packs on their backs. An officer stepped forward and called out in French, 'Until to-morrow, Messieurs les Français; then we shall see.' What are we to infer from all this? That the retrograde movement is not pronounced, and that we shall soon be in contact with the enemy's right wing.

For Napoleon the fog of war was beginning to clear. Three days later the French infantry crossed the Ukra, and by 26 December three bloody combats were in progress. Nevertheless, the destructive battle that Napoleon was seeking failed to develop. The Prussians retreated before Ney, the Russians before Lannes and Davout, and as the weather got steadily worse the French army was ordered into cantonments. Bessières returned thankfully to the cavalry of the Guard.

In his absence the Chasseurs à Cheval had made a fine start to the campaign under Nicholas Dahlmann, their deputy colonel;[7] on Christmas Day he had led them in a charge which routed a Russian regiment and captured three cannon, for which Napoleon promoted him to general of brigade.

One of Dahlmann's troopers had sustained a particularly odd wound, even for a Guard Chasseur, having been hit by a Russian shot that was at the end of its flight. The slight hole that it made in his arm began to heal, but after nine days it began to suppurate, causing him great pain, and after a certain amount of probing a small metal splinter was taken out. It proved to be the tip of the man's sabre, which the Russian projectile had broken off.

★   ★   ★

The French army was not left in peace for long. On 12 January the Russian commander was replaced by General von Bennigsen, who moved to attack the French left, but the speed of Napoleon's concentration forced him to retire into East Prussia. The French followed, and on 6 February Murat found the Russian rearguard halted at Hof.

Murat was riding at the head of Auguste de Colbert's light cavalry brigade, followed by dragoons and d'Hautpoul's cuirassiers, when he sighted the Russian position. It was an extremely strong one. Twelve battalions of infantry were formed in squares behind a stream, supported by a horse artillery battery, three regiments of cavalry and Cossacks. The whole area was marshy, and the only bridge over the stream was so narrow that cavalry could only cross it riding four abreast. In short, everything was in the enemy's favour, and Murat would have been well advised to wait for Soult's infantry, which was close behind him. Without even waiting for his dragoons and cuirassiers, he ordered Colbert to attack with his two regiments of light cavalry.[8]

Colbert was a brave officer and a brilliant tactician, but he had been given an impossible task; in the heat of the moment he chose to execute a needlessly complicated manoeuvre. As his column passed over the bridge he tried to deploy by ordering it to form line in inverse order of battle; in other words, with the rearmost squadrons taking the right of the line.

On the parade ground it would have been simple enough: on marshy ground and under fire it proved disastrous. The leading squadrons faltered and were raked by musketry and cannon-shots; in confusion the brigade fell back towards the bridge. What next took place was later described to Colbert's son by General Digeon, who was following the light cavalry at the head of a dragoon brigade.

> Your father charged again with his second regiment, only to encounter the same obstacles as before; this time he was charged by Russian kurassiers and put in total disorder. I arrived behind him with my brigade. I'd hardly crossed that nasty little bridge when I saw a dismounted French hussar and asked him where his general was. 'Oh, the general, he's absolutely —————d.' he replied. 'And so is his horse.' I charged in my turn, and soon met the same fate as your father: I was firmly repulsed.[9]

By this time Soult's infantry were in sight and d'Hautpoul's four cuirassier regiments had arrived on the scene. D'Hautpoul, as usual, was burning to charge, all the more so since one of his regiments had been repulsed with Digeon's dragoons. In two charges led by Murat and d'Hautpoul the cuirassiers smashed all resistance by brute force, jabbing at the enemy faces with their sword-points, breaking down an infantry square, pressing their powerful horses through the line of guns and riding down the gunners. A panic-stricken Russian dragoon regiment fled at the gallop, scattering two more battalions in its flight. As the French infantry deployed the rearguard dissolved, leaving behind 800 prisoners and nine cannon.

For General d'Hautpoul it was a fine piece of work to add to his service record. To use the French expression, d'Hautpoul was an antique character, proud of his ancient name and insatiable for glory. He was nearing the end of his career. At 52 he was the oldest divisional commander in the French cavalry, and Napoleon liked his horse generals to be in the prime of life. D'Hautpoul had been a soldier for 36 years, and the prospect of retirement can hardly have been an attractive one; no doubt he was hoping to die in action at the head of his squadrons, as so many French cavalry officers of his generation had done. If so, he was soon to be disappointed.

Two days after the action at Hof, von Bennigsen drew up his army north-east of Preussisch Eylau, a village on the road to Koenigsberg. He was well prepared to fight. Having served in the Russian army for over 30 years, the stiff and autocratic Hanoverian had great faith in the courage and staying power of Russian infantry. Expecting the French infantry to attack in its usual dense columns, he deployed his own in three lines almost four miles wide, with cavalry on each wing and 300 guns in front.

At any other season the marshy country round Eylau would have made deployment difficult, but in February 1807 the bitter East Prussian winter was at its height. Lakes, streams and swamps were all covered by thick ice, and everything lay under three feet of snow. The battlefield was a vast white landscape, on which massed cavalry might charge full out.

When the main battle began on the 8th Napoleon was without his three best corps commanders, for Ney, Lannes and Davout had all been detached. Since none of the famous Storm Marshals was available, the brunt of the fighting fell on the infantry of Soult and Augereau. To counter a Russian attack on Eylau, Augereau's corps moved forward in a snow-storm, with one of Soult's divisions in support; unable to see where it was going, the head of the column lost direction, turning what should have been a frontal assault into a stumbling oblique march. Suddenly 72 Russian guns opened up with grape-shot; then Russian cavalry charged down-hill before the wind to sabre Augereau's men. In 15 minutes over 5,000 were killed or wounded.

In the cemetery south of Eylau, which had almost been captured by a Russian column, Napoleon spoke briefly to Murat, who was in attendance at Imperial Headquarters. Murat immediately rode away to lead one of the most astonishing cavalry charges ever made.

There had been no time for formal orders to be given or received. According to some sources the Emperor merely asked Murat, 'Are you going to let those fellows eat us up?' According to others he said, 'Take all your available cavalry and crush that column.' Whatever his instructions, Murat left Imperial Headquarters at the gallop, looking more like a mediaeval boyar than a French marshal, in a long-skirted green coat and fur-trimmed bonnet.

Half a mile away Generals Klein and Milhaud waited at the head of their dragoon divisions. If the troopers of their rear ranks had looked over their shoulders they would have seen the regiments of Grouchy's dragoon division drawn up behind them. To Grouchy's left, the snow-flakes drifted down on the helmets of d'Hautpoul's cuirassiers. In rear of Grouchy was Bessières with the cavalry of the Guard.

As Reserve Cavalry commander, Murat did not normally have authority over the Guard's mounted regiments, and the circumstances which led them to support his movement are obscure; but since the snow-covered ground at Eylau provided the French cavalry with the finest field of manoeuvre that it had ever had, perhaps Marshal Bessières found the temptation to charge impossible to resist.

Approaching from the direction of Eylau, Murat began to ride across the front of the leading dragoon division, then suddenly wheeled his horse and galloped towards the Russian lines. The French cavalry spurred after him, 70 squadrons rolling in three waves over the snow. As the dragoons met Russian cavalry, d'Hautpoul's division by-passed them and rode on, breaking through the first line of enemy infantry, then through the second line. Before the Russians could re-form they were hit by Grouchy and Bessières, whose impetus carried them on to the third and last line.

The charge had gone too far. As the Grenadiers à Cheval reined in their blown horses, a Russian officer stepped forward and called on them to surrender. Louis Lepic, the Grenadiers' deputy colonel,[10] pointed with his sword to the troopers at his back. 'Look at these faces!' he shouted. 'Do they look like men who would surrender?'

Unable to advance further, Murat's horsemen began the long ride back. On tired horses, they were forced to cut their way through the first two lines of infantry, which had re-formed behind them. Luckily the Russian muskets were damp with snow, and many misfired; even so the French cavalry suffered heavy losses. When Grouchy's division regained its lines it had lost over 400 horses, and the route taken by d'Hautpoul's division was marked by a trail of bloody corpses and severed limbs. Even the French bulletin described the scene of the cavalry action as a horrible sight.

Nevertheless, the colossal gamble had succeeded; the disaster that might easily have followed Augereau's defeat had been averted. 'The day had been saved by Murat and Bessières,' wrote General Zurlinden. 'It was wonderful to see those two Marshals risk their lives as though they had everything to gain by it, as if they were Volunteers of the Lot instead of Marshals of the Empire.'

They had done it at a terrible cost, and each of them had lost an old comrade. In Bessières' case it was Nicholas Dahlmann, deputy colonel of the Guard Chasseurs, who was wounded by a piece of grapeshot and died a few days later. Son of a cavalry trumpeter, Dahlmann had joined the Mounted Guides in 1796, and served in every rank from trooper to general of brigade.

Russian grapeshot also finished d'Hautpoul, who was carried with a shattered leg to a nearby château, where it took him six days to die. 'He is universally mourned,' the Bulletin announced. 'Few soldiers have had a more glorious end. His division of cuirassiers has covered itself with glory.'

III

After Eylau, von Bennigsen retired towards Koenigsberg, and the weather improved. According to Thomas Aubry, however, morale was very low in the French cavalry.

> The country was ruined from top to bottom, and bare of inhabitants: burnt villages, nothing to eat, all the roofs stripped of thatch to feed the horses, roads impassable because of the thaw . . . Three of our NCOs blew their brains out.[11]

In these conditions the French system of living off the country inflicted great hardships. 'During the whole of this terrible campaign,' Aubry relates, 'the 12th Chasseurs received not one single distribution, either of rations or of forage.'

On 17 February the army went back into winter quarters. Normally the French trooper enjoyed his winter cantonments; but in East Prussia, Aubry tells us, it was a wretched experience.

> We passed the rest of the winter in cantonments, ill-provisioned and suffering many privations. The country was like a desert; no inhabitants, not a human face to be seen, not a single woman (which is always depressing for a soldier). We were deprived of wine, suffering from hunger, reduced to collecting up crusts left by the Russians . . . But at last the first days of spring arrived, and our horses started to nibble the grass that was pushing through the earth. I must say the spring sunshine did us good, and we were overjoyed at the prospect of a new campaign.[12]

On 14 April a great cavalry review was held at Elbing in East Prussia. Wearing his colonel's undress uniform of the Guard Chasseurs, Napoleon arrived on the parade at his usual gallop, followed by a glittering cavalcade of Marshals and staff officers. Before the regiments carried out their manoeuvres he inspected them at the dismount, frequently stopping to talk to a veteran; during the inspection of the 11th Chasseurs, he asked a troop commander how many of his men had been killed in the recent campaign.

'Six, Sire,' Captain Josselin replied.

'How many wounded?'

'Four officers and thirty men, Sire.'

'Taken prisoner?'

'None, Sire!' said Josselin proudly.

'That's good! That's what I like to hear! Kill or be killed!'[13]

Pleased by the splendid turn-out of a Carabinier NCO named Chambrotte, Napoleon asked him where he came from.

'Sire,' said Chambrotte, 'when I look at the squadron standard, for me that's the steeple of my parish.'

Delighted with this answer, Napoleon turned to the Carabinier colonel and asked him why he had not recommended this brave fellow for promotion.

'Because he can neither read nor write, Sire,' the colonel replied.

'Is he a good soldier?'

'Yes!' barked the NCO, before his colonel could speak. 'Steadfast!'

'Then I will make you an officer,' Napoleon promised him.[14]

Even on this splendid occasion, the losses suffered at Eylau were all too apparent. The Grenadiers à Cheval were down to 742 men, many of whom were riding German remounts instead of their famous black horses. Although two squadrons of the newly-formed Guard Dragoons had been added to Bessières' command, the Guard cavalry was only 2,000 strong.

When the fighting re-started in the spring, however, the Reserve Cavalry mustered all of 18,000 sabres. It included 12 cuirassier regiments instead of the usual eight, the third division under General Espagne having arrived from Italy.

Born at Auch, the ancient capital of Gascony, Espagne was a fine-looking man six feet tall. He had had an unusually wide experience of the cavalry arm, having been a sergeant of dragoons, a captain of hussars, colonel of the famous 8th Cavalry, and commander of the Carabinier brigade. On 10 June his cuirassiers made a bloody début at Heilsberg, where von Bennigsen held a strong position surrounded by streams and deep ditches.

Since Napoleon had no immediate use for Murat's cavalry, the hero of Eylau was obliged to cool his heels while Soult's infantry worked round the Russian lines. This took longer than Murat expected; his patience finally ran out.

Espagne's division was drawn up in column of regiments, with the 6th Cuirassiers in front. According to Colonel de Gonneville, then a young lieutenant in the regiment, the first indication that they were about to charge was Murat's arrival at the gallop.

The Grand Duke of Berg approached from our right rear, followed by his staff; bending forward on his horse's neck, as he passed by General Espagne he flung at him only one word that I could hear – 'Charge!'[15]

It seemed quite wrong to de Gonneville that so brief an order should send 15 unsupported squadrons of heavy cavalry to the attack, and to make things worse they had to ride through a ravine by twos and fours, then re-group under fire only 200 paces from the Russian front line. If a neighbouring body of enemy cavalry had had the intelligence to charge, it could have cut Espagne's regiments to pieces, but with typical lack of initiative the Russians sat breathing their horses while the cuirassiers re-formed.

Six times that day de Gonneville's regiment charged against Russian cavalry. Colonel d'Avenay's sword was covered with blood and even Murat was moved to remark on it. 'Pass my regiment in review, Your Highness,' d'Avenay suggested. 'You'll see that every trooper's blade is the same as mine.' At the end of the day three of the regiment's 22 officers were dead and 14, including d'Avenay, had been wounded. Collecting his shaken troopers, de Gonneville passed a miserable night.

> The baggage had not come up, so we had no bread or anything to eat. I had a little tea brewed in a piece of canister-shot case . . . The day was spent burying our dead and organizing the living as best we could; we made up two weak squadrons.[16]

Next day a rumour went round the division that Murat had been severely reprimanded for committing the cavalry too soon; when Napoleon rode through the 6th Cuirassiers' lines, de Gonneville noticed that the Grand Duke of Berg followed him wearing 'a tolerably sheepish air'.

It took Espagne's division several days to recover its nerve. Four days after Heilsberg, as the Reserve Cavalry marched towards Koenigsberg, the leading squadrons of the 4th Cuirassiers entered a wood. De Gonneville's regiment was about to follow when the troopers of the 4th came riding back in disorder. De Gonneville immediately halted his squadron, expecting it to be charged by a legion of Russians at any moment. 'The 7th and 8th Cuirassiers also formed up at a gallop and we waited. Nothing came. It was a panic!'

★   ★   ★

On 14 June Napoleon closed the campaign by the great victory at Friedland, fought appropriately on the anniversary of Marengo. In Murat's absence the cavalry was put under the command of Grouchy, an arrangement which General de Nansouty did not like. Nansouty was at his most unco-operative, and badly lacking in judgment; when he first took up position the Carabinier brigade was posted behind a hedgerow, and on the right flank the muzzles of the front rank's horses were practically touching it. On Grouchy's orders Nansouty moved his division to reinforce Marshal Lannes, who was under great pressure, but the cuirassier general was uneasy in this new position, which he thought might be out-flanked.

Soon afterwards, returning from a charge, Grouchy was amazed and outraged to see the cuirassier regiments of Nansouty's division moving rearwards at a grand trot, leaving a dangerous gap in Lannes' battle line. Galloping after the departing cuirassiers, Grouchy bellowed at Nansouty to bring them back.

Nansouty obeyed.

IV

When the campaign ended, the armies fraternized while the Emperors met at Tilsit. Except with the half-mad Cossack hetman Platov, who was said to take his personal sorcerer into battle, Napoleon's Marshals had much in common with the devious and boastful generals of the Tsar. The Grand Duke Constantine went about with Marshal Murat, clearly enjoying the company of the inn-keeper's son; they were often to be seen riding side by side behind Napoleon and Alexander, laughing like madmen.

The goodwill extended even to the other ranks. When the French and Russian guards regiments attended a joint banquet, Dorsenne's grenadiers went into dinner arm-in-arm with their recent enemies, looking almost dainty beside Alexander's towering guardsmen.

By the Treaty signed at Tilsit the Tsar agreed to enforce the Continental blockade and Prussia was bound to pay enormous reparations to Napoleon, who confiscated her territories west of the Elbe and her Polish provinces. The French Emperor stood at the height of his power, though he had no illusions that the peace would be a lasting one. As part of his insurance for the future, he was planning to increase the French cavalry to unprecedented numbers, provided he could obtain enough horses.

For the regiments on foreign service the acquisition of remounts was relatively easy. For the depôt commanders in France it was much more difficult, not least because of the French civil servant's traditional reluctance to authorize any kind of payment. Faced by a request to provide money for horse purchase, French officials played for time by setting up an enquiry that could last for months.

Fully aware of this, Napoleon issued a typical directive. 'If a regiment has 300 men at its dépôt and only 12 or 15 horses, by all means instigate an enquiry; but first of all provide 300 horses.'

Meanwhile the call-up of young Frenchmen to the colours continued. Within a few months of peace being signed an officer at the dépôt of the 5th Hussars was writing to his colonel:

> You know that there are 250 hussars here counting the artificers, that the next conscription will provide 415, and that within a month 380 remounts should arrive here before joining the *escadrons de guerre*. So in a few months' time you will have more than 1,200 white pelisses, with whom I hope we shall do great things.

⋆　　⋆　　⋆

Nothing better illustrates the French cavalry's spirit at the close of 1807 than an incident which occurred at Breslau, the capital of Prussian Silesia. Towards the end of the year, a dinner given by the French dragoon colonel Lamothe was attended by some of the city's most charming Prussian and Polish ladies; a number of dashing French cavalry officers were also present, including Auguste de Colbert and the colonel of the 3rd Hussars, and a good deal of champagne was drunk.

As dessert was about to be served a French dragoon orderly arrived, bearing a document which required the signature of General Fournier, one of Lamothe's guests.

'Right, my lad,' said Fournier, who was in an expansive mood. 'I'll give you one that you won't rub out in a hurry. Stand at the end of the room there and hold it up for me, if you're not afraid.'

'Afraid, General? I don't know the word,' the dragoon assured him. Walking to the end of the room, he turned to face Fournier and held up the paper with a steady hand. Armed with a pistol provided by his host, Fournier took careful aim at his target and put a bullet through it; then, to everyone's delight, he announced that the dragoon's conduct had earned him a 40-franc reward.

The man never moved, and continued to hold out the paper at arm's length.

'If you'd like to add your initial, General,' he said hopefully, 'I'm ready for it.'

Fournier added a bottle of wine to the 40-franc reward instead.[17]

4

Lasalle

I

According to General Charles Lasalle, no French hussar ought to live beyond the age of 30. When the Polish campaign ended he was already 32.

Born in Metz of a good family, Lasalle was an outstanding example of the double culture, a combination of Teutonic martial instincts and Gallic charm. Because of his devastating good looks and scandalous reputation women found him irresistible, and he took full advantage of the fact. For all his womanising, however, he was capable of deep affection; in his early twenties he fell madly in love with Joséphine Berthier, wife of the Marshal's younger brother and four years Lasalle's senior. In 1803, after Berthier had divorced her, Lasalle married her and treated her children as his own.

To his men, Lasalle was everything a French cavalry general ought to be: expert with a horse and a sabre, devoting his life to smoking, drinking, fighting and making love. They were fond of recounting his famous *brimades,* such as the time at Salamanca when he had had four hussars seal off the narrow street through which the pots of night soil were carried away, and thrown the town's sewage disposal system into utter chaos. Or the occasion when, riding through Perugia late at night, he had halted his column outside a mansion where a ball was in progress and urged his horse up the steps into the ballroom. He had then accepted a glass of punch, made his horse pirouette in time to the music, waved to his admiring troopers through a window and ridden back to join them, all without ever having left the saddle.

Next to Kellermann, Lasalle was the most gifted horse general in the French army, a dashing opportunist with an infallible *coup d'oeil*; but his career, like Kellermann's, had been a mixture of brilliant exploits and

60

bad luck. In the First Italian Campaign he had been unstoppable both on and off the field, charging down a rocky hillside at Rivoli to demoralize the Austrian centre, riding with 25 troopers through the Austrian lines at midnight to sleep with an Italian marchesa. In Egypt, where he commanded the 22nd Chasseurs, he had been deeply unhappy, writing gloomy letters back to France complaining that he had no friends in the regiment and that all his hair was falling out. Taken prisoner with the rest of the army there, he had returned to France in 1800, but missed the battle of Marengo.

After four years as colonel of the 10th Hussars he was promoted general of brigade and given a dragoon command; as a result his talents were wasted in the Austerlitz campaign. Then in 1806, at the head of his Infernal Brigade of hussars,[1] he proved himself one of the best advance guard generals in Europe.

To the local inhabitants in Prussia, his brigade's nickname seemed highly appropriate. Whenever one of his units arrived at a town, two parties were organized to comb the place, one to requisition food and drink, another to search for horseshoes and nails. Lasalle himself went straight to the magistrate's office to confiscate all the maps of the district. By the time that he rode out, everything of use to a light cavalry brigade had been transferred to his supply waggon and his troopers' saddle-bags. Unlike most other French cavalry generals, however, he did not loot: he took only the necessities of war.

For his services in the Jena campaign he was promoted general of division and given twelve regiments of hussars and chasseurs.

As a light cavalry *divisionnaire* he had no equal. Famous for the relentless fury of his pursuits, he never tired his horses by useless galloping on the battlefield. 'Look at those mad sods,' he would murmur to an aide de camp, as enemy cavalry galloped to attack his trotting regiments. 'Let them wear themselves out.' Keeping his division at the trot, when the right moment arrived he would hold his pipe in the air and press his horse into a triple gallop; just when the enemy's horses were beginning to tire they were hit by Lasalle's troopers riding full out.

Despite his flamboyance and madcap exploits Lasalle was a strict and sometimes pitiless disciplinarian; on one occasion he kept two hussar regiments halted under artillery fire as a punishment, with himself mounted in front of them. He knew every trick or bad habit that impaired a cavalry unit's ability to march and fight, such as over-clipping fetlocks, riding in wet boots, returning damp sabres to the scabbard; he was hard on any man whom he caught over-loading his horse, cutting firewood with his sabre, or exposing his musketoon to the weather. He

demanded absolute obedience, in return for which he worked tirelessly
for his men's welfare.

In the terrible winter of 1807 he organized supplies of candles and
charcoal, fur coats and blankets. Taking over the local mills, he formed
his men into night shifts, making them grind corn, mill flour, and bake
bread. Troopers who had been cobblers in civilian life were set to work
repairing the division's boots and mending the horses' harness. Flour
and rye were fermented to make a tonic which the men hated having to
drink, but which Lasalle insisted was doing them good. In short, he did
everything possible to ensure that his division consisted of fit, well-
armed troopers, riding healthy horses, and carrying four spare horseshoes and 60 nails in their saddle-bags.

The results were disappointing. At Eylau his division was kept
inactive on the French left; at Heilsberg it was dispersed by cavalry
charges and artillery fire, forcing Lasalle to take refuge in an infantry
square. When the Polish campaign ended his command was reduced to
two brigades and attached to the corps of Marshal Davout.

His career seemed to have reached a dead end, since Austria, Prussia
and Russia had all made peace and the English would only fight at sea.
Lasalle needed the stimuli provided by action and danger; without them,
the handsome young general's extravagant gaiety alternated with fits of
black depression. He knew that he had earned Marshal Berthier's
enmity by cuckholding his brother; now he began to suspect that
people close to the Emperor who envied his success were working against
him.

For the time being he consoled himself with Joséphine, who had
travelled from Paris to join him, and other delights of the flesh. At
Elbing and Warsaw a serviette was often to be seen fluttering from a
flagpole fixed to the balcony of his house, signifying that his officers were
welcome to dine at his table, on which 20 *couverts* had been laid. Once
the places were all occupied, the serviette was removed.

These dinner parties helped to keep up his officers' morale, morale
which left a good deal to be desired. Poland was an unpopular station
even in peace-time. The country had few resources, the hunting was
poor, and game was almost non-existent; moreover the Russian-hating
Poles had much goodwill towards the French army, consequently
requisitioning was forbidden. Lasalle was longing to be gone. Garrison
life did not suit his temperament, and the climate was ruining his wife's
health. Worst of all he had earned the Emperor's disapproval.

During the cavalry review at Elbing, Lasalle had asked him for command of the Guard Chasseurs, but Napoleon considered him too head-

strong and ebullient for such a post. So far from accepting the decision gracefully, in the summer of 1807 Lasalle repeated his request in writing, a pushing action that Napoleon did not like. Both requests having failed, Lasalle began to sulk and to complain openly at the reduction of his division. Most unwisely, he wrote a sarcastic letter to the Minister of War, pointing out that he had recently held 'the most brilliant post in the army', and actually daring to imply criticism of the Emperor.

My presence at the head of so few troops being of little use, I beg you to give me leave to go to Paris, or alternatively a command more suitable to my rank . . . I do not think that His Majesty has cause to complain of my services in the last campaign . . . (yet) for the first time since I have served under his orders His Majesty has not cited my name in his report.[2]

Apparently bent on committing professional suicide, he next applied for a posting to the colonies. In the spring of 1808 he was posted back to France instead, to take command of a cavalry force that was assembling at Poitiers and lead it to Spain.

Spain was officially France's ally, but the alliance was not popular with the Spanish people; the regiments at Poitiers were destined to join a French army of occupation that was being organized.

For Lasalle it was hardly an exciting command. Apart from the 10th and 22nd Chasseurs, the cavalry at Poitiers consisted of provisional units and *régiments de marche*, totally unlike the crack formations he normally led.[3] Even supposing that Spain declared war, which seemed unlikely, there was not much glory to be gained from fighting the Spanish army, which was one of the most backward in Europe.[4] But policing Spain was at least preferable to stagnating in Poland. Handing his wife into a carriage, Lasalle drove across Europe in high spirits, inviting to dinner the officers of the French hussar regiments he found stationed along his route.

He could well afford to do so. On 10 March 1808 he was made a Count of the Empire, with two dotations totalling 50,000 francs a year.

II

In March there were over 120,000 French troops in the Peninsula,[5] commanded by Murat from headquarters at Madrid. The Spanish king and his family were virtual prisoners in France, and Spain seethed with rumours that Napoleon intended to put a Bonaparte on the throne. In early May, after an abortive rising at Madrid, resistance councils and volunteer units began to form all over the country.

To hold his communications with France, Murat stationed 25,000 men between Burgos and San Sebastian; mostly conscripts, they were under the orders of Marshal Bessières, newly-created Duke of Istria.

Bessières' main task was to keep open the road between Burgos and Madrid; his greatest fear was that Spanish insurgents would move across it, cutting him off from Murat and cutting Murat off from France. He was still nervous in an independent command, and he missed the guidance of Roussel, his old Chief of Staff, who had been decapitated by a Russian cannon-shot at Heilsberg. When Lasalle came riding into Burgos at the head of his light cavalry, Bessières was very glad to see him. Apart from being an old friend, Lasalle was just the man Bessières needed to discover the intentions of the enemy.

From Burgos the cavalry fanned out south and west, into a parched landscape from which many of the local people had fled. Some places were completely deserted, ghost towns where the only sound to be heard was the croaking of ravens in church belfries. The 2nd Hussars spent four days in an empty village without ever managing to learn its name.

Although he now commanded the whole of Bessières' cavalry, for the time being Lasalle led the advance guard, which comprised the 10th and 22nd Chasseurs, 2,000 infantrymen and six guns. On 6 June he reached Torquemada, 40 miles from Burgos, to find armed Spanish peasants defending a bridge over the river Pisuerga. The bridge was barricaded with carriages and furniture, making what the insurgents thought was a formidable obstacle; but they reckoned without the fury that the sight of armed civilians always aroused in French soldiers of the period.

The action was short and bloody, and the French gave no quarter. Lasalle was as angry as his men, for underneath the gallant manner and the elegant uniform was a ruthless *homme de métier* who had been brutalized by ten years of warfare. On the battlefield, an enemy soldier who threw down his weapon might expect to be spared by Lasalle's troopers; at Torquemada, a peasant who tried to surrender received a sabre slash across his face. The Spanish fled in terror, leaving the town at the mercy of the French. It was burnt to the ground. Handing the postmaster a sum equal to 6,000 francs, Lasalle told him to rebuild his posthouse and rode on to Palencia, where he established his headquarters.

Twenty-five miles to the south-west of Palencia lay Valladolid, seat of Don Gregorio de la Cuesta, the Captain-General of Castile. Cuesta had no regular troops except for 300 cavalrymen and only four guns, but he had organized 5,000 local men and issued them with arms. When the news of Torquemada reached him he collected his forces and moved north-east to meet Lasalle, who kept himself well informed of Cuesta's movements. On 11 June Lasalle mounted his horse, lit his favourite pipe, and marched towards Valladolid, picking up two brigades of infantry on the way. The following day he rode in sight of Cabezón, where Cuesta's volunteers were drawn up in a single line on the river bank.

As at Torquemada, the Pisuerga was spanned by a long stone bridge, on which Cuesta had very unwisely placed his four guns; even more unwisely, he had posted his cavalry in front of the bridge, on the bank nearest the approaching French. When Lasalle saw these dispositions he immediately ordered his men to attack.

The massacre of Torquemada was repeated. Cuesta's band dissolved, leaving 400 dead, all four guns and 4,000 muskets behind them. Reporting his casualties as 12 killed and 30 wounded, Lasalle rode on to occupy Valladolid.

Cuesta was not yet finished. The 68-year-old Spanish general was a brave and stubborn man, and in spite of his defeat the Castilian peasants were still willing to fight for him. Realising that they needed regular troops and artillery to back them up, Cuesta sought help from General Joaquin Blake, who was organizing four divisions into the Army of Galicia.

The Irish-born Blake was no less brave than Cuesta, but unlike Cuesta he was a realist. Pointing out that he had only 30 guns, and Cuesta none at all, he protested that to march against the French even with their joint forces was madness. Using his seniority, Cuesta insisted on adding the Galician regulars to his Castilian volunteers.

From Valladolid Lasalle had returned to Palencia, where he was joined by Madame Lasalle and their little daughter.[6] For the next three weeks he sent his patrols out into the countryside and his couriers galloping back to Burgos. By 7 July Bessières knew that his nightmare had become a reality; an army of 20,000 Spanish was moving to drive a wedge between Burgos and Madrid.

Murat was no longer in command at the capital, having left for his new kingdom of Naples. Bessières therefore sent an urgent call for help to the Emperor in France, who acted at once. Ten seasoned infantry battalions under General Mouton, recently arrived at Bayonne from Germany, were given marching orders for Spain; three squadrons of Guard cavalry were seconded to Bessières from Madrid. As soon as they were all under his hand, Bessières marched to join Lasalle.

On 13 July the whole force moved out of Palencia with three days' bread ration in the men's packs and five days' supply of biscuit in the waggons. The advance was led by Lasalle's chasseurs, followed by 20 battalions of infantry, the three squadrons of Guard cavalry and 32 guns. As dawn rose over the wheatfields of the Tierra de Campos the marching columns must have made an impressive sight; but since 13 of the infantry battalions consisted entirely of conscripts, Bessières knew that his force was not so impressive as it looked. In blazing heat his men marched south-west to Ampudia, where they took a few hours' rest. At two o'clock next morning, wearing his best uniform, Bessières rode out to fight the first independent battle of his career.

At several points along the line of march the advance guard found the bodies of French soldiers who had been tortured and mutilated by the insurgents. Bessières ordered his troops to look at them as they passed, hoping that the sight of these gruesome remains would stiffen morale. Presently Lasalle's scouts reported that the enemy was drawn up east of the town of Medina de Rio Seco; Bessières rode forward to assess the ground.

Ahead of him the road ran up a gentle incline towards the town. To the left of the road, three of Blake's Galician divisions were formed in line on the forward slope. A mile behind them, but to the right of the road and on the reverse slope, Cuesta had posted Blake's fourth division and the Castilian volunteers. In other words the two bodies were stationed at seven and two of the clock-face, with nothing to guard the open space on Blake's left flank but two regiments of horse.

With 20,000 men in line, Cuesta outnumbered the French by three to two; nevertheless Bessières decided to attack. On the French right, Mouton's battalions began a long advance towards Cuesta's reserve; on the left, infantry under Merle marched to engage Blake. Lasalle was in the centre of the French line, at the head of the 10th and 22nd Chasseurs. Suddenly he led these two regiments full out up the slope and into the cavalry on Blake's flank. After a brief sabre fight the enemy squadrons scattered; wheeling to the left, Lasalle's 800 troopers fell on Blake's infantry. The first two battalions collapsed; threatened by the advance of Merle's division, the whole of Blake's line gave way. Lasalle rode away to report to Bessières.

He arrived at a critical moment. On the French right, Mouton's infantrymen were fighting for their lives against Cuesta's reserve, which had suddenly come to life. Enveloped by 300 Spanish cavalry, a company of the 4th Light had been practically destroyed. Galloping forward to assess the situation, Bessières found himself completely out of his depth: even Mouton's staff, according to a young aide de camp, could see that the Marshal did not know what to do.

When Marshal Bessières arrived before our division, we were struck by his air of indecision. Having just made his charge on the left flank, General Lasalle rode up with his sabre dripping blood. The plight of our voltigeurs demanded a quick decision. General Mouton was pressing for one. General Lasalle told Marshal Bessières, 'It needs a charge!' Without waiting for an answer, he put himself at the head of a squadron of Guard dragoons, some Polish light horsemen of the Guard, and fifty *gendarmes d'élite*.[7]

These Guard squadrons were in the presence of their Colonel-General, and they were not supposed to charge without his authority. Perhaps Bessières gave the squadron leaders some approving gesture that Mouton's aide failed to notice; perhaps the sight of Lasalle with his sabre in the air carried them away. Willingly or not, Bessières watched his mounted reserve riding to the attack, led by the man whom Napoleon had twice refused a command in the Guard cavalry.

At the head of his three squadrons, Lasalle routed the Spanish horse, giving Mouton's shaken infantry a chance to rally. They were alarmingly slow to take it. Fortunately Merle's victorious infantry arrived from the left to threaten Cuesta's right, and Lasalle seized the opportunity to lead a further charge with the 10th Chasseurs. The Spanish broke and streamed away down the road to Benavente, where many of them were caught and sabred by the French cavalry.

The victory was complete, but it had been narrowly won. Had it not been for Lasalle and Merle, General Cuesta might well have defeated a Napoleonic Marshal in the field.

★   ★   ★

Napoleon was sure that Bessières had won a decisive victory and established Joseph Bonaparte on the Spanish throne. He was quickly disillusioned. A week after Rio Seco, General Dupont surrendered his army of 18,000 to the Spanish at Bailén; on 21 August Junot was beaten at Vimeiro by Portugese insurgents and the newly-arrived English, who shipped his army back to France by sea. King Joseph abandoned Madrid, Burgos was evacuated; by the autumn of 1808 the remaining French forces in Spain had withdrawn behind the river Ebro.

Furious at the check to his plans, the loss of territory, and the immense damage done to French military prestige, Napoleon marched into Spain with three crack army corps, four divisions of cavalry and the Imperial Guard.

III

Burgos and Madrid were swiftly re-taken. With the Emperor in command, Lasalle looked forward to winning fresh laurels in a glorious campaign, but Fate decided otherwise. His friend Bessières was replaced by Marshal Soult, who had no particular liking for ambitious young cavalry generals; feeling that the new corps commander's reports were failing to do him justice, Lasalle complained about it in a letter to Joséphine:

> In the most recent report on the fighting at Burgos I was not mentioned . . . My two regiments of chasseurs surpassed themselves and made a horrible carnage among those disgusting Spaniards, yet no-one said anything about them. I saw sabre wounds eighteen inches long, and severed arms. It was magnificent. *Eh bien!* Not a word about us, so what's to be done? . . . I'm afraid this injustice is due to the change of Marshal.[8]

To add to his depression Joséphine had gone back to France, and she never wanted to campaign with him again. 'She is a coward now,' Lasalle joked, though secretly he was proud of the way she had tended the wounded at Rio Seco. For a brief moment during the battle, she and her little daughter had been in Spanish hands, and no doubt she had decided that Spain was too dangerous a place for them. Also, perhaps she preferred not to see at first hand the brutality of which her handsome husband was capable.

Fortunately there was plenty of work to keep him occupied. Somewhere in the peninsula the English redcoats were at last within reach, and Napoleon was determined to destroy them, if only they could be found in time. At the head of four regiments Lasalle rode deep into Andalusia, sending back model reports on the local Spanish forces.

> I have just caught a peasant who was taking a letter from General Galluzo to the alcalde of this village. Galluzo's headquarters are in the inn at the village of Nuevo. The stones underneath the arches of the bridge there have been removed and the parapets have been lowered; holes have been pierced at intervals and filled with powder. It is impossible for a vehicle for pass, and difficult even for a man riding a horse. The batteries are all on the left bank. I am sending a reconnaissance under one of my aides de camp to Puente del Conde, wrongly marked on the map as Puente del Cardenal.

The Emperor, however, was not interested in General Galluzo; he was only interested in finding the English. By the middle of January 1809 he was not even very interested in them. On the 17th he handed the command in Spain to Marshal Soult and returned to France; the following month Marshal Bessières was recalled to Paris, leaving General Lasalle to advance his career as best he could.

Lasalle was beginning to think that he might very well die in Spain, and his letters to Joséphine became increasingly mournful.

> I read this morning that Cathérine followed Peter I when he went to the wars; I grumbled for a bit, and complained to myself about your lack of courage, but then I realised I was wrong to do so. What would become of my daughter who you tell me is so lovely. For her I can make every sacrifice, and the greatest of all is not to be with you, my beloved Joséphine.[9]

On 2 March he wrote out his will, leaving each of her three sons one of his Imperial titles[10] and an income from his rents; he also recorded his intention to adopt them as his own children. In view of his absence from France, he wrote, he had no way of knowing whether these arrangements were good in law; if not, he desired the will to be given to the Emperor for execution, 'begging him to add this last favour to those which His Majesty has constantly conferred on me'.

*   *   *

Lasalle spent the last few weeks of his service in Spain attached to the corps of Marshal Victor, which assembled at Talavera at the beginning of March. A pre-war professional, Victor had served for ten years in the ranks of the French artillery; he was an old hand at Spanish campaigning, having led an infantry brigade in Catalonia in 1794.

His orders were to cross the Tagus and invade Portugal in conjunction with Marshal Soult, which was not an easy task. Soult's corps was 200 miles away to the north, while immediately to Victor's front lay a Spanish army commanded by Cuesta. Totally unlike the Castilian bands that he had led in 1808, Cuesta's force consisted of three regular infantry divisions, 5,000 cavalry and 30 guns; he was confident that he could beat Victor, whom he outnumbered by almost two to one.

Victor was equally confident. In background and appearance he was the exact opposite of Cuesta, but the middle-aged ex-gunner and the white-haired old nobleman had certain things in common; in addition to being mediocre generals, they were both brave and stubborn men. On 28 March they fought each other on a plain south of the town of Medellin.

Nine years earlier, Victor had commanded the French left in the fighting withdrawal at Marengo, and the lessons he had learned there proved invaluable at Medellin. For two hours the outnumbered French retired before an arc of advancing Spanish infantrymen, who called out that they would show no quarter. General Lasalle may well have felt thankful that he had put his affairs in order. His four cavalry regiments were on the left of Victor's line and in the worst position on the battlefield, for the Spanish advance was forcing them back into a trap formed by a loop of the river Guadiana.[11] His squadrons retired at a walk, stopping every fifty paces to turn and face the enemy. Each time they made the *demi-tour* a mass of Spanish horse led by lancers broke into a trot, hoping to catch them as they manoeuvred. Fortunately the Spaniards did not have the courage to charge, owing to the astonishingly cool behaviour of Lasalle and his men.

After every change of direction, Lasalle's officers dressed their lines as calmly and deliberately as if they had been on parade at the regimental depôt; meanwhile, as one of them describes in his memoirs, the general rode slowly back and forth in front of his division 'with a lofty and fearless air'.[12]

Finally the hard-pressed French infantry reached the line on which Victor had decided he must stand. The first troops to arrive were on the French right, which was covered by Latour-Maubourg's division of dragoons. When the Spanish were almost on top of Victor's artillery, the French dragoon general charged; it was exactly what Cuesta, riding with three cavalry regiments on the Spanish left, had been hoping for. Intending to take the dragoons in flank the fierce old man threw his horse into a gallop, and his regiments followed him; then suddenly they wheeled their horses without having struck a blow and rode away, unhorsing Cuesta in their flight.

Lasalle immediately led his squadrons against the cavalry in front of him and cut it to pieces. The Spanish infantrymen, who had fought with some bravery for nearly five hours, began to waver; as the French line advanced at the *pas de charge* they broke and ran.

Keyed up by the strain of the long withdrawal the French cavalry was in a particularly murderous mood, and butchered the fugitives for miles. More than once that day Lasalle's troopers spurred towards dark shapes in the distance, having mistaken them for Spanish soldiers. They turned out to be unusually large vultures, which were flocking to the area in hundreds.

General Lasalle always regretted that the French press under-estimated the number of Spaniards killed at Medellin, which he himself put at 14,000.

*　　*　　*

After the battle Victor ordered his corps into cantonments round Mérida, although the spring campaigning season had only just begun. Lasalle was detached to Guarena, where he spent ten frustrating days. He could see little chance of further fighting in Estremadura, and none whatever of advancement. With the Emperor's departure Spain had become a side-show once more; furthermore it was not just to exercise the horses that Imperial Headquarters had moved from Valladolid to Paris in six days. For months the rumour that Austria was mobilizing had been current in Spain, and no-one doubted that a great new campaign was being planned. Lasalle seemed to have been forgotten.

Then on 7 April a courier from corps headquarters brought him a letter from his friend Pierre Sémélé, who stated that General Merlin was on his way to Mérida to take over Lasalle's division, and carrying orders for Lasalle to report to Paris. He hardly dared believe it. 'I see a hope of crushing you against my heart,' he wrote to Joséphine, 'and the children as well. I shall be more use in Germany than I am in Spain, where everything is nearly over.'

He was afraid that his orders would arrive too late. Guarena was 1,000 miles from Paris, where Bessières was already organizing transport for the Guard to Strasbourg and checking the height of the infantry packs; it was even further from Strasbourg, where no doubt the staff at the Hotel de la Lanterne were hiding the best glasses, and covering up the mirrors, against the arrival of the French light cavalry.

Marshal Berthier was already there. On 10 April, from Strasbourg, he was writing to the Minister of War:

> The reserve of cavalry, which will be commanded by the Marshal Duke of Istria, will comprise two divisions of light cavalry commanded by Generals Lasalle and Montbrun, a division of heavy cavalry commanded by General de Nansouty, composed of six regiments having 12 pieces of artillery, and a division of six provisional regiments of dragoons.

IV

On 29 April, at Burgos, General Thiébault was awakened by clanking scabbards and the sound of heavy objects being dragged up the stairs outside his bedroom. Getting out of bed, he lit a candle and saw that it was three o'clock in the morning. Opening the door, Thiébault found Lasalle and his senior aide de camp struggling with several crates of the best local wines.

After the two old friends had spent the day together, Thiébault celebrated with a small dinner party. One of Thiébault's guests was the politician P.-L. Roederer, who came from Lasalle's birthplace of Metz; he was delighted to meet the famous young cavalry general from Lorraine, who made a deep impression on him. 'I knew he was one of our best light cavalry generals,' he wrote. 'I had heard of his courage and his intellect. But I was 100 leagues away from realising what great qualities he had.'[13]

Over dinner Thiébault told Lasalle that it was very dangerous for him and his aide to be travelling alone through Spain, but Lasalle pointed out that an escort would only slow him down.

'I'm six weeks behind in the German campaign,' he explained, 'and the Emperor has given me a superb division. I shall be desolate if he starts without me.' He intended only a brief stay in Paris: 'I shall arrive at 5 in the morning, order a pair of boots, give my wife another infant, and be on my way.'

Roederer agreed with Thiébault that he should take an escort, adding that a man who could render France valuable service had a duty to take care of himself.

'But I've lived a full life,' Lasalle argued. 'What's the point of living? To earn a reputation, get ahead, make your fortune? Well, I'm a general of division at 33, and last year the Emperor gave me an income of 50,000 francs.'

'Then you must live to enjoy it,' Roederer replied.

'Not at all,' said Lasalle. 'To have achieved it, that's satisfaction enough. I love battles, being in the noise, the smoke, the movement; so long as you've made your name, and you know your wife and children won't want for anything, that's all that matters. For myself, I'm ready to die to-morrow.'

At 10 p.m., when the general's carriage arrived, five German chasseurs presented themselves; Thiébault explained that they would act as escort.

'But I've already told you,' Lasalle protested, 'I don't *want* an escort.'

'But *I* want you to have one,' said Thiébault.

Swearing amiably in German at the troopers, Lasalle told them that if they tried to go with him he would mount the postilion's horse and charge them. Thiébault ordered them to ride with the carriage as far as

Celada, fifty paces in its rear.

Eighteen days later General Lasalle joined the French army at Vienna. His first thought was to provide suitable female company for the officers of his new division.

5

1809

For the renewal of the war with France, Austria was able to put 300,000 front-line troops in the field, but the mounted arm had not fully recovered from its losses at Austerlitz. Moreover the Austrian cavalry was thinly spread; 44 squadrons were serving in Poland and another 44 in Italy, leaving only 164 for the German campaign.[1] The kurassiers still wore the demi-cuirasse,[2] which made them vulnerable in a mêlée, and the light cavalry lacked the spirit and aggressive scouting techniques of the French.

Morale, however, was high, and Austrian soldiers had great faith in their new Commander-in-Chief, the stern and brilliant Archduke Karl. At 37 he was one of the most experienced generals in Europe. He was also, as befitted an Emperor's son,[3] one of the most chivalrous; his favourite dictum, which he had incorporated in the revised drill manual, was 'Ein Kriegsmann muss ein Ehrensmann seyn' – A man of war must be a man of honour.

Twice in his career he had been frustrated by the cumbersome machinery of the Empire; in 1799, when the Aulic Council's indecision had prevented him from exploiting his victory at Stockach, and again in 1805, when the necessary orders to join the Allies had arrived too late for him to fight at Austerlitz. In 1809 there were no such impediments. Despite the intrigues of the Empress and his subordinate Hiller, who both hated him, he had been given formal authority over the War Council. Combined with his royal status, his tremendous reputation, and the fact that he had had no part in the blunders of 1805, this authority put him in a position of unprecedented power. Unchallenged in the Kriegsrath, supreme as Generalissimus of the finest army that Austria had ever put in the field, he seemed not only dedicated to his task, but uniquely equipped to carry it out.

He made a bad start to his campaign. On 10 April he marched into

Bavaria with 200,000 men and split his force into three; Bellegarde was left on the north bank of the Danube with 50,000 men, while Karl's main body and 60,000 under Hiller crossed the river. On the 21st Hiller was beaten and forced back on Landshut; the following day Karl himself was defeated at Eckmuhl.

Although Eckmuhl was mainly an infantry affair, the French Guard cavalry fought a sharp action against Austrian kurassiers, which Captain von Grueber describes in his memoirs.[4] Attacked by a Grenadier à Cheval, von Grueber managed to block a sword thrust, but the man's fist struck him on the chest. A blow from a Mounted Grenadier's fist, the Austrian discovered, was almost as effective as a sabre cut; blood spurted from his nose and mouth, and for a moment he was blinded and virtually helpless. The surgeon who later examined him told him that he would need at least six weeks to recover; he was back in the saddle in three.

★   ★   ★

After the check at Eckmuhl the Archduke crossed to the northern bank of the Danube, leaving nothing between the French army and Vienna but Hiller's three beaten corps. Bessières was sent after them with a mixed force consisting of cavalry and von Wrede's Bavarians.

Bessières, who had assumed command of the Reserve Cavalry in Murat's absence, displayed no sign of his old hesitation. Indeed, he seemed to have inherited Murat's recklessness along with his post, and when the retreating Austrians suddenly turned to attack von Wrede the situation looked extremely serious. An aide to General Jacquinot, commanding the cavalry advance guard, was sent galloping to warn the Marshal, whom he found sitting down to lunch at Neumarkt.[5] Bessières was at his most charming and out-going.

'Tell your general that the more Austrians there are, the more prisoners we shall take,' he said gaily. Then, knowing that the young aide was from the Midi, and would understand the Quercynois patois, he gripped him by the arm and added, '*Anen lous esponti coumo de froumatché de Rocamadou!*'[6]

It was a boast worthy of his flamboyant predecessor, since he had only 14,000 men against Hiller's force of perhaps 40,000; fortunately the Austrian commander learned soon afterwards of Karl's defeat at Eckmuhl, and broke off the action to continue his retreat. At the beginning of May he crossed the Danube to unite with Karl and Bellegarde.

As the two armies were now separated by the river, the French marched unopposed to Vienna, which lies on the Danube's southern bank. On 11 May 20 howitzers began to bombard the city, despite an Austrian delegation's protests that the Archduchess Elizabeth was in residence at the capital and feeling far from well. On the 13th Vienna surrendered, enabling Napoleon to cross to the Danube's northern bank, where he expected Karl to offer him battle.

The Archduke did not intend to oppose the crossing: on the contrary he was anxious to let Napoleon proceed to his own destruction. The Danube was swollen by rain and the currents were strong; as soon as the French army had crossed Karl planned to launch stone-filled barges up-river, smashing the bridges in Napoleon's rear. The French army would then be trapped on the plain of the Marchfeld with a river at its back.

In 1809 the Marchfeld's only features were a handful of villages, four of the execrable Austrian roads, and a stream called the Russbach. There was no other water, except in the ditches that encircled the villages, no swamps or woods. On this tremendous field of manoeuvre, which was ideally suited to massed cavalry charges, Karl intended to check the career of the House of Hapsburg's arch enemy and to destroy his army.

II

The French army made the crossing in two stages, using the island of Lobau as a stepping-stone. A bridge was built from the Vienna bank to the island, which divides the Danube into two branches; then a floating bridge supported by pontoons was laid from Lobau to the northern bank. At 6 p.m. on 20 May the first French infantry division arrived on the Marchfeld, followed by Lasalle with his four light cavalry regiments and Espagne's division of cuirassiers. Soon afterwards a section collapsed on the *grand pont,* as the bridge from the Vienna bank into Lobau was called. General Marulaz, who commanded the light cavalry division immediately behind Lasalle, found his force split into three; one squadron of the 3rd Chasseurs was on the Marchfeld, the rest of that regiment was crossing from Lobau, and the remaining regiments of the division were still on the Vienna bank. The bridge was not repaired until 3 o'clock next morning.

To maintain its foothold on the Marchfeld it was vital for the French advance guard to hold the villages of Gross Aspern and Essling, which were just over two miles apart. Connected by a trench, these places were natural strongpoints, surrounded by copses and ditches. Most of their houses were built of stone. North-east of Essling was a public granary, three stories high, which could house several hundred men; Aspern had a cemetery encircled by a stout wall.

The French left, based on Aspern, was commanded by Marshal Masséna, whose infantry occupied the village. The space between the village and the Danube was filled by the light cavalry of Marulaz, who was under Masséna's orders.

Although the French cavalry patrols had failed to make contact with the enemy, Napoleon rightly believed that the fate of what Karl referred to as 'our House' was about to be decided on the Marchfeld. The Archduke had, in fact, already issued his Order of the Day for the approaching battle, a stirring proclamation which exactly matched the mood of his men.

> Soldiers, we shall fight a battle here to-morrow. On it will depend the existence of the Austrian monarchy, the throne of our good Kaiser Franz, the fate of each one of you. The Fatherland, the Monarchy, your parents and your friends all have their eyes upon you, sure of your courage and your strength . . .

Early on the 21st the sky to the north-west of Vienna was lit by a dull red glow. Masséna, watching from the tower of Aspern church, knew that it was made by the camp fires of a great army.

★   ★   ★

As the sun came up over the Marchfeld, Marshal Bessières saw 105,000 Austrians moving to the attack, their white uniforms blurred against the morning mist. One hundred and sixteen battalions advanced towards Aspern and Essling, flanked and supported by 148 trotting squadrons and nearly 300 guns. Over the heads of the columns floated the colours of Austria's finest regiments: Erbach, Jordis, Froon and Rohan: Klebeck, Argenteau, Zettwitz, Stein. The bands played Turkish music, the men cheered and sang as they marched. Three of the five huge columns moved against Aspern; two more marched for Essling, supported by a mass of horse.

Bessières had taken post mid-way between the two villages, with Lasalle's light cavalry and Espagne's cuirassiers ranged in four lines behind him. He was using his 32 squadrons as a screen, waiting for the main body of the French army to cross the Danube and form up in his rear, but in the early afternoon of 21 May things began to go seriously wrong. Weakened by the fast-moving river, the *grand pont* ruptured for the second time. Napoleon's army was thus split into two halves which

were separated from each other by the Danube: and the weakest half was
on the Marchfeld, where Karl was opening the battle. At 3 p.m. Hiller
attacked Aspern, and the two days of carnage known as the battle of
Aspern-Essling began.

On the French left, where Masséna's 17,000 men faced 36,000
Austrians, Marulaz charged repeatedly against infantry which was
trying to work round behind Aspern and cut the defenders off from the
river. Marulaz was a 40-year-old veteran, a fine tactician and one of the
toughest generals in the French cavalry; but though he succeeded in
delaying the infantry's advance he could not stop it.

In the centre Austrian artillery opened up on the halted ranks of
Bessières' cavalry. When a piece of shot struck the tip of General
Espagne's cocked hat, knocking it slightly askew, the Gascon cuirassier
general calmly put up a hand and adjusted it.

'The sods won't make it salute them again to-day,' he muttered. . . .

Since every French musket and cannon on the Marchfeld was needed
to defend the villages, Bessières was forced to hold the centre without
infantry or artillery, and to assist the French right as well. With Lasalle
and Espagne he furiously attacked the Austrians who threatened
Essling; but without artillery support he could make no headway against
the enemy infantry. If a few horse batteries had been available to pour
grapeshot into their massed ranks, the French cuirassiers would
perhaps have broken them; but there were no horse batteries to spare. As
it was, the Austrians received the cavalry charges with absolute steadi-
ness, holding their fire until the French squadrons were only ten paces
away.

> Even when they had completely enveloped them, the French horse-
> men could not penetrate the Austrian battalions, which bristled with
> bayonets. Without worrying about what was happening behind them,
> without giving a foot of ground, the Austrians presented everywhere a
> front of iron, and the French were forced to cede the corpse-covered
> ground to the cavalry of Prince Lichtenstein.[7]

The French right was commanded by Marshal Lannes. No-one in the
French army fought better under pressure than the famous Gascon, but
on the first day of Aspern-Essling he was stretched to the limit, trying to
contain 23 enemy battalions and 32 squadrons with only one division.
Nine years before, at Marengo, Lannes had accused Bessières of
compromising him by making half-hearted charges; as the battle for
Essling developed, Lannes apparently decided that Bessières was doing

it again. Summoning his aide de Marbot, he ordered him to tell Bessières to 'charge right home'.

As Marbot galloped away he was hoping that his horse might be hit, so that he would be unable to deliver such an insulting order. Finding the Marshal surrounded by his senior officers, Marbot asked to be allowed to talk to him in private, but Bessières told him to speak out.

'Excellency,' said the unhappy aide, choosing his words very carefully, 'Marshal Lannes directs me to tell you that he orders you to charge right home.'

Bessières was outraged. 'Is this, sir, how you speak to a Marshal?' he demanded. 'Order? Charge home? I shall have you disciplined for this!'

'Marshal,' Marbot replied, 'the more my words strike you as harsh, the surer you must be that I am only carrying out Marshal Lannes' orders.'

Bessières immediately launched Lasalle into action, but his regiments were checked by the fire of Austrian infantry formed in squares. Galloping to the front of the cuirassier division, Bessières himself led Espagne's sixteen squadrons to the attack.

'You're going in again, cuirassiers!' shouted an admiring French infantryman.

'Yes, we're going in,' Espagne remarked grimly to an aide de camp. 'But I doubt if we'll be coming back.'

By-passing Lasalle, Bessières broke through the first line of Austrian infantry and took its guns. Avoiding a second line of squares he pressed on to a third line, but as the charge began to lose its impetus enemy cavalry counter-attacked. Espagne's squadrons were tired and heavily out-numbered. Three of the cuirassier colonels were killed; Espagne was hit in the stomach by a piece of grapeshot and unhorsed. With blood running into his boots the six-foot cuirassier general struggled to his feet, then fell dying to the ground. His body was borne away, wrapped in his cloak, to Lobau.

At this critical moment Lasalle charged again at the head of a single chasseur regiment and rescued Bessières, who was surrounded by uhlans. Hatless and with both his pistols fired, Bessières rallied the heavy cavalry regiments and led them forward, but a fresh wave of Austrian cavalry threw them back.

Fortunately the bridge had been repaired, and towards 7 p.m. Nansouty arrived on the Marchfeld with a fresh cuirassier brigade. It was sorely needed. Espagne's division had lost a third of its effectives; Lasalle's light cavalry was exhausted; the 24th Chasseurs had been practically destroyed. Bringing Marulaz in from the left, Bessières led the French cavalry back to the battle.

The vast battlefield was an enormous mêlée of 15,000 horsemen, French and Austrian, charging each other with fury, advancing in ordered ranks, falling back in confusion, then rallying to charge again[8].

Seeing that he had no hope of gaining a decision that day, Karl called a halt to the slaughter, and the armies bivouacked for the night. Bessières and Lasalle could hardly raise their sword arms: Marulaz had had a horse killed under him for the twenty-sixth time in his career.

Lannes was still master of Essling, but Masséna had been forced to relinquish half the buildings in Aspern. That night, hearing firing on the left, Marshal Lannes went to investigate and encountered Masséna and Bessières. When the latter demanded an explanation for the order to 'charge right home', Lannes saw his chance to rub salt into the wound.

'Has the Emperor not told you that you are under my orders?' he asked.

'He has told me that I must conform with your wishes,' Bessières replied.

'In military circles, Monsieur,' Lannes informed him, 'one does not conform. One obeys!'

Bessières wanted satisfaction, which Lannes was quite willing to give him, but Masséna out-faced them.

'For two Marshals to draw swords on one another before the enemy would be a disgraceful thing,' he said, 'and I will not allow my men to see it. I am your senior, and you are in my camp. I order you, in the Emperor's name, to separate at once.'

Next day Napoleon crossed the Danube with a fresh infantry corps, Nansouty's second brigade, and the Imperial Guard.

III

On the second day of the battle the bloody and confused cavalry combats were repeated, Bessières and Lasalle charging at the head of cuirassiers and light cavalry through a storm of grape and musketry, then falling back before counter-attacks of enemy horse. Essling was taken and re-taken several times. Lannes, with both knees shattered by a round-shot, was carried off the field. Marulaz was hit in the thigh by a musket-ball, but stayed in command of his division.

The Austrian infantry had never fought so gallantly. When the ensign of Chasteler's regiment was killed the colour was snatched up by Lieutenant Cazan, who was hit almost at once; as he lay dying he handed it on to Sergeant Pap. In one critical moment the Archduke Karl himself seized a colour and led its regiment to the attack. During the noon assault on Essling the grenadier battalions of four crack infantry regiments made five rushes against the burning houses, thrusting their bayonets into the loop-holes when their ammunition was spent.

In spite of it all the French line began to go forward, until the *grand pont* over the Danube was broken again, this time by Austrian barges and fire-ships. Hearing that his line of retreat was thus threatened, Napoleon ordered a retirement into Lobau. To protect the retreating army the French cavalry made further sacrifices, Bessières charging at the head of six cuirassier regiments, Lasalle and Marulaz fighting Lichtenstein's cavalry in a mêlée.

As the French line receded Karl ordered Baron Dedowitch to make the final assault on Essling. Dedowitch knew that there were still many Frenchmen in the village, but he was convinced that they must soon abandon it, before the wings of the Austrian army closed in to cut them off; in his view a futher attack on Essling would result in heavy and needless casualties. All this he told the Archduke.

'For the eighth time,' Karl replied, 'you will attack with your division, or I will have you shot.'

Dedowitch put himself at the head of his regiments, and the village was finally won.

Covered by Legrand's division, the Reserve Cavalry and the Imperial Guard, the French army passed slowly over the pontoon bridge into Lobau. Lichtenstein was quite prepared to go after it with his cavalry,[9] begging Karl's permission to have six kurassier regiments swim the river on their horses and turn Napoleon's retreat into rout. 'Happily for us,' von Grueber observed, 'the Archduke would not sanction this brave but foolhardy idea.'[10]

Until the *grand pont* was repaired the French army was crowded on the island of Lobau with totally inadequate medical facilities for the 20,000 wounded. For three days the men ate horsemeat stew cooked in cuirasses, seasoned with gunpowder because there was no salt to be had; according to Marshal Masséna it had an excellent taste. Oats being unobtainable, the cavalry horses were fed on grass.

Lannes was taken to Vienna, where he died. Ten days after the battle the dead were still unburied on the Marchfeld, which had a hellish aspect with its smoking villages and charred corpses. Von Grueber never forgot the terrible and moving sight of dead French cuirassiers lying rotting in the torrid heat:

> lying where our artillery fire had mown them down, regiment after regiment, the sun reflected in the mirror of their cuirasses. What a striking sight they made, all those corpses in their gleaming shrouds!

Each one of us silently gave thanks to Almighty God for having escaped the death that so many others had met there. In the bravest of men there is always the instinct to survive.[11]

Speaking of the battle three years later,[12] Napoleon ascribed his defeat at Karl's hands to the weather. 'How could I prevent the Danube rising six feet in one night?' he asked. 'If it hadn't been for that, it would have been all up with the Austrian monarchy.'

★   ★   ★

For the next six weeks every available soldier from Italy, South Germany and the depôts in France was sent to reinforce Napoleon's shaken army on the Danube. The cavalry was badly in need of men, horses and equipment. The three cavalry divisions which had fought throughout the battle had lost over a third of their strengths; on 1 June Marulaz paraded 1,029 all ranks and Espagne's old division 1,530. Lasalle, who had started with 2,431 sabres on 21 May, was reduced to 1,439. 2,000 cavalrymen had lost their horses; every two mounted troopers leaving the depôts in France were ordered to lead a third horse, fully harnessed.

As usual, the wounded cuirassiers had thrown away their armour as they left the battlefield. To re-equip them Napoleon ordered the War Ministry to send with the utmost dispatch 1,000 complete cuirasses, helmets and cuirassier-pattern swords to the depôt at Schonbrunn, and 500 more of each item to Passau. General de Nansouty took the opportunity of asking Napoleon to issue some of these helmets and cuirasses to his Carabiniers, who still wore no armour, and whose bearskins gave very little protection against sword cuts. The Emperor refused, claiming that Nansouty was trying to force his hand by making the Carabiniers lead all his charges, instead of using his three brigades in strict rotation. Nansouty was furious and retaliated by being extremely un-cooperative towards the new commander of the 3rd Cuirassier Division, who was one of Napoleon's favourites.

Espagne's successor was General Arrighi, a 31-year-old Corsican who had previously commanded the Guard Dragoons.[13] Conditioned by Bessières' high standards and the strict Guard discipline, Arrighi found the more casual cuirassier methods hard to understand, especially when the trumpets sounded Boots and Saddles. When this occurred, only the regiment which was due to lead the column hastened to form up; the rest of the men went calmly on with whatever they had been doing. Some even continued eating their meal, while others shaved themselves, using their breastplates as a mirror.[14]

A number of cuirassier officers, having left their cuirasses behind on the Marchfeld, put in expense claims for loss of effects. Napoleon would not allow them. In his view a French officer's cuirasse, like his sword, should only be taken by the enemy along with the officer himself.

IV

Fortunately for Napoleon the Archduke Karl was strangely inactive after Aspern-Essling, possibly because of his ill-health.[15] Thus unhindered by the enemy, by the beginning of July Napoleon had assembled in Lobau an army of 180,000 men and over 700 guns. At 10 p.m. on 4 July, while a violent thunderstorm raged over the Danube and rain fell in torrents, the French army crossed the river to the northern bank. For the cavalrymen, who went on foot leading their horses, it was a nerve-racking experience. The pontoon bridge used by the 8th Chasseurs had sunk below the racing waters under the weight of the passing regiments; they had nothing to guide them but the tops of partly submerged posts.

The following day Karl's army, 140,000 strong, was drawn up in a ten-mile arc on the Marchfeld, with its centre on the village of Wagram. The French succeeded in taking Aspern and Essling, which were thinly held, but a movement to advance over the Russbach came to nothing. The armies bivouacked on the field.

The morning of 6 July dawned hot and sultry. Although the day promised so much in the way of noise and movement, General Lasalle was in one of his gloomy moods. When the Emperor passed by his division Lasalle did not address him, but spoke instead to a secretary who was following a few paces behind. Handing him a document, Lasalle asked him to take charge of it, adding that he had never before asked a favour of the Emperor. According to General Savary, the document was a petition on behalf of Lasalle's children, which he had written out the night before.

The cavalry regiments that had borne the brunt of the fighting at Aspern-Essling were posted on the wings. Lasalle was on the French left, under the orders of Marshal Masséna. Arrighi's 3rd Heavy Cavalry Division was on the right, attached to the *corps d'armée* of Davout. His cuirassiers had been mounted since 4 a.m. By the time the battle began at noon they had been halted for several hours in the blazing heat with nothing to eat or drink, and many of them were quite unfit for action. Davout's corps was the toughest in the army, but even 3rd Corps veterans were unnerved by the sight of 16-stone cuirassiers vomiting blood and fainting in the saddle. Arrighi himself was heard to say that he would gladly exchange a bottle of his best rum for a drink of muddy water from the Russbach.

Arrighi was used to taking his orders from Bessières, and he was apprehensive about serving under Davout, who had a reputation for making unreasonable demands on cavalry commanders. His fears were justified by Davout's first order, which required him to charge over what he regarded as very difficult ground. Arrighi was a brave and capable officer, but he was not a reckless one, and he was anxious to win the trust of his new division; furthermore he had more confidence in his cavalryman's *coup d'oeil* than in the judgment of Davout, who possessed the worst eyesight in the French army. Hoping that the order might be counter-manded, he bided his time; but when a second aide arrived from Davout to repeat the order he drew swords and advanced.

The charge was a disaster. Hindered by a line of Austrian kitchen sheds, the leading squadrons were checked and decimated by enemy fire. The 7th Cuirassiers encountered a ditch which the Austrians had used as a latrine trench. Some troopers who fell into it emerged demoralized and covered in filth, whereupon the entire regiment panicked. The colonel and all his senior officers having been put out of action, command of the 7th devolved on the 22-year-old squadron leader Michel Ordener,[16] who had to draw his pistols and threaten to shoot his men before they rallied.

In the centre of the field the cavalry fared little better. Nansouty had begun by forming his division in line; then for reasons best known to himself he ordered one cuirassier brigade to a new position, leaving Defrance's Carabinier brigade isolated and without adequate support. When Defrance subsequently launched the 1st Carabinier regiment against an infantry square, the leading squadron of the 2nd regiment charged with it, when it should have waited for the right moment to provide the second shock. Before they could close with the enemy Defrance's squadrons were forced to change front by threatening cavalry, and were crippled by flanking fire. Defrance and the Colonel of the 2nd Carabiniers each had two horses killed under them.

When his second horse was hit, Defrance was thrown to the ground and injured so badly that he was carried off the field. His sword, which had been struck from his hand and twisted by a round-shot, resembled a huge corkscrew.[17]

In his 16 years of service Marshal Bessières had ridden unscathed through nine campaigns, leading dozens of charges without receiving so much as a scratch. On the second day at Wagram his luck ran out. To clear the ground for a massed battery with which Napoleon intended to smash the enemy centre, Bessières went forward at the head of Nansouty's six regiments. Attacking the Austrian squares drawn up between the villages south of Wagram, the heavy cavalry created a gap in the enemy infantry positions and pressed on to charge the guns behind. The Carabinier brigade was suddenly checked by a cavalry counter-attack, and as Bessières tried to rally it he was struck by a round-shot that zigzagged along his thigh like a thunderbolt, ripping open his breeches to the knee and tearing his pistol barrel from its stock. His horse was killed instantly, and Bessières was thrown from the saddle so violently that everyone who saw it felt sure that he was dead.

Mounted on his white charger Euphrates, Napoleon commanded the centre in person that day. Seeing the commotion round the fallen Marshal he knew at once that one of the high officers was down.

'Who is it?' he asked.

'It is Bessières, Sire,' someone replied.

Bleeding and unconscious, Bessières was liften up and taken away. *'Général,'* Napoleon called to Nansouty, *'à vous la bataille!'*

Nansouty, however, was a poor substitute for the Duke of Istria, whose loss seemed to reduce the cavalry of the centre to paralysis. At the head of the Guard cavalry, General Walther waited for orders, and when the Guard Chasseurs and the Polish Light Horse finally charged, the Grenadiers à Cheval and the Guard Dragoons failed to support them.[18]

While the battle was reaching its climax on the Marchfeld, a fresh Austrian corps under the Archduke Johann was marching slowly from Pressburg towards Wagram; but at 3 p.m. Karl decided that he could wait for it no longer. With his centre blasted by over 100 massed guns and his right threatened by Masséna, the Archduke ordered his army to retreat.

On the French left the light cavalry attached to Masséna prepared for a final effort. As the Austrian infantry fell back before Leopoldau, Marulaz swept forward with his division and General Lasalle drew in his reins. The battle was nearly over, and while Marulaz had excelled himself, breaking three infantry squares and taking 11 guns, Lasalle had done practically nothing. But there was still a little time left.

In the distance, Lasalle could see a line of shakos moving above a hedgerow, and he knew at a glance who their wearers were. Even a soldier of two days' service, to use one of his favourite expressions, would have realized what a fine target they made; Hungarian infantry on the move, not even in square, whose musket barrels had been thickening for hours.[19]

Behind him, breathing their horses, were several squadrons of the 1st Cuirassiers, which Bessières had seconded to Masséna just before he was hit. 'Follow me!' Lasalle ordered their commanding officer, and pressed his horse into a gallop. The troopers who had once charged with d'Hautpoul spurred after him.

Shortly afterwards, in the plain a little to the north of Leopoldau, a Hungarian grenadier shot him between the eyes. Summoned by a grief-stricken aide de camp, Surgeon-General Larrey explored the wound gently with his finger, then went away to help the living.

On the hideous battlefield, where Nansouty's division alone had left over 1,100 dead and dying horses, Larrey found many strange cases to add to his notebook. Perhaps the strangest case of all was that of a Grenadier à Cheval, who had been grazed by a cannon-shot. The shock was so great that he was struck dumb, and remained so for the rest of his life.

Jacques Chevillet, a young trumpeter of the 8th Chasseurs, was badly wounded by a bursting shell that had left his right arm hanging by a strip of flesh.[20] For several hours he lay helpless on the battlefield, pinned beneath the carcase of his horse. Eventually he was found by two of his comrades and taken to Essling, where a lieutenant of his regiment asked a number of surgeons to attend to him. They were all too busy. When his wound was finally treated next morning it was nine hours old.

Chevillet gave his severed arm to an Austrian peasant and asked him to bury it under a tree in his garden. 'I hope they will give me a pension so that I can come and live with you,' he wrote his father in Pontoise. 'If not, then my only hope is the Hôtel des Invalides.' His chief regret was that he could no longer play the trumpet or the clarinet.

Another cavalryman who closed his active career at Wagram was Pierre Daumesnil, the Guard Chasseurs' deputy colonel. The wound that cost him his leg was his twenty-third. After the limb was amputated he recovered in the Esterhazy Palace at Vienna, claiming that the operation had at least separated him from a sore which had been plaguing him for years. 'What are you complaining about?' he asked his servant, who was devoted to him. 'I'll only have one boot for you to polish now.'[21]

But apart from Daumesnil, there were not many French soldiers able to make jokes after Wagram, where Napoleon had pushed his army to the limit of its endurance. The cavalry was never quite the same afterwards. Drunkenness and indiscipline increased, especially in the light cavalry; for three years after Wagram the 6th Hussars remained on the worst possible terms with the 8th Chasseurs, with whom they were brigaded, and duels amongst the officers were not unknown.

The days of smashing victories and swaggering leisure were over. The glamour had gone from the business, the leaders were getting older and indifferent, the enemies of France were growing wiser and more difficult to beat. Cavalrymen who remembered the gusto of the sunlit Italian campaigns and the exalted mood of 1805 became increasingly disillusioned, and whenever Lasalle's death was discussed round the mess-tables of the French hussars, someone was bound to close the subject with the words, 'He died at the right time.'

The only French cavalrymen whose lot improved after Wagram were the survivors of the Carabinier brigade, who were finally issued with helmets and cuirasses. They were also given white uniforms. 'It will make a fine costume,' wrote an NCO of the 2nd Carabiniers to his father. 'Monsieur Nansouty, our general – or rather the father of our division – has promised us we shall be *cuirassiers d'élite*.'[22]

★   ★   ★

At the end of July the Archduke Karl handed over command of his army to Lichtenstein in Bohemia. He never commanded in the field again.

On the 23rd, at Paris, a letter was delivered to the Countess of Lasalle's residence at 54 Rue Basses-des-Remparts de la Madeleine. It had been written at Vienna three weeks earlier, evidently in haste.

I am going to bed for two or three hours, *ma bonne amie*, after having had the honour of dining with His Imperial Highness the Viceroy...[23] The whole army is assembled, and in two or three hours we shall see who is going to reign on the Danube. We have five or six hundred pieces of cannon and are willing as angels. Goodnight, *mon amie*; you are in my thoughts.[24]

V

Following the battle of Wagram, Austria once more made peace; but in the Peninsula the war dragged on, absorbing the energies of several of Napoleon's best Marshals and over 160 squadrons of the French cavalry.

In the autumn of 1809 two Spanish armies opened an offensive in Castile, Areizaga marching for Madrid with 50,000 men while 30,000 more under del Parque moved on Salamanca. A French force led by General Marchand tried to stop del Parque, who defeated it on 18 October at Tamamès. Occupying Salamanca, del Parque continued his advance with the object of cutting the French lines of communication between Valladolid and Madrid.

The local commander at Valladolid that autumn was General François-Etienne de Kellermann, who fully recognized the danger. Ordering Marchand to hold the vital road junction of Medina del Campo, Kellermann assembled all his available forces at Puente del Duero; but on hearing that Areizaga's army had been routed in a battle south of Madrid, del Parque began to retreat.

Kellermann was after him. The pursuit began on 26 November, Kellermann riding ahead with Lorcet's light cavalry brigade and six regiments of dragoons. The French infantry followed by forced marches. At a village near Salamanca it was learned that del Parque had taken the direction of Alba de Tormès, 15 miles to the south-east.

Aware that the enemy had gained several hours start, Kellermann pressed on with his cavalry alone. No contact was made on the 27th. At first light on the 28th the march was resumed, and at mid-day the light cavalry took the lead, Kellermann following an hour's ride behind with his dragoons. Early in the afternoon, Lorcet sent back word that he had found the whole of del Parque's army at Alba de Tormès, where Kellermann arrived with his dragoons at 3 p.m.

On the nearest bank of the River Tormès, screened by 1,200 cavalry, three of del Parque's infantry divisions were drawn up in two lines totalling 18,000 men; two more divisions were assembling on the farther bank.

Kellermann's force in hand consisted of a mere 3,000 sabres and four light guns.[25] His infantry was only ten miles away, but by the time it arrived the main Spanish body would have crossed the river and taken up a far stronger position. Against these overwhelming odds, Kellermann decided to attack.

While the light cavalry and two dragoon regiments charged the enemy wings, Kellermann himself led two more dragoon regiments against the centre with his usual faultless timing and at his usual breakneck speed. The Spanish cavalry broke; the first line of infantry was cut to pieces.

As the dragoons of Kellermann's leading wave fell back his last two regiments, formed in squadron column, charged the enemy's second line. Except on one flank the Spanish fled in panic, jamming the narrow bridge which was their only means of escape, hurling their packs and muskets into the ravine formed by the river.

'It was the most singular cavalry action I witnessed in my entire career,' wrote one of Kellermann's officers. 'Rarely can so many corpses have been seen covering so small an area.'[26]

Fortunately for the Spanish, darkness was falling and they were able to withdraw, leaving behind them five standards, nine guns and over 4,000 muskets. It took del Parque four weeks to re-assemble his army, which had lost 6,000 men as a result of Kellermann's action. Some 3,000 had been killed or taken prisoner on the field; 3,000 more had deserted.

The French losses were eight killed and 57 wounded. It was a brilliant addition to Kellermann's service record and the traditions of the French cavalry, but Kellermann realized that it was nothing more.

'The resistance of this stubborn nation is exhausting us,' he wrote. 'Cutting off the Hydra's heads on one side achieves nothing, since they merely appear somewhere else. It would take the strength of Hercules himself to settle this business – if it can be settled at all.'[27]

6

Castles in Spain

Bâtir châteaux en Espagne (lit. to build castles in Spain)
– to formulate useless projects, to entertain false hopes.
French-English dictionary.

I

In 1810 Marshal Bessières was 41 years old and one of the most famous soldiers in Europe. He had served in all the great campaigns of the Empire, held the highest command in the French cavalry, and won an independent battle in Spain. He possessed large estates, an attactive wife, a healthy son and a fascinating mistress, on whom he spent the bulk of his substantial income. Since he had made a complete recovery from his Wagram wound, the only cloud on his horizon was the hostility of the Emperor.

For years Bessières had held a special place in the Emperor's affections, partly because he was an old companion of the First Italian Campaign, to which Napoleon looked back with increasing nostalgia as the years went by, and partly because of his intense loyalty. Following the divorce of Josephine, Bessières' sense of loyalty put him in a very difficult position.

Through his friendship with Eugène, Bessières had always been close to the de Beauharnais family, and he naturally sympathized with the broken-hearted Empress. So did the members of his inner circle. The Marshal regularly attended Laure Junot's *soirées*, where the divorce was strongly criticized; he also continued to call on Josephine at Malmaison. Napoleon made his resentment of these visits brutally clear.

His decision to remarry put Bessières in an even worse position. Napoleon wanted a son; he also wanted an alliance with Austria, mainly to counterbalance the growing coolness of the Tsar. He had been amazed and impressed by the Austrian army's heroic conduct during the bloody battles on the Danube; in 1810, hearing someone make a slighting remark about Austrian soldiers, he turned to the speaker and said, 'Evidently you were not present at Wagram.' By marrying a German Hapsburg he hoped to gain not only a male heir for his Empire, but Austrian divisions for his army as well.

As a devoted friend of Josephine, Bessières was appalled to learn that she was about to be replaced by a Kaiserlik princess; in the meantime, Napoleon continued to treat him with a coolness bordering on contempt. In the spring of 1810, at his château of Grignon, Bessières was host to the Emperor and a distinguished party which included two Queens, several Marshals and the King of Bavaria. Napoleon had been to Grignon several times; on the last occasion, as he had described it to Eugène, he and Bessières had played together like 15-year-old children.

This time it was very different, Napoleon being deliberately rude both to Bessières and his gentle wife. For a parlour game that he wanted to play one evening, he asked Madame Bessières to provide a piece of ribbon, but she had none to hand. When one of the ladies present finally produced one, Napoleon told his hostess, 'While I've been kept waiting for this, you could have cut up one of your gowns.'

When Bessières presented his aides, Napoleon pretended to recognize one of them as an officer who had given him wrong information during the Austrian campaign. Bessières assured him that the officer he meant was not at the château, but Napoleon affected to disbelieve him, and succeeded in making the aide uncomfortable for the rest of the evening. When the company went in to dance the King of Bavaria stood to one side, since he was 55 years old, over-weight, and an indifferent dancer. He was also father-in-law to Josephine's son.

'King of Bavaria,' ordered the Emperor, 'dance!'

On 11 March Napoleon and Marie Louise were married by proxy in the church of St Augustine at Vienna. The Archduke Karl himself represented the absent bride-groom and escorted the bride to the Austrian frontier. Thomas Aubry, on leave from the 12th Chasseurs, caught a glimpse of her as her carriage was leaving Braunau, and thought she looked charming. Laure Junot, on the other hand, declared that she had ungainly breasts and shoulders, no grace, the gaze of a Kalmouck and a typically Austrian mouth.

Bessières was made Governor of Strasbourg for 48 hours so that he could welcome the new Empress to France. Early in 1811 he was posted to Spain.

II

From his old headquarters in Castile Bessières commanded a corps of 30,000 men, which included an infantry division of the Young Guard and a brigade of Guard cavalry under Louis Lepic. His task was to keep the roads to France open, and to contain the insurgents of Leon and Navarre. The Spanish resistance units were far stronger than they had been in 1808,[1] and his provinces were swarming with guerillas. No officer carrying a dispatch was safe unless he had an escort of 200 men; a ration convoy needed an entire battalion.

Bessières had no enthusiasm for his new command, and in addition to his military problems he was worried about Laure Junot, who had followed her husband to Spain. Learning that she had just given birth to a son at Salamanca, Bessières urged her to put herself under his protection.

> Here you can have an escort back to France whenever you need one, if you should decide to go home without waiting for Junot; also you have here a good friend who will guard you and look after you. Come, I beg you, for your sake and your child's.

Laure replied that she would only leave with Junot, whose corps was part of Masséna's harassed Army of Portugal.

Having invaded Portugal with the main intention of destroying Wellington's British, Masséna had been checked by the impregnable lines of Torres Vedras. By March 1811 his army was retreating into Spain, moving back through country which it had recently stripped and plundered in the usual Napoleonic fashion. Masséna's men were in a wretched state, and urgent requests to send them food, ammunition, clothing and reinforcements arrived every week at Bessières' headquarters in Castile.

Bessières was no friend of the man who had fought beside him at Aspern-Essling. When it came to supplying the needs of his own troops, Bessières was ready to strip his provinces of food, horses and public money; but he was not anxious to do it for Masséna, whose notorious habit of lining his own pocket disgusted him. In Bessières' view the misfortunes of the Army of Portugal were mainly due to its ageing commander, who no longer rode on horseback, and who went everywhere accompanied by an attractive young woman dressed in French dragoon uniform.

Personal feelings aside, Bessières had his own needs to consider. His corps area was huge, and since he was guarding the lines of communication with France his responsibility was great; possibly he felt completely justified in sending Masséna the minimum amount of support. If that was the case, it is a pity that he did not say so.

According to his aide de Baudus, clearly a partial witness, the news that the Army of Portugal was retreating into Spain threw the Duke of Istria into a fever of activity. Dispatch riders were sent galloping to Salamanca and Ciudad Rodrigo, warning the local commanders to collect everything that Masséna's soldiers would need after their long and punishing campaign. De Baudus himself rode to see Masséna and assured him that Bessières would send him all the cavalry, infantry and artillery he wanted. Masséna replied that he lacked only for food.

At the end of April de Baudus again saw Masséna at Salamanca. This time Masséna told him that he had enough infantry and guns, but too few horses. As soon as de Baudus returned with this news to Valladolid, Bessières ordered all available cavalry to assemble. Next day he rode out at the head of 2,000 horsemen, including 800 Guard troopers under Lepic, plus enough horses to draw six batteries of artillery. On 1 May this force joined Masséna at Salamanca. When Masséna saw the reinforcements that Bessières had brought he was astounded; two weeks earlier he had asked Bessières in writing for 1,200 to 1,500 horses, 15 to 28 guns, and an infantry division. 'He'd have done better to send me a few thousand men,' he remarked bitterly to his aide de camp, 'and stayed where he was himself.'

Four days later, at Fuentes d'Onoro, Masséna fought his last battle. Under General Montbrun, whom many regarded as a possible successor to the great Lasalle, the French cavalry vigorously attacked Wellington's infantry; according to a British eyewitness Montbrun's troopers were all drunk and fought like madmen. Finally the moment came to throw in Lepic's élite squadrons of the Guard. An aide was sent spurring to Lepic with the order to charge, but the deputy colonel of the Grenadiers à Cheval would not obey it, pointing out that the Guard cavalry took its orders only from the Duke of Istria. Unless their Colonel-General ordered it, Lepic insisted, no man under his command would so much as draw his sword from the scabbard.[2]

Ten staff officers were dispatched to find Bessières; when it was too late, he was discovered at a nearby swamp, gravely inspecting a causeway. Masséna's chance of beating the Duke had gone, and at the end of the day he ordered his army back to Salamanca.

★   ★   ★

In spite of his extraordinary behaviour at Fuentes, Bessières was retained in his command; but apparently realizing that he had gone too far, he sent de Baudus 800 miles to make his excuses to the Emperor.

When de Baudus found him he was at Cherbourg, scattering handfuls of snuff[3] and in a furious temper. De Baudus was shocked to hear the way Napoleon spoke of Masséna, the hero of Rivoli and Zurich. 'He is used up, he isn't fit to command four men and a corporal! But Bessières! Bessières is in his prime! What was his reason for not giving his infantry to the Army of Portugal? How could he have managed things so badly for me?'[4]

Describing his missions to Masséna, de Baudus blamed the defeat at Fuentes on the French Sixth Corps commander, who had been apathetic throughout the battle.[5] 'Go away,' the Emperor retorted angrily. 'You are too young to argue about such things.' Later de Baudus heard that the Emperor had disliked the way he had answered his questions, and thought that he was lying.

For the time being Bessières remained in Castile, sending a stream of letters full of advice to his colleague Marmont, who had taken over Masséna's army. The man who had once been so sarcastic about Bessières' promotion to Marshal was now a Marshal himself, and Bessières addressed him by his title so punctiliously that Marmont began to suspect him of sarcasm.

Marmont, who had spent much of his career administering provinces, evidently believed that commanding in Spain was basically the same as governing Illyria; his first request to Bessières was for 10,000 shoes and half a million francs. Bessières replied that he was sending the shoes but not the money, explaining that he did not have a sou in his treasury. He did, however, have contractors' bills for two million and 2,000 sick men of the Army of Portugal on his hands. Their presence had trebled his hospital expenses. Meanwhile his own men had been without pay for from four to eight months, and he had no transport and very little grain. 'Such is my situation, my dear Marshal.'

He warned Marmont that the Army of Portugal's Intendant General was embezzling the ration money and that one of its contractors had been run out of Madrid for swindling; he also strongly advised him against crossing the Tagus in case he had any illusions about assisting Marshal Soult. 'You will leave half your artillery on the road, and after eight days you will have lost a third of your cavalry. Such is the terrain, my dear Marshal, on which you march.'

Marmont still regarded Bessières as a glorified escort commander, whose natural caution made him quite unsuitable for an independent command; nevertheless Bessières' assessment of the situation was absolutely right, and he did not hesitate to write to Paris in a similar tone. 'We occupy too large an area,' he informed Berthier. 'We spend our resources unnecessarily and without result; we cling to dreams. We should concentrate our resources and regard two-thirds of Spain as a vast battlefield.'

Shortly after this dispatch reached Imperial Headquarters he was replaced by General Dorsenne and recalled to France. His arrival at Paris convinced many people that the long-awaited war with Russia was about to begin. It was said that Napoleon expected it to last for three years; that Murat would return to his old post at the head of the Reserve Cavalry; that his wife Caroline would be made Queen of a new state embracing most of European Russia and all of Poland.

The rumours were premature. In the autumn of 1811 Bessières went home to Prayssac, where the valley of the Lot was at its most inviting, with leaves turning golden on the chestnut trees and good food cooking in goose fat over slow wood fires. In Quercy when the leaves fall, runs the local saying, Gargantua is at home, feasting on beef stew with chestnuts, *omelette aux truffes,* wheat cakes hot from the ashes, and *paté de foie gras.* It made a welcome contrast to the heat and desolation of Old Castile. Bessières stayed with his father for several days, while people came flocking from all over Quercy and Aquitaine hoping to catch a glimpse of the famous Marshal. It was their last chance to do so.

From Prayssac he returned to Paris to prepare the Guard. The Emperor had forgiven him for Fuentes; when he left for Holland that September he paid Bessières the striking compliment of putting his infant son in the Marshal's care. 'Go often to see him,' Napoleon wrote from Boulogne, 'and take all the necessary measures for his safety. Inform Madame de Montesquiou that in any eventuality it is to you that she must address herself, and you whom she must keep informed.'

III

During Bessières' absence in Spain, Napoleon had been working to improve his cavalry's efficiency; in particular he wanted to restore the heavy branch to its old ascendancy. To this end nine new regiments had been formed.[6] Armed with lances, and wearing uniforms that included a crested helmet, they were known as Chevaux-légers Lanciers, or Light Horse Lancers.[7] On campaign they would be attached to the heavy cavalry divisions, for the purpose of carrying out such tiring non-combative duties as outposts, picquets, escorts and reconnaissances Even general officers of the heavy cavalry would be expected to use chevaux-légers for such tasks, so that their cuirassier regiments would always be ready for battle, with men and horses in the best possibl condition.

On the battlefield, cuirassiers would no longer pursue a beaten enemy;
as soon as the enemy broke, the lancers would take over. The cuirassiers
would halt, dress their lines, and advance at a steady pace, ready to make
further charges when necessary.

To make the cuirassier regiments even more effective, Napoleon
increased their armament. For years he had been dissatisfied with their
lack of firepower. Once cuirassiers had dismounted, they were practically defenceless against musketry; and it was an absurd state of affairs,
the Emperor declared, when three or four thousand brave men could be
held up on the march, or surprised in their cantonments, by two
companies of infantry. He therefore ordered the War Ministry to
remedy this by giving cuirassier troopers a musketoon or short musket;
at the same time carbines similar to those used by the light cavalry could
be issued to the chevaux-légers.

This order was amended by General Clarke, the Minister for War,
who informed the Emperor that carbines were not in use in the French
light cavalry and never had been, at least not since 1763; what the
French light cavalry insisted on calling a carbine was in fact a musketoon.
Furthermore, since a carbine had a rifled barrel it used a *balle forcée*, or
belted bullet, and this made it a very unsuitable weapon for a mounted
man. In view of this he proposed to issue musketoons to cuirassiers and
chevau-légers alike, but as a total of 25,000 musketoons would be
required the chevaux-légers would have to be satisfied with foreign ones.

Several cavalry experts took the opportunity of pointing out to
Napoleon that cuirassiers should also be given a pair of serviceable
trousers and a more manageable sword. The trousers would replace their
tight breeches and stiff jack-boots, which were extremely elegant on
parade but hopelessly impractical on campaign. Once the breeches were
wet it took three or four days to dry them out, and the boots rubbed the
horses' flanks into sores. As to the long sword with its heavy Klingenthal
blade,[8] the cuirassiers themselves had been complaining about it for
years, mainly because it was difficult to parry with, which was a grave
disadvantage in the mêlée.[9]

A committee of enquiry was formed. Questionnaires were sent out to
the heavy cavalry regiments and the advice of General de Nansouty was
taken, as a result of which it was decided to issue a more suitable sword.
The smart breeches and stiff knee-boots were retained.

Figuratively speaking, stiff breeches were not confined to the cuirassier regiments, for in French cavalry slang the term *culotte de peau
renforcé* signified an extremely tough character. No-one deserved the

1 Jean-Baptiste Bessières, from the portrait by Guérin

2 François-Etienne de Kellermann

3 A trumpeter of the
Grenadiers à Cheval
of the Imperial
Guard, from a
watercolour by
Maurice Orange

4 French hussar
trooper circa 1796

5 French heavy
cavalryman of the
Revolutionary period
and the early
Consulate

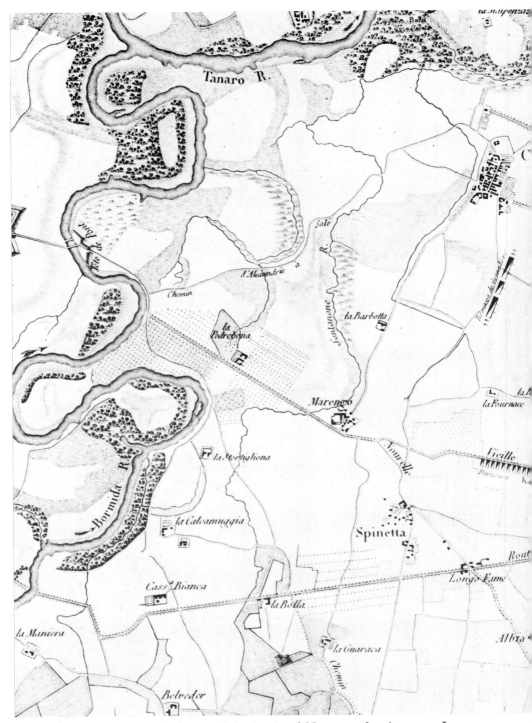

6 This highly detailed map of the battle of Marengo, fought on 14 June 1800, was published in France in 1826. Just above Cassina Grossa the first half of Kellermann's heavy cavalry brigade, formed in column, is shown

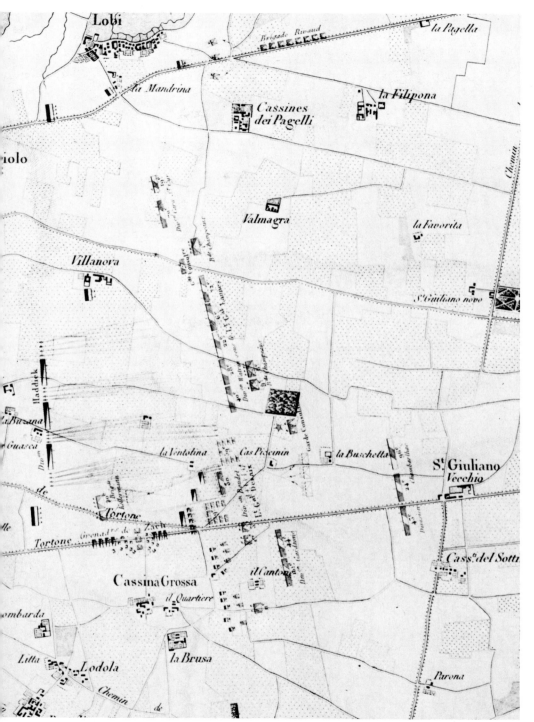

breaking through the column of Austrian grenadiers. A short distance away the rest of Kellermann's brigade, formed in line, prepares to charge Austrian cavalry to its front.

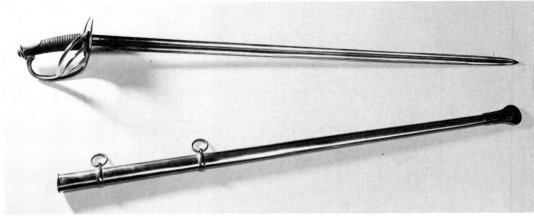

7 French heavy cavalry sword fitted with a blade manufactured at
Klingenthal in 1813.   (Author's collection)

8 French hussars demonstrate the art of living off the country. Both men
have the braids of plaited hair which hussars of the Revolutionary and early
Empire periods wore on each side of the face. The forage cap worn by the
man on the right was used during grooming parades and on fatigue duty, and
as an off-duty head-dress. The sword shown here is the light cavalry sabre,
known as *le bancal* (the bandy-legged one) because of its shape. It was
supposed to last for fifty years, but on campaign it was damaged by various
malpractices, especially the cutting of wood for bivouac fires.   (Author's
collection)

9 Kellermann's charge at the battle of Marengo, from the painting by Bellangé. Kellermann is the officer just to the left of centre, holding his sword at boot level

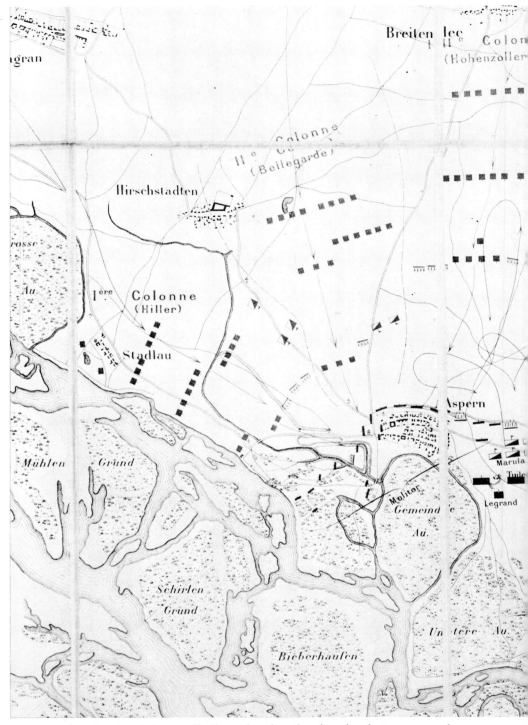

10 The battle of Aspern-Essling, showing the situation between 4 and 5 p.m. on 21 May 1809. Arrowed lines indicate forward movements and the French cavalry charges

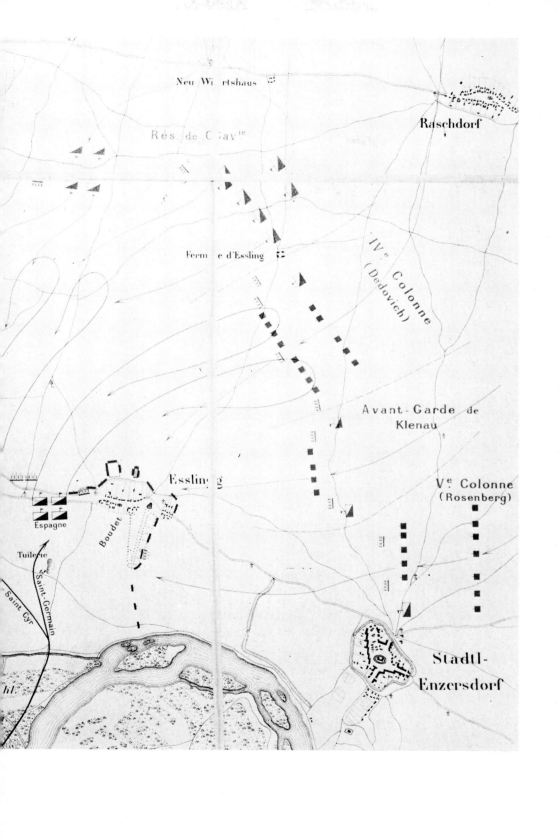

Neu Wirtshaus

Raschdorf

Rés. de Cav.ie

Ferme d'Essling

IV.e Colonne
(Dedovich)

Avant-Garde de
Klenau

Essling

V.e Colonne
(Rosenberg)

Espagne

Boudet

Tuilerie

Saint-Germain

Saint Cyr

Stadtl-
Enzersdorf

11 The correct 'seat' as taught to French cavalry recruits

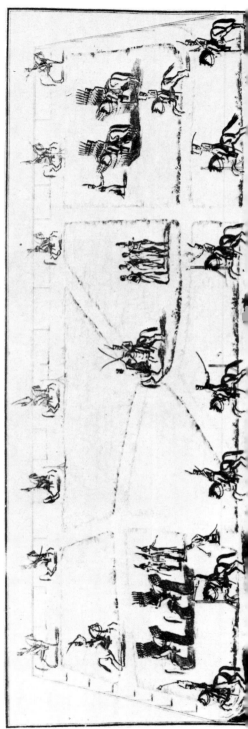

12 French cavalry school exercises, from an early 19th-century print

13 French Hussar officer 1806

14 French 9th Hussars trooper 1806. It was
not usual for light cavalry regiments of the
Line to wear plumes on active service. Those
who did so, especially in action, were said to
be *faisant faquins*, or showing off

15 The Prussian garrison marches past General Lasalle at the surrender of Stettin

16 General Lasalle at the
battle of Wagram, from the
painting by Edouard
Détaille

17 Preceded by Guard
Dragoons, Napoleon rides
through the streets of
Moscow

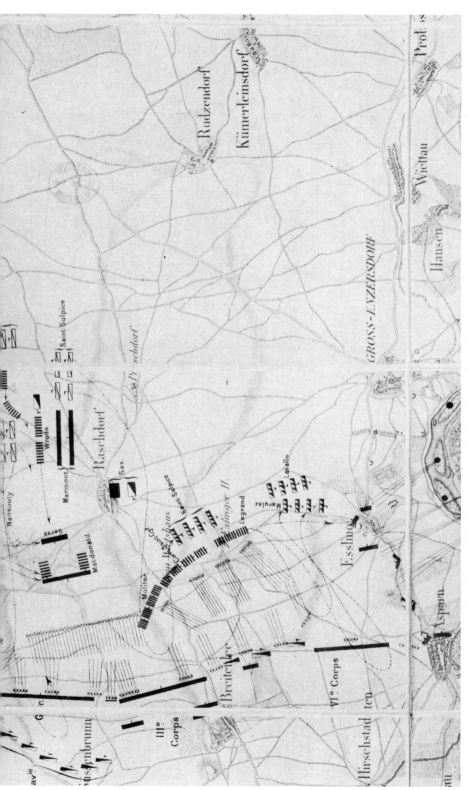

18 The battle of Wagram towards the close of the fighting on 6 July 1809. Earlier positions are indicated by unshaded symbols. The body of cavalry marked 'Arr.' south of Markgrafen Neusiedl is Arrighi's 3rd Heavy Cavalry Division

19 French cuirassiers salute the body of General Auguste de Caulaincourt on the field of Borodino. The stretcher bearer in the crested helmet is a Carabinier

20 French cavalry in the Retreat from Moscow

description more than General François Bourcier, organizer of the French remount depôts.

In the early years of the Empire, Bourcier had refused to accept any horse for the French cavalry that was a day over eight years old or half an inch under the regulation heights, but as one campaign succeeded another his standards had become increasingly flexible, due to the Napoleonic army's staggering wastage of cavalry and draught horses. As the quality of French cavalry regiments declined with the loss of veterans and the intakes of conscripts, so did the quality of their mounts.

For the inadequate supply of acceptable native animals, the directors of France's horse-breeding establishments were partly to blame. For years they had been retaining for breeding purposes first-born males and females, which were almost invariably genetically weak specimens, and allowing couplings between fathers and daughters, and brothers and sisters. Even before the Jena campaign of 1806 Napoleon had spoken of France having been denuded of horses, and for several years after it Prussia and Hanover were the main sources of supply; in the month of March 1807 12,700 horses were despatched to the French army by the Potsdam remount depôt alone. Not even the combined resources of the Empire and the conquered states, however, could satisfy the insatiable demand for fit horses aged between five and eight. By November 1810 the French cavalry had only 58,000 horses for 78,000 troopers, and since the cavalry was at that time 8,000 men under strength the total deficiency of horses was 28,000. In 1811 Napoleon calculated that France should be able to provide another 25,000 horses; only 18,000 were forth-coming. At the end of the year there were 500 dismounted troopers at the depôt of the newly-formed 5th Chevaux-légers and not a single horse.

For the campaign of 1812 huge quantities of horses were levied from Poland and East Prussia. Many of them were not strong enough to carry the burdens required of them. Including a rider and his equipment, but excluding the two days' rations for man and horse which were generally carried, these burdens totalled nearly 130 kilograms in the heavy cavalry and $102\frac{1}{2}$ kilograms in the hussars and chasseurs. These weights automatically increased in bad weather, when clothing and saddlecloths were wet, and many troopers added to the load by carrying personal possessions, though this was strictly forbidden.

The poor condition of these horses was aggravated by the bad habits of the inexperienced conscripts who rode them, and some of them were unable to gallop for more than five minutes at a time.

IV

By the end of 1811 the gigantic preparations for Napoleon's invasion of Russia were well in hand, but the command of the Reserve Cavalry was still vacant. In the four years that had elapsed since he had held the post, Marshal Murat had become a source of increasing irritation to the Emperor. Even during the years of his greatest achievements, Napoleon had had plenty of grounds for complaint against his brother-in-law; the bad taste which showed itself in Murat's outlandish uniforms, the arrogance which often resulted in premature action, the wastefulness and inefficiency of his methods.

In making Murat King of Naples, Napoleon had expected him to act as his viceroy, especially since he owed his throne solely to the fact that he was Caroline Bonaparte's husband; but once he was established on it Murat began to act as though he were an independent sovereign by Divine Right. By the beginning of 1812 Napoleon was so angry with him that he refused to communicate with him except through Queen Caroline or Marshal Berthier.

In view of the approaching war with Russia, however, a reconciliation was inevitable, for when it came to inspiring French troopers for the charge, as Napoleon well knew, not even Kellermann could match the innkeeper's son from La Bastide. No matter now inadequate his orders, no matter how unsuitable the ground over which he chose to attack, nothing aroused the French cavalry's lust for blood and victory with such devastating effect as the sight of Marshal Murat with his cane in the air.

As for Murat, the thought of someone other than himself being appointed to lead the tremendous force of cavalry that was assembling proved unbearable. 'Sire, I shall die if you do not summon me!' he finally informed the Emperor, who was pleased to keep him in suspense until the last possible moment.

'I brought him round by using anger and sentimentality in turn,' was Napoleon's comment on Murat's return to obedience. 'That's what you need with that Italian Pantaloon.'

$$\star \quad \star \quad \star$$

For his colossal new undertaking Napoleon had drawn fighting men, not only from France and her allies, but from the armies of former enemies as well. The polyglot Grand Army contained corps of Italians, Bavarians, Saxons, Westphalians, Prussians, Austrians and Poles. There were also several divisions of Wurttembergers, plus regiments of Spaniards, Danes and Swiss. The cavalry numbered 80,000 men in more than 100 regiments, of which only half were French; apart from the Polish ones, which always fought particularly well against Russians, the foreign ones were of doubtful value. This was especially true of the southerners; yet strangely enough, and contrary to all expectations, the cavalry mounts which would prove best able to survive the horrors of 1812 were the unprepossessing little horses from the arid plateaux of Portugal.

The Guard cavalry having made its usual levy of veterans from the line regiments, Bessières had 6,000 troopers under his hand, including nearly 2,000 lancers.[10] Of the rest, 11 divisions of light cavalry were needed for reconnaissance with the *corps d'armée*, leaving 40,000 sabres for Murat's Reserve. Napoleon had no illusions about their quality. 'When I put 40,000 men in the saddle,' he confided to General Dejean, [11] 'I know perfectly well that I don't have 40,000 good cavalrymen; but the enemy will learn from their spies and the Press that I have 40,000 cavalry, and it's the moral effect that counts.'

For the first time in its existence the Reserve Cavalry was formed in groups of divisions, each group constituting a mounted corps. The first three corps, commanded by Nansouty, Montbrun and Grouchy, were the backbone; each of them had one division of light horse and two divisions of heavy cavalry, and except for a few light cavalry units all their regiments were French. The fourth corps, commanded by Victor Latour-Maubourg, consisted of a division of Polish lancers and four good regiments of Saxon and Westphalian kurassiers.[12]

Throughout the spring of 1812 this mass of horse, and the great army to which it belonged, was marching towards the concentration line in Poland. On 26 May orders were issued for a general advance to the River Niemen, and the combined host moved forward in echelon on a front of 150 miles. By mid-June, wearing his colonel's undress uniform of the Guard Chasseurs, the Emperor was travelling past cheering columns on the dusty road to Kovno.[13] On the 22nd, at Gumbinnen, he proclaimed to the army that Russia's destiny was at hand, and that he was about to carry the war into her territory. On the 23rd, wearing a Polish lancer's helmet and cloak, he was reconnoitring the Niemen, where the cavalry bivouacs stretched for 12 kilometres along the western bank. Next day the regiments trotted to join their divisions, and without any formal declaration of war the invasion began.

'What a magnificent spectacle it made,' wrote General Morand, 'with gold and steel sparkling under the rays of a June sun, as the French cavalry deployed its lines.'

That day the 9th Cuirassiers of Nansouty's corps crossed the Niemen 900 strong. Six months later the regiment rode back across the river with 83 men.

7

Russia

'The French have never understood how to manage their cavalry.'
– General Désiré Chlapowski, chef d'escadron in the Polish Lancers
of the Guard during the 1812 campaign.

I

The Guard cavalry marched at its usual steady pace of six kilometres to
the hour, and under its usual strict discipline. During the hourly ten-
minute halts the horses and their loads were carefully inspected; whenever the route passed over hard or stony ground the men dismounted.

The Reserve Cavalry was not so fortunate. To guard against Cossack
raids, Murat ordered the men to be constantly alert and under arms
during the daylight hours, with the horses saddled and bridled. This was
a punishing system, for daylight lasted a long time; dawn broke at two
in the morning, and by ten at night it was still light enough to read. All
the units of the huge columns were made to assemble at the same time;
consequently some regiments waited for up to four hours before they
could move off, and their fully loaded horses were exhausted even before
the march began.

The way led through gloomy forests and over shifting sands. Uniform
colours disappeared under a coating of fine sand and dust, and veterans
complained that the heat was worse than it had been in Egypt. Both
water and forage were scarce. Fed on green crops and thatch taken from
village roofs, horses began to die of colic; as usual the heavy cuirassier
mounts were the first to go. 'Our horses have no patriotism,' Nansouty
remarked drily to Murat. 'The men will fight without bread, but the
horses won't fight without oats.' Even the men were dying, however,
many of them from sunstroke. One month after the invasion began, the
9th Cuirassiers depôt at Mainz was ordered to send all available men and
horses immediately to the front.

The nights were almost as hard as the days. Fed by the resinous local
wood of Russian Poland, bivouac fires gave off acrid smoke but very little

heat. The light cavalry was employed on rigorous night marches, on which Lieutenant Michel Combe of the 8th Chasseurs found it impossible to keep awake. Flanked by two sturdy troopers to stop him falling, Combe thrust his feet into the stirrups, built up his cloak into a pillow on the saddle bow, folded his arms on it, and went to sleep.

★   ★   ★

With his army shrinking at an alarming rate, Napoleon wanted a quick and decisive victory, but the Russians steadily retreated eastwards, fighting vigorous rearguard actions to wear the enemy down. When Smolensk was stormed on 17 August Napoleon refused to let his army rest, and the advance towards Moscow went on. Senior cavalry officers were appalled. 'Another six days' march,' General Belliard warned the Emperor, 'and there will be no cavalry left.'

Whenever time allowed, the Russians burnt everything in the French Army's path. 'Fine towns like Vyazma were only piles of ashes when we arrived,' wrote Thomas Aubry. 'So were others, whose names I don't remember.' His regiment was part of the crack 2nd Cavalry Corps, commanded by General Montbrun, whose three divisions had crossed the Niemen over 10,000 strong; by the end of August they were reduced to a total of 3,859.

Tall and powerfully built, '*le beau Montbrun*' was one of the most impressive officers in the cavalry, with a tremendous reputation and a resounding word of command. He was still regarded as Lasalle's natural successor, which was a sad reflection on the younger cavalry generals. Lasalle, after all, had died at thirty-four; Montbrun was already forty-one and troubled by gout. Unlike the chivalrous Lasalle, who had been adored by his men and liked by most of his superiors, Montbrun was an incorrigible looter and a difficult subordinate;[1] when his temper was up not even the Emperor could control him.

Soon after crossing the Niemen, Napoleon gave him a direct order to take his corps to Wilna and seize the enemy magazines; unfortunately Murat was not informed of this, and when he saw Montbrun about to move off with his corps he demanded an explanation. When Montbrun explained his orders Murat declared that he had no knowledge of them and ordered him to dismiss. Montbrun hesitated, pointing out that he ought not to disobey the Emperor, but Murat insisted.

Soon afterwards, accompanied by Murat, Napoleon rebuked Montbrun in front of his corps for disobeying an order, saying that he was not fit for a field command and would be better employed on the lines of communication. Montbrun waited in vain for Murat to intercede. Finally he drew his sword, reversed it, caught it by the point and sent it whirling through the air; then he galloped off the parade shouting, 'You can all go to the devil!' As the Emperor rode away he was white with anger, and Montbrun's officers were certain that he would be replaced. Next day, however, he resumed command of 2nd Cavalry Corps as though nothing had happened.

To make up for his loss of face, Murat complained several times to Napoleon that Montbrun was not using his cuirassiers properly.

II

By the end of August the Russian army was growing tired and demoralized by the long retreat and there was friction in the high command, especially between Bagration and the 'foreigner' Barclay de Tolly. To restore his soldiers' morale, and to stop the French reaching Moscow, the Tsar turned to Kutusov. Sixty-seven years old, Kutusov could no longer ride a horse, and he was said to sleep for eighteen hours a day, but he was still a hero to the army and the people. When his appointment to the chief command was announced, Moscow blazed with light in his honour.

Seven days later his army stood for battle between Moscow and Smolensk, formed in dense masses along a two-mile front strengthened by redoubts. In preliminary fighting on 5 September the French took the advanced redoubt of Schevardino. There was no general action on the 6th, but late at night firing was heard in front of the positions won by Prince Eugène's Italian Corps; accompanied by de Baudus, Marshal Bessières rode over to the French left to see what was afoot. De Baudus expressed surprise that the Emperor had not gone to see the situation for himself.

'He's in a lot of pain,' Bessières explained. Aware that his Marshal knew as well as anyone what went on in the Imperial tent, de Baudus was depressed by this disclosure; for weeks past he had noticed that Napoleon, once so tireless in the saddle, rarely rode a horse.

Soon after midnight the French cavalry mounted up without trumpet calls, formed squadron column, and trotted to its positions; Grouchy on the left, Nansouty on the right, Montbrun and Latour-Maubourg in the centre. At 6 a.m. the artillery bombardment began, and the infantry of Eugène's corps went forward to open the battle of Borodino.

Even in this holocaust, which Napoleon himself described as the most terrible of all his battles, there were flashes of the old flamboyance. Murat went into action wearing a green velvet tunic and yellow boots, making a conspicuous mark for the Russian skirmishers, and keeping up the French infantry's morale merely by his presence. When Russian cavalry attacked the Italian Corps, Eugène sought temporary refuge in a French infantry square, and as the colonel came forward to receive him he asked, 'Whom am I with?'

'Monseigneur, you are in the centre of the 84th,' the colonel replied, 'and as safe as if you were in your palace at Milan.'

As at Wagram, Napoleon's tactical method was the human battering-ram, supported this time by 400 massed guns; and as at Wagram things went badly for the French cavalry. Halted in closed ranks for most of the battle, the divisions that formed the Reserve made a perfect target for the Russian guns. On the left, where Grouchy's troopers sat for nearly six hours with their swords on their shoulders,[2] one brigade commander[3] received three mortal wounds at once. Grouchy's horse was killed under him, and as he mounted another a piece of grapeshot struck him full in the chest. Luckily, it was at the end of its flight.

On the French right, Nansouty's corps was also halted under a punishing fire. When Captain Charles Oriot of the 9th Cuirassiers praised a sub-lieutenant for his cool behaviour the young man replied, 'I've no complaints, Captain; all I'd like is a drink of water.' As he finished speaking a cannon-shot cut him in two. Almost immediately afterwards Oriot's horse was killed, and as he mounted a fresh one the cuirassier who held the bridle for him was struck dead by a shell.

It was the same with Montbrun and Latour-Maubourg. In addition to all the other difficulties which faced the commander of a cavalry corps that day, General Victor de Latour-Maubourg had to cope with the problems caused by having a mixture of German and Polish regiments under his orders. During the bombardment a shot wounded the horse of General Thielmann, the German commander of the Saxon heavy cavalry brigade, and as he was mounting a replacement one of Latour-Maubourg's Polish staff officers ordered the colonel of the Saxon Garde du Corps to move his regiment to a new position.

The movement had hardly begun when Thielmann arrived on the scene and countermanded the order, not knowing that it had come from the corps commander. When Thielmann angrily rebuked him for daring to give orders to one of his regimental commanders, the Pole replied that he had been unable to find the general at his post; he then rode back to corps headquarters. Drawing his sword, Thielmann rode after him like a madman, and in front of Latour-Maubourg and his staff announced that if the Pole were not removed he would run him through at the next opportunity. Then, loudly declaring that he was not going to be insulted or ordered about by adjutants, he returned to his brigade. As he rode along the front of it his aide Graf von Seydewitz was killed by a shot which also brought down an orderly trumpeter and three horses.[4]

Under a hail of cannon and howitzer fire, the light cavalry division of Montbrun's 2nd Corps lost 800 horses; Thomas Aubry's troop of the 12th Chasseurs, being posted in the middle of the regiment, was one of the worst hit. The senior NCO on the right flank was killed by a cannon shot just as Aubry was holding his sabre against the man's chest to align the front rank, and Aubry was splashed with his blood. The NCO who replaced him was also blown to pieces, and the next NCO in line had three horses killed under him.

Determined to find a better position for his light cavalry division, Montbrun galloped towards it followed by a handful of his staff officers. On the way, a shot killed the horse of Colonel Séruzier, who commanded the corps' light artillery, and Montbrun turned back to see if he was hit. As he did so a *boulet de trois* struck him in the side. Carried to an ambulance, he died as it was being removed.

The Russian guns continued to do terrible execution; according to one French observer a regiment of German kurassiers had become a favourite target, and the air was filled with the flying splinters of their helmets and cuirasses.

To help fill the gap caused by Montbrun's removal, Napoleon sent his aide General de Caulaincourt to 2nd Cavalry Corps, which was to assist Eugène's assault on the Raevsky Redoubt. Just after one o'clock he rode to the head of Wathier's division and led three cuirassier regiments to the charge. Caulaincourt was killed almost at once, and Wathier's regiments were driven back by a storm of musketry. Their retirement hindered the advance of Defrance's Carabiniers[5] and the supporting movement of Latour-Maubourg's German kurassiers. The Saxons nevertheless succeeded in riding into the Redoubt, which was taken and held by the French infantry. Caulaincourt's dead body was carried on a bloody cloak to the rear.

'Whoever ordered the cavalry to make this extraordinary attack committed an unforgivable error,' wrote a French chasseur officer.[6] 'There is no glory in using cavalry prematurely for a job that does not suit it, nor in causing its best leaders to be killed.'[7]

At 3 p.m. the Russians began to retire. It was the crucial moment that Napoleon had so often described and so often recognized on other battlefields: the moment for reserves to be thrown in headlong to smash a yielding enemy into rout. Up at the front Ney and Murat had already seen it, and sent General Belliard back to Napoleon to ask for the support of the Imperial Guard. Napoleon merely gave them 30 pieces of light artillery, while Marshal Bessières went galloping across the battlefield to find out if the Guard's time had really come.

'You'll have to send the Guard in to finish it,' General Rapp urged the Emperor.

'And have it destroyed?' he replied. 'Supposing there is another battle to-morrow, what shall I fight it with?'

Bessières came back to report that the enemy retirement was well under way, and that it would be pointless to commit the Guard. It was precisely what Napoleon wanted to hear. The Guard did not attack and the Russians withdrew in good order, leaving the French to clear up the ghastly battlefield. The dead were piled in mounds eight corpses high and 50,000 wounded, including Rapp and Nansouty, waited for whatever help Larrey and his 36 surgeons could give them.

Montbrun's obituary was the most laconic ever published in the bulletin about a senior cavalry general. 'We have lost General of Division Count Montbrun,' it announced, 'killed by a cannon-shot.'

He was replaced by General Horace Sébastiani, who had previously commanded Montbrun's light cavalry division. Forty-two years old, a veteran of Marengo and Austerlitz, Sébastiani was a most attractive officer; his devastating good looks and fascinating manners, as a contemporary put it, had caused an insurrection in the salons and boudoirs of Paris. Partly because he was Corsican, and partly because he had rendered useful services in the *coup d'état* of Brumaire, he was one of Napoleon's favourites. This was just as well, because apart from an outstanding talent for leading sabre charges his conduct left much to be desired. In July his regiments had been surprised and badly mauled at Drissa; in August he had allowed his 3,000 troopers to be surrounded by a force of 12,000 Russian cavalry. After Borodino he was dispatched in pursuit of Kutusov. Completely deceived by a thin screen of enemy horse, Sébastiani led his corps 80 kilometres beyond Moscow to the south-east, while the Russians retired in safety to the south-west.

'General,' Napoleon told him, 'with you we march from one surprise to the next.'

★   ★   ★

From Borodino to Moscow the cavalry marched under better conditions. The roads were wide enough to take ten carriages abreast, and shaded on each side by a double row of birch trees. The men, however, were still on short rations, their regular diet consisting of potatoes and biscuits, baked in the ashes of the bivouac fires. Now and then it was supplemented by horsemeat; but except for the heart and liver, which tasted rather like chicken, it was so tough and stringy that many men could not eat it.

On 13 September the army bivouacked within sight of Moscow. Hundreds of brightly-painted domes and spires, topped by ornate crosses linked by thick gilded chains, were outlined against the reddish tints of sunset. It was a welcome sight for Napoleon's weary soldiers, and to Lieutenant Michel Combe of the 8th Chasseurs it proved irresistible. Deciding to take some unauthorised leave, at five in the afternoon Combe and a brother officer mounted their horses and rode towards the city. On the way they encountered the cavalry division commanded by General Bruyère, who asked them who they were and where they were going. Expecting to be put under arrest, they told him the truth, whereupon Bruyère ordered them to ride on into Moscow and enjoy themselves. 'If you can!' he added.

They soon discovered what he meant. Apart from a party of French gunners dragging artillery through the empty streets, the only human beings they encountered were three dead drunk Russians, sleeping in a cellar full of the finest French and Spanish wines, and an old crone.

When the French army entered Moscow next day, however, the inhabitants began to emerge from their hiding-places. Prostitutes wandered freely through the streets, for the magistrates and the police had quit the city. The better-class shopkeepers had also fled, leaving shops stocked with food that Captain Oriot estimated would last an occupying army for at least two years. Oriot was amazed at the size of Moscow. For five hours he explored the place, marvelling at the sumptuous mansions with their fine gardens, the wide streets and multi-coloured walls. He was looking at a doomed city. That evening most of the buildings he had admired were in flames, and the lead sheets from their roofs were crashing down into the streets.

Starting on the Solianka the fire raged for three days, destroying four-fifths of Moscow's pinewood dwellings and all but 200 of its stone buildings. Books could be read by the glare ten miles away, and for days afterwards Michel Combe's cloak smelled of smoke. When it was over, any food and valuables that had survived were looted by citizens and French soldiers alike. For 80 francs a grenadier of the Guard sold Combe a superb pelisse lined entirely with Siberian fox fur, which was rare even in Russia. Comparing it with similar but inferior garments that he had seen for sale in East Prussia, Combe valued it at over 1,000 crowns.

From the ruined city the bulk of the cavalry was ordered to Winkowo, which was aptly nicknamed Starvation Camp. Very few supplies were sent from Moscow, and to get a handful of chaff for their starving horses Murat's troopers had to make a daily journey of over 20 kilometres. The French and Russian outposts were very close together, but by mutual consent the two sides left each other in peace. On one occasion Murat actually visited the Russian lines to complain that their outposts had been placed too far forward, and the Russians obligingly withdrew to the positions that he indicated.

Meanwhile Napoleon waited at Moscow for the Tsar to negotiate, and the Tsar waited for winter. Already the nights were turning chilly. Oriot brooded over the words of a Russian guards officer, sent to parley after Borodino, who had been entertained by the officers of the 9th Cuirassiers. 'We knew as well as you did that we should be beaten,' he had said. 'But the winter will be our salvation. Your courage cannot withstand cold and hunger. Believe me, I know my country's climate, and I hope you never experience its malignant power.'

On 18 October the Emperor decided that he could wait no longer. On the 19th his army set out on its long march back to the Niemen, 550 miles to the west.

According to the 26th bulletin, it was fine marching in the crisp October air. 'The inhabitants of Russia do not recall such a season as we have had for the last 20 days. The army is in an extremely rich country, which may be compared to the best in France or Germany.'

The chosen line of march was via Kaluga, so as to avoid the country that had been wasted during the advance to Moscow; but on 24 October Kutusov fought Eugène's Italian Corps at Malo Jaroslavetz, and the French were forced back to the pillaged northern route. On the evening of Eugène's action, de Baudus was at Imperial Headquarters, which had been set up in a wretched house at Ghorodnia. In his memoirs he paints a vivid picture of the depressing scene; the silent Emperor, head in hands, sitting in a badly-lit, windowless room while Murat, Berthier and Bessières stood before him waiting for orders. None were given.

At 7 o'clock next morning Napoleon rode to inspect the scene of his stepson's battle, and was nearly captured by Cossacks. As they issued from a wood the Cossacks were taken for French cavalry because of their neat formation, but a staff officer recognized them just in time. 'They are Cossacks!' he cried.

'That's not possible,' Napoleon told him. 'They would not dare!'

'Yes, Sire,' shouted Rapp, seizing the Emperor's bridle. 'They are Cossacks!'

Charging at the head of the service squadron, Rapp was thrown heavily to the ground as a lance struck his horse; fortunately Bessières arrived with the heavy cavalry of the Guard and drove the Cossacks away. Seeing a man wearing a green uniform and armed with a lance, a Grenadier à Cheval promptly gave him a sword thrust; he was horrified to discover that the 'Cossack' was an aide de camp to Marshal Berthier, carrying the lance of a man whom he had just killed. Happily the sword thrust was not fatal.

★   ★   ★

After the previous day's fighting Malo Jaroslavetz was a grim sight. The streets were full of charred corpses, grotesquely mutilated by the artillery wheels that had passed over them. According to the French bulletin, over 1,000 of the Russian dead were grey-uniformed recruits with barely two months' military service. 'The old Russian infantry is destroyed,' the bulletin announced. 'Only the first rank is composed of soldiers; the second and third ranks are militia.' Meanwhile the march was continuing, through the pleasant country so reminiscent of the Fontainebleau district. 'It is beautiful weather and the roads are excellent. It is the end of autumn. This weather will last eight days longer, by which time we shall have arrived in our new positions.'

The temperature, however, was dropping, and the Cossacks were getting bolder. French cavalry no longer regarded '*La Cosaquaille*' with contempt. On the battlefield Cossack irregulars were notoriously unreliable, quick to ride away at the first hint of defeat: but now that the enemy was retreating they were in their element, able to find their way through unfamiliar territory without maps, guides or any knowledge of the local dialect. Nothing the French might do could shake off these Arabs of the North, as Larrey aptly called them. French staff officers, in particular, took good care to avoid them, and acquired the bad habit of questioning local inhabitants for information, rather than riding a few kilometres to get it at first hand.

'The Cossacks waged partisan warfare with incredible energy and bitterness,' wrote Michel Combe, 'falling suddenly on any detachment that left the main route; issuing like packs of furious wolves from thick woods, then vanishing back into them on their splendid little horses, having done us the greatest possible damage, and without ever giving quarter.'[8]

On 27 October the thermometer plunged; soon afterwards it began to snow. Roads, fields and ditches having disappeared, the route was only recognizable by hummocks of snow made by the corpses underneath. Every afternoon a bizarre scene occurred between 3 and 4 o'clock.

Without orders men began to straggle away to left and right of the line of march to search for food in the neighbouring villages. Except for the halted rearguard, the white landscape that had recently been filled with thousands of shuffling figures was deserted.

Many firearms had been thrown away, and many more were unusable through neglect. It hardly mattered, for in November the cold became so intense that frozen hands could no longer hold weapons. De Baudus recalled the time, years before, when Eugène had been uneasy about Napoleon's quarrel with the Pope, and the possibility of France's Head of State being excommunicated. 'Why, what do you suppose would happen?' Napoleon had chaffed him. 'Do you think the weapons would fall from my soldiers' hands?'

Unable to stand nine degrees of frost, the few remaining Norman horses in the cuirassier regiments perished, and as the weather worsened the many southerners in the army ceased to have any military value. One night encampment in 22° of cold destroyed the Neapolitan cavalry contingent; the Bavarians died in hundreds. Discipline was affected even in the Guard.

'These veterans were given the name of Grumblers,' wrote de Baudus, 'and towards the end they well deserved it by virtue of their behaviour, even towards their own officers.' The rest of the army had always disliked soldiers of the Guard, partly because of their arrogant attitude towards officers and men of the Line, partly because they always got the best rations and billets. In Russia the dislike turned to contempt.[9] That November the army reached Smolensk to find that the expected issue of rations would not take place; the Guard had got there first.

In the first ten days of November 30,000 horses died, and without horses to draw them many guns had to be abandoned. Cavalrymen disembowelled their dead mounts and lay down in the warm entrails to sleep, but the pains caused by their shrinking boots kept them awake. Once the boots were removed they could not be put on again.

There was no longer enough cavalry to lead or connect the columns, and reconnaissance was limited to one kilometre. By 14 November only 500 men in the Guard cavalry were still mounted; they dared not use their stirrups, because had they done so their feet would have stuck fast to the frozen metal. Some of the dismounted troopers had cut holes in the middle of their saddlecloths and wore them like ponchos; de Baudus, however, saw one Grenadier à Cheval whose outer garment was a fantastic patchwork of multi-coloured cloth. On one foot he wore a boot, on the other fragments of material and pieces of his shabracque, bound together with strips of copper. Apart from his sword, his most carefully guarded possession was a square of linen which he used both as handker-chief and tobacco-pouch, washing it clean whenever he could find a fire to dry it by.

Apart from horseflesh the army ate black puddings made from horses' blood, and soup consisting of cart grease and gunpowder mixed with melted snow. In most men the will to survive extinguished all feelings of comradeship and pity. An infantryman who charged five francs for a drink from his pitcher of spirits refused to deal with one man, saying, '*Eau-de-vie* would be wasted on you; you're dying.' Stunned by a fall from his horse, an officer regained consciousness to find that he had been stripped naked. Soldiers who succeeded in building a fire sat round it on frozen corpses and swore at anyone who tried to join them; except for the fortunate General G-----, even senior officers were turned away.

General G----- had lost his brigade, his horses, his servants and all his baggage, but he had managed to save a cooking-pot. This was a priceless asset, since those who had been lucky enough to find something to eat had nothing in which to cook it. For the loan of his pot the general required the best seat at the fire and a generous portion of whatever was cooked in it. Next morning the pot was scrupulously cleaned and returned to him. Slinging it once more round his shoulders, he set out on the day's march with his supper guaranteed.

★   ★   ★

By the end of November it was so cold that even the pursuing Cossacks had dismounted. Since everyone had taken clothing from the dead, it was impossible to tell a man's rank or regiment, and except in the rearguard all discipline had collapsed. Many men refused to go further, hoping to be captured and given food. Birds fell frozen from the tree-tops. Men who saw a fire 30 or 40 paces away would stretch out their hands towards it, as if they could feel its warmth, then suddenly drop dead. Their shoes and clothing were immediately searched for scraps of food.

On 25 November the terrible four-day crossing of the Berezina began. Russian artillery played on both banks, ploughing great holes in the huddled masses that waited to cross the river and jamming the bridges with corpses. 'You had to clamber over them,' Michel Combe recalled. 'They were slippery with blood, and if you had fallen you would have been trampled underfoot and crushed to death. You had to make your way forward sword in hand, sabring without pity, keeping as near to the middle of the bridge as possible and pushing on with your head lowered like an angry bull's.'[10]

The French hussar officer Victor Dupuy had the good fortune to fall in behind a statuesque Carabinier officer mounted on a powerful horse, and rode close behind him to safety. But for this man's help in clearing the way, both Dupuy and his feeble horse would have perished.

Thanks to the Prussian Army's superior care of horses, the 2nd Prussian Hussars still had a high proportion of mounted men.[11] Using their sabres, it took them five hours to ride the last 180 steps to their crossing-point.

By the 28th nearly 30,000 men had passed over the river, but thousands more were waiting to cross. On the 29th a horde of Cossacks approached. The bridges were set on fire, and many men who were in the act of crossing died in the flames.

Six days later Napoleon handed over the army to Murat, who led it as far as Wilna. Wilna was almost the last station on the army's Calvary; 50 miles further on the survivors crossed the River Niemen into the havens of East Prussia and the Grand Duchy of Warsaw.

III

'Ordinary men died,' the Emperor observed about the 1812 campaign. 'Men of iron were taken prisoner. I only brought back with me men of bronze.'

Even the men of bronze, however, were utterly exhausted. Marshal Berthier was on the verge of a breakdown, Ney seemed strange and withdrawn, Bessières found it difficult to concentrate. 'I don't look for glory now,' wrote Prince Eugène. 'The price is too high.'

He had, however, retained his sense of humour. From Gumbinnen in East Prussia he wrote his wife that, for a joke, she could tell the ladies of Paris that half their acquaintances would be coming back without noses or ears. The joke would not have appealed to General Rapp; but for the healing skills of a Polish barber he would have lost his nose and two of his fingers as well. Meanwhile, Pomeranian housewives had stopped emptying buckets outside their back doors, for fear of the faceless *mutilés* of the Grand Army who were said to be lurking in the woods.

With the remnant of the Guard, Bessières returned to Elbing, scene of the French cavalry's magnificent parade in 1807. While his men refreshed themselves with *eau-de-vie* and Baltic herrings he stayed with the wine merchant Habeck. An old friend of the French army, Habeck was one of the few Prussians who had not turned against it in its hour of defeat.[12]

Bessières was highly dissatisfied with the Guard. Less than ten of its officers, he wrote, were fit to belong to it, and the experiment of promoting Guard NCOs to be officers in the Guard, rather than in the line regiments, had proved to be a great mistake.

★　　★　　★

Another cavalryman who recovered from the Russian campaign at Elbing was Captain Oriot of the 9th Cuirassiers, who changed his shirt there for the first time in seven weeks.

★　　★　　★

Michel Combe ended the campaign in style, travelling from Wilna to Koenigsberg in an open carriage. Despite 25° of cold he thoroughly enjoyed the experience.

> The weather was superb. We glided along on a surface of ice like an express messenger, in other words doing at least four leagues an hour. Wrapped in a rug, with my feet also wrapped up inside their boots and my face protected, I watched enchanted as the snow-covered country-side flew past on either side of me. We arrived at Koenigsberg at 9 in the morning, and got down in the Grand Place at the Hotel de Paris.[13]

For Lieutenant Combe, who enjoyed his creature comforts, East Prussia's ancient capital seemed like Paradise; at 8 o'clock every morning, an hotel servant brought a bottle of Madeira and half a dozen hot pastries to his bedside. . . .

At the end of the year his regiment went into cantonments in Silesia with 75 men left out of 800. Not all of them were fit for service. One captain kept knocking on the local townspeoples' doors, begging for food and asking if Cossacks had been seen in the neighbourhood.

The 8th Chasseurs were by no means a unique case, insofar as casualties were concerned. The 4th Chevaux-légers had come out of Russia with 17 men, the 9th Cuirassiers with 39 horses out of 970. It had taken 12 years to create the cavalry that had ridden to Austerlitz, and six months to destroy it.

8

Fields of Carnage and Glory

'Since the greater part of her soil is cultivated with
the use of oxen, France does not produce born horsemen.'
– *Flavien d'Aldéguier, former riding instructor at the
Saumur cavalry school.*

I

During his stay at Koenigsberg in 1812, Michel Combe saw the driver of
a Prussian army wagon deliberately knock a hobbling French cuirassier
into the gutter, and as he passed by the fallen trooper the driver lashed
out at him with his whip. It was typical of the Prussian Army's attitude.
Now that the French Army was so weak, Prussian soldiers thought only
of avenging the disasters of 1806 and the humiliating peace.

Napoleon was confident that he could beat them again, even without
drawing on the 200,000 troops serving with the French armies in Spain.
'A great part of the army is lost,' he told Marshal Kellermann at Mainz
in December 1812. 'But in a few months' time I shall have another
300,000 bayonets at my command.'

He was almost as good as his word. By calling up the class of 1814
prematurely he increased his infantry to a total of 200,000, and the
recruits were soon taught how to use their bayonets. With astonishing
speed a powerful force of artillery was created. To turn recruits into
efficient artillerymen – especially layers – took more time than Napoleon
could afford, but Europe's most famous gunner still had his talent for
improvisation. Naval gunners serving on the warships lying at French
ports were transferred to the army; cannon were obtained by drawing on
the huge reserves in the arsenals of Strasbourg, Metz and Antwerp;
horses were provided by the remount depôts.

General Bourcier, the legendary organizer of the French remount
service, was ordered to give the artillery's requirements top priority, and

113

obeyed with his usual ruthlessness and efficiency.[1] As a result the cavalry had to take inferior replacements. There were no longer any of the famous heavy cavalry-type mounts in Normandy, except for a handful in the canton of Le Merlerault; consequently the cuirassier regiments re-forming at Frankfort and Stettin had to be content with Hanoverian horses, and so had the cavalry of the Guard. Manpower was another problem, since it took almost as long to train a cavalryman as it did to train a gunner. To reinforce the line cavalry, a few regiments were brought back from Spain, and all officers and men of the mounted gendarmerie who were fit and not too old for active service were posted to the army.

At the end of February 1813 Marshal Bessières arrived at Paris to reorganize the Guard. Its cavalry was a skeletal force, consisting of 773 men and 821 horses; the Grenadiers à Cheval mustered only 127 men, and the Chasseurs 260. By Imperial decree, Bessières was ordered to increase both the Chasseurs and the 2nd Lancers to 2,000 men, and the Grenadiers à Cheval to 1,500:[2] but even after the Garde à Cheval of Paris had been incorporated in his regiments barely half these figures had been reached, and there was no time to do more.

On 17 March Prussia declared war.

★   ★   ★

Napoleon was still master of western Germany. With the Prussians and Russians concentrating at Dresden, his first task was to unite his new army with the survivors of 1812, who were lying west of the lower Elbe under the command of Prince Eugène. At the end of March, Bessières was ordered to assemble all his Guard cavalry at Frankfort. 'I hope we shall meet again,' the Marshal told a friend before he left Paris. 'But with so many young soldiers in the ranks, the high officers must not spare themselves.'

It was not only in the lower ranks, however, that the quality of the French army had declined. Many of the senior officers were still shaken by their Russian ordeal; in one division all decisions had to be taken by the commander of its light cavalry brigade, who had only just been promoted from colonel. The malaise had even spread to the General Staff, as Bessières found out during the advance through Germany.

Whenever the Emperor changed his headquarters in the field, the Guard sent an advance party on ahead to prepare whatever place he was moving to, and as this party left very early in the morning it had to be given its orders on the previous night. On 27 April the Emperor was at

Erfurt. He intended to move on the following day, but by 10 o'clock that night no orders for the advance party had been issued. General Berthezène, interim commander of the Guard's infantry, sought guidance from Marshal Berthier and General Duroc. They could not give him any, because the Emperor had already retired for the night, and neither his Chief of Staff nor the Grand Marshal of the Palace dared to disturb him.

In desperation Berthezène explained his dilemma to Bessières. The Marshal went at once to the Emperor's quarters, obtained the necessary orders, and gave them to Berthezène with his own hands.

Three days later Napoleon's advance guard encountered enemy forces at Weissenfels and pushed them back towards Leipzig. The retreating allies took up strong positions defending the defiles of Poserna and Rippach, which the French attacked next morning.

Marshal Bessières was in low spirits that day. At first he refused to eat any breakfast, saying that he had no appetite; he was coaxed into changing his mind by de Baudus, who pointed out that a long day's fighting lay ahead of them. 'Well,' said Bessières morosely, 'if a cannon-shot is going to carry me off to-day, I suppose it had better not find me empty.' As soon as the meal was over he gave de Baudus the key to his portfolio and asked him to fetch his wife's letters. When de Baudus returned Bessières threw them on the fire.

Soon afterwards they rode out together to the White Swan, the Weissenfels posting house, where Imperial Headquarters had been set up. De Baudus noticed that his Marshal's face had lost all its colour.

To open the action Ney's infantry stormed the village of Rippach, but when they tried to advance beyond it they found the plain covered by allied cavalry. At 12.45 a messenger arrived at Weissenfels to report that Souham's division was held up by Cossacks and enemy batteries, whereupon Napoleon ordered Bessières to support Ney with the cavalry of the Guard.[3] Accompanied by a small mounted escort, Bessières galloped forward to reconnoitre the ground.

The Marshal's little cavalcade included his aide Alexandre de Bourjolly, his Mameluke servant Mirza, and a Guard cavalry NCO named Jordan, who had served Bessières as orderly for several years. As the party rode along the high ground bordering the Leipzig road it came into the range of a Prussian battery that was just coming into action. The first shot it fired hit Jordan and decapitated him.

Moments later Bessières reported to Ney, who was watching the Prussian cavalry that covered the plain in front of him. The hero of the Moskowa greeted him brusquely. As at Borodino, Ney had asked the

Emperor for support, and as at Borodino the Emperor had merely sent up Marshal Bessières.

'You've come on your own, then,' Ney grunted. 'Look, if your cavalry was up here, there'd be a good job for it to do.'

Bessières promised to fetch it, pointed out to Ney the spot at which it would arrive, and rode away.

According to de Baudus, the death of Jordan had deeply affected his Marshal. As he passed by the headless body, Bessières reined in his horse and said, 'I want this young man buried. The Emperor won't like it if he sees a dead under-officer of the Guard here, because if this position is re-taken the enemy will recognise his uniform and think that the Guard has retreated.'

As he finished speaking the Prussian battery fired again. The shot ricochetted from an adjacent wall and struck Bessières, smashing his riding hand and throwing him to the ground. When de Bourjolly got to him he was dead. His watch, which had not been hit, had stopped at ten minutes to one.

Marshal Ney arrived on the scene shortly afrerwards. In Ney's philosophy it was right for soldiers to die on the battlefield, and better for Marshal Ney to be mourning a comrade than for one of his comrades to be mourning Marshal Ney.

'That's our Fate,' he said quietly, as he gazed down at the corpse in its brilliant uniform. 'It's a good way to die.'

In the Emperor's view, however, Fate had picked a very inconvenient moment; in the interests of morale he decided not to announce the famous Marshal's death until after the approaching battle.

'Did you know Bessières long?' he asked Baron Fain that evening.

'Yes, Sire,' the secretary replied. 'His death will grieve the army, which loved him. He was a loyal friend to Your Majesty, a devoted servant.'

'You could also say he was an honest man,' the Emperor answered. 'I need a victory to make up for such a blow.'

Despite Baron Fain's epitaph, at the time of his death Bessières was loved only by the Guard. The rest of the army still blamed him for the defeat at Fuentes, and for the Guard having been held back at Borodino. But however unpopular he had become, he was still admired for his courage and his tremendous service record, which few men in the French army could equal. Since the day when he had joined Pérignon's cavalry legion of the Pyrenees he had campaigned in Egypt, Poland and Russia, twice in Italy, Austria and Germany, and three times in Spain.

'He was one of our old companions of Italy,' wrote Marshal Marmont in his memoirs, 'and the army felt his loss. I felt it more than most, on account of the memories we shared. Though I was separated from him for a long period, and had some grounds for complaint against him, we had made up our differences and revived our old friendship. A man of good heart and spirit, he always gave the Emperor sound advice.'

No-one knew that better than the Emperor himself. 'He was as valuable for his *coup d'oeil* and his great experience of the cavalry arm as for his personal qualities,' he explained to Marie-Louise. To the heart-broken Duchess of Istria he wrote, 'The loss this causes you and your children is great, without doubt, but mine is greater still.'

For the Marshal's widow, who had never had the least suspicion that he was unfaithful to her, his death was a double blow, for on opening his bureau she found proof of his liaison with Virginie Oreille, a young dancer of the Opera ballet. It was largely because of his infatuation with this lady that Bessières, whose yearly income totalled 263,000 francs, left debts of over a million.[4]

*   *   *

The Emperor was soon to lose another old companion of Italy, and an even older comrade than Bessières: Andoche Junot, Duke of Abrantès, whose friendship with Napoleon had begun at the siege of Toulon in 1793.

When Junot had arrived to take up his command in the 1812 campaign, men who had not seen him for several years had been shocked by the change in him; they scarcely recognized the slim, devil-may-care cavalryman they remembered in this heavily-built, stoop-shouldered, slow-moving man who was not yet 41. His conduct in Russia had matched his appearance; during the advance to Moscow, a Russian force that was virtually trapped had been able to withdraw largely because Junot had handled his corps so sluggishly, he who had once led 300 horsemen in a headlong charge against 10,000 Turks, and been given the nickname of The Tempest.

After the Russian campaign he was made Governor of Illyria, but his behaviour grew increasingly eccentric and it was plain that he was going mad. Eugène was ordered to send him home by the Emperor, who wrote that Junot must be removed without delay from the land where he was creating 'so painful a spectacle'; at the same time Napoleon insisted that his old friend be given all the courtesies that became his rank.

In the summer of 1813 Junot set out for Burgundy, wearing his magnificent uniform of Colonel-General of Hussars. ('If the post had not existed,' the Emperor had once told him, 'I should have had to create it for you, Monsieur le Sabreur.') For part of the journey he travelled outside his coach, sitting up on the driver's box; but not before they had taken away his sword.

Soon after reaching his father's château at Montbard he threw himself from an upstairs window to prove that he could fly, and died within the week.

II

The day after Bessières' death Napoleon won the victory that he needed at Lutzen, but the French cavalry was not strong enough to exploit it. To disguise its weakness Napoleon had organized it into an impressive number of regiments, but many of these so-called regiments were hardly the size of a normal squadron, and some of them had almost as many officers and NCOs as men. General Defrance's division consisted of ten dragoon regiments and the 13th Cuirassiers;[5] its total strength was 11 squadrons. The Reserve Cavalry comprised five corps.[6] On paper they looked formidable, with effectives of over 40,000 men and 96 guns; but out of 10,000 troopers in Sébastiani's corps only 5,000 were fit for battle. The rest were Marie-Louises, as the new conscripts were called.

For all its defects, the Napoleonic system of cavalry training had always managed to teach a young recruit the basic essentials; how to keep his seat, handle and care for his horse and accoutrements, recognize the trumpet calls, and perform most if not all of the 18 manoeuvres in the drill book. In 1813 there was not time enough even for that. As Marshal Marmont put it, all that the cavalry conscripts of 1813 knew about their trade was whatever they had been able to pick up during the ride from the regimental depôts to the frontiers. Some of them, however, had served an even shorter apprenticeship; having marched into Germany on foot, they only met their horses on the eve of going into action.

The cuirassier recruits complained bitterly about the weight of their helmets, swords and cuirasses, and could barely manage to charge in column at the trot. The conscripts in 5th Cavalry Corps were the youngest and most ill-trained soldiers that General Pajol had ever seen in his life.

Some had only mounted a horse for the first time in their lives two weeks previously. Most of them did not know how to handle their horses or their weapons; it was all they could do to hold the reins in one hand and a sabre in the other. They had to use both hands to execute a movement to right or left.[7]

There was little time to train them, for after Lutzen the French army pursued the allies eastwards towards the Elbe. The Russians having conducted the retreat in their usual pitiless fashion, the countryside was devastated, and in Saxony, whose king was still Napoleon's faithful ally, the people were destitute.

Louis Rilliet, a young Swiss who was serving as a sub-lieutenant in the 1st Cuirassiers, felt desperately sorry for them. 'Once I was quartered with a bourgeois,' he wrote, 'and while I drank wine and ate meat this poor man, seated at the same table with his family, drank water and ate potatoes.' The friendliness of the Germans amazed him. 'They give you a better welcome than a Frenchman ever does; and when you leave next morning, well fed and rested, instead of asking you for anything they thank you for behaving so well towards them.'

In his memoirs, written without the boasting that mars so many contemporary French accounts, he vividly describes conditions in the 1st Cuirassiers, which in d'Hautpoul's day had been one of the finest cavalry regiments in Europe. During one halt he saw a veteran captain of the regiment sitting surrounded by troopers' saddles, which he was repairing and adjusting with his own hands. The young Swiss envied him his knowledge. Rilliet was only 19, and his military service consisted mainly of two years at the cavalry school for officer-aspirants at Saint Germain; he regretted that he had not been taught more about care of horses.

When an officer knows how to care for a horse, and treat it for the innumerable little injuries that happen every day, how to shoe it, adjust and correct the saddle and equipment, he can render the greatest service to his troop.[8]

Three weeks after Lutzen Napoleon won another battle at Bautzen, pushing the allies back over the Elbe: but again his cavalry failed to exploit the victory, and even its conduct on the field was critized. 'It is with sorrow that I inform Your Highness,' Marshal Macdonald reported to Berthier, 'that only the cuirassiers have done their duty.' He might have added that, at one stage of the battle, three cavalry regiments had been kept halted under enemy artillery fire for over six hours.

Fortunately an armistice was arranged after Bautzen, giving the French cavalry a chance to train up its recruits. According to Victor Dupuy, commanding a squadron of the 7th Hussars, the results were encouraging:

We did not attempt to turn out stylish horsemen, just reliable troopers who could handle their weapons properly. To achieve this, we made them trot and gallop without stirrups, carrying arms and baggage. To begin with they rolled about in the saddle and even fell off, but they soon acquired the confidence that they needed. We called these young soldiers, who had been mounted and equipped by their communes, the Hussars of the Don.[9]

For three months the French cavalry was kept hard at work. Rilliet, whose regiment formed part of 2nd Cavalry Corps, was irritated by what he regarded as General Sébastiani's 'pitiless' inspections.

I called them pitiless, not because he was unpleasant – on the contrary, he was a most charming man. But he never over-looked the slightest detail . . . We younger officers considered him too critical, telling each other that his passion for detail was a fault, and that a general officer ought not to concern himself with such trivia. Experience has taught me otherwise. Cavalry can only survive by paying attention to details which have to do with care of horses. Scrutinising us as he did, General Sébastiani was merely proving that he had an expert's knowledge of the cavalry arm.[10]

★   ★   ★

When the armistice ended Austria joined the coalition against Napoleon, and an army of 130,000 men under Schwarzenberg entered the lists. Schwarzenberg, however, was a poor substitute for the Archduke Karl. At the end of August Napoleon smashed the allies again at Dresden, taking 15,000 prisoners. The battle was fought over two days in drenching rain, and many of the enemy cartridges failed to go off. Even so the French cavalry made a poor showing; only after Latour-Maubourg had put 50 of his escort lancers into the first rank of his cuirassier regiments could the heavy cavalry make any impression on the Austrian squares.

Except at Dresden, things went badly for the French in August, due to the blunders of Napoleon's subordinates. Oudinot was beaten at Gross Beeren and Vandamme's corps was all but destroyed at Kulm. Marshal Macdonald, commanding three *corps d'armée* and Sébastiani's cavalry, was routed by Blucher on the Katzbach. In Sébastiani's corps the light cavalry division lost half its horses and most of its artillery; even his cuirassiers abandoned some of their guns. Sébastiani had the news of the Emperor's victory at Dresden read out to raise his men's morale, but while some of them shouted '*Vive l'Empereur!*' others shouted '*Vive les pommes de terre!*'

Following these defeats, which forced him to abandon his plans to march on Berlin, Napoleon was in a black mood for days, and even vented his anger on the cavalry of the Guard. Seeing Edouard de Colbert at the head of his lancers, Napoleon asked him if he was satisfied with them, to which Colbert replied that both men and horses were in fine fettle. The lancers of Berg, which had recently been seconded to him, were some of the finest troops he had ever had under his orders.

'Yes,' said the Emperor sarcastically, 'since they happen to be foreigners, you *would* be satisfied with them.' Then turning to Nansouty he remarked, 'I find it absurd that French generals should have a preference for foreign troops.' When Macdonald and Sébastiani rejoined him, Napoleon galloped up to General Saint Germain and asked him angrily, 'How is it that the cuirassiers let their guns be captured?'

'Sire,' the hard-bitten cuirassier general replied, 'if we'd been guarding them ourselves we should still have them now – and others to offer to Your Majesty as well.'

Even more serious than the loss of guns was the wastage in manpower. By the beginning of the autumn Napoleon's cavalry was reduced to 35,000 men, and now that the Austrians had arrived it was outnumbered by three to one. Against the troopers of Austrian Uhlan regiments, who were armed with lances, the French conscripts were helpless, and to make matters worse the Cossacks had abandoned their usual harassing tactics to fight in the open. On 16 September they actually surprised French cavalry in full manoeuvre.

'It was utter rout,' wrote Michel Combe. 'The plain was covered with fugitives who were massacred by the Cossacks. They did not even try to defend themselves, but let themselves be killed with their sabres on their shoulders.'[11]

Marshal Murat was tired of leading charges with such unpromising material, and he saw no point in fighting the Austrians; indeed, provided they would guarantee his throne at Naples he was even prepared to join them. 'Everything is going badly,' he wrote on 19 September. 'The army longs for peace. Only the Emperor resists the general mood.'

This was not quite true. Unlike the Reserve Cavalry commander, Sub-lieutenant Rilliet had been greatly heartened by the victory at Dresden and by the change in the weather. Now that the rain no longer fell in torrents life in the 1st Cuirassiers was much improved, and Rilliet was even beginning to enjoy the bivouacs. Whenever the regiment bivouacked under reasonable conditions, quarrels were made up or forgotten and the spirit of comradeship became uppermost. Officers and men worked side by side, building fires, cooking meat and vegetables for the evening meal, collecting dry straw to sleep on.

After a long day in the saddle, sleep came easily to the men of the 1st Cuirassiers.

> Many times, when I was roused to serve on a night patrol, it put me in a quiet and even solemn mood to look at the long lines of peacefully sleeping men, oblivious of the night, heedless of the fact that in a few hours time they might be causing or suffering death. Sometimes, when we were on high ground, one could see another line of fires on the horizon. They were those of the enemy, who were probably sleeping just as peacefully as us, wishing us no more harm at this strange hour than we did them. There is nothing stranger than war![12]

Rilliet's morale improved further when he heard that the Emperor would review the division at the end of September. Apart from the honour of parading under the great man's eye, the regiment could expect to receive the usual quota of promotions and decorations, and Rilliet's anticipation was heightened by the knowledge that Lieutenant Dehayes intended to make a personal appeal. Dehayes, who had recently been widowed, was worried about his children's future; he hoped that Napoleon might help him to educate one of his sons.

The review was held on 28 September. When Napoleon asked the colonel of the regiment if he had any favours to ask, the colonel bowed but did not speak. 'Then I allot the regiment five crosses of the Legion,' said Napoleon with a shrug. 'Four legionaries' and an officer's.' He began to pass down the lines and in due course came to Dehayes.

Unfortunately the lieutenant had lost his nerve and was completely tongue-tied. The inspection ended: but as the Emperor rode on to the next regiment Dehayes spurred his horse and rode after him. Suddenly aware that he was being followed by a strange officer, Napoleon halted his inspection of the 5th Cuirassiers and asked him what he wanted. Dehayes finally found his voice and explained his problem.

'What rank are you?' the Emperor asked.

'Lieutenant, Sire.'

'Since when?'

'For the last eighteen years.'

'Then you are a bad character,' Napoleon told him brusquely.

'If I was a bad character, Sire,' Dehayes argued, 'you wouln't have taken me into your Guides, when you were General-in-Chief of the Army of Italy.'

On hearing that he was talking to a veteran of '96, Napoleon immediately sent for Dehayes' colonel.

'What do you know of this officer?' he demanded.

'He is a brave man, Sire,' the colonel answered, 'and worthy of Your Majesty's interest. I was going to propose him for one of the crosses Your Majesty was good enough to award us.'

'You have no complaints, then, Colonel, to make against him?'

'None, Sire.'

'Well,' said Napoleon tartly, 'I've got plenty to make to you.' Turning back to Dehayes he took him by the arm and said, 'Console yourself, *mon vieux*. I'm giving you the Cross, I'm making you a captain, and I'm putting *both* your sons into the *lycée*.'

III

As the autumn wore on Napoleon's allies began to desert him. The rulers of the puppet states that Napoleon had created in Germany believed that the Empire's days were numbered; when Metternich invited them to keep their territories by changing sides most of them accepted. Troopers of the French regiments that had been brigaded with German ones lost many old friends when the Bavarians and Wurttembergers rode away, and the 10th Hussars said good-bye to their comrades in the Baden Dragoons with tears in their eyes.

Abandoned by all but the King of Saxony, Napoleon retreated westwards from Dresden, hoping that he could still beat the three allied armies[13] in detail. On 16 October two of them attacked him simultaneously at Leipzig.

On the first day of this extraordinary battle infantry conscripts fought like veterans while veteran cavalry regiments ran away. Routing Pahlen's Russian horsemen, Latour-Maubourg's cuirassiers broke an infantry square and took 26 guns, but Murat subsequently led them into marshy ground where they were demoralized by artillery fire. Charged by Guard Cossacks and Russian hussars they turned bridle and fled at the gallop. Separated from his regiment, Sub-lieutenant Chalendar led a handful of cuirassiers back to the French lines; as he approached an infantry battalion in square the commander of it stepped forward and shouted to him, 'Go back, Monsieur! We are about to receive cavalry!'

Chalendar was astonished, because the infantry were at ease with their muskets by their sides; but presently a Prussian cavalry regiment came charging into view. Waiting until it was only a few dozen paces away, the battalion commander calmly ordered his men to take aim. At the first volley the Prussians pulled their horses round and rode away.

A much more determined charge was made by Hungarian horse on Sébastiani's 2nd Cavalry Corps, which included the celebrated Carabinier brigade. Rilliet describes the unexpected outcome.

> We were in column of regiments. The 1st Carabiniers were in front and General Sébastiani was to the right of this regiment: all at once a mass of enemy cavalry, mainly Hungarian hussars, rode furiously down on the Carabiniers. 'Bravo!' cried the general, laughing and waving the riding crop which was the only weapon that he deigned to use. 'This will be charming; hussars charging the Carabiniers!'[14]

Rilliet thought that the huge Carabinier troopers need only draw their long swords to frighten the enemy away,[15] but he was mistaken. When the Hungarians were 100 paces from them, the 1st Carabiniers turned about and rode back on to the 2nd regiment; both regiments then fled, taking the leading squadron of the 1st Cuirassiers with them.

Sébastiani arrived at a triple gallop, and Rilliet had never seen anyone in such a furious temper as the handsome Corsican, nor had he ever heard a distinguished general use such bad language. 'Order a picquet of cuirassiers to protect those Carabiniers!' he roared. 'Those ————s! Those ————ing ————s!'

When the day's fighting ended the Carabiniers tried to take up quarters at a farm that was already occupied by the 5th Cuirassiers. The cuirassiers would not let them in. 'Pass on, Carabiniers, there's nothing for you here,' they shouted. 'If it's hospitality you want, try the Hungarian hussars!'

On the 17th, which was spent mostly in skirmishing, reinforcements arrived to swell the ranks of the allies, who disposed 300,000 men against 130,000 French. When the battle began again next day Napoleon's army occupied a huge semi-circle, the bulk of the Reserve Cavalry being drawn up four miles south of Leipzig. As Rilliet mounted up that morning he noticed that the cuirassier who held his horse seemed in low spirits.

'It's a fine morning,' the young Swiss remarked cheerfully.

'Yes, Lieutenant. But a lot of men who are watching the sun rise to-day will never see it set.'

'That's true,' Rilliet agreed. 'But it won't apply to you or me, I'm sure.'

'Let's hope so,' the trooper answered.

The division was hardly formed up when it was surrounded by

Cossacks, and though they dared not attack they could not be driven off. Presently Rilliet heard a cannon-shot whistling through the air, and immediately afterwards he felt something on his face. He put up a hand and brushed it away.

Next moment I saw two men lying on the ground. One of them was a trooper of the leading rank, a fine chap from Paris called Gonthier. The same shot had struck the cuirassier in the rank behind him, and it was the man who had brought me my horse half an hour before. It was his brains that I had felt on my face.

A moment later the lieutenant who commanded the troop next to Rilliet's had his horse killed under him.

A former NCO of the Guard, he calmly removed the saddle, bridle and portmanteau, hoisted it all on his shoulders, and set off to look for another horse. It seems he didn't find one, for we never saw him again. I took over command of his troop, which consisted of 22 men, and when we reached Leipzig that night there were only six left. All the others were dead, wounded or dismounted.[16]

For the first time in his career Napoleon had been decisively beaten in battle; by the following day his army was in full retreat. As Rilliet rode away from Leipzig he found himself next to a white-cloaked cuirassier who was groaning with pain; when Rilliet asked if he was wounded he replied that he had just had his arm cut off.

'Are you mad?' Rilliet demanded. 'Why didn't you stay in Leipzig?'

'Because the enemy will be there to-morrow.'

'Well, what of that?' said Rilliet. 'They are not savages; you will be cared for. Besides, there are French surgeons still working there.'

'Lieutenant,' the trooper told him, 'I'd rather snuff it than mix with scum.'

★ ★ ★

Outdistancing the pursuing allies, Napoleon's army marched for the Rhine, cutting its way through a force of Bavarians at Hanau. The enemy were commanded by von Wrede, whose cavalry proved even more unreliable than Murat's.

As one Bavarian regiment rode into action it encountered two squadrons of Gardes d'Honneur,[17] formed up at the halt with their sabres on their shoulders. Half-trained and ill-mounted, these young troopers had no idea what they should do, but luckily two squadrons of Guard Chasseurs were drawn up behind them. 'Hold your ground and point your sabres,' the Chasseurs shouted. 'If you budge, you're dead!'

The advice was well taken. According to Rilliet, who witnessed the incident, the Bavarians had arrived on the scene like thunderbolts; suddenly confronted by a handful of youths who were fighting their first campaign, they turned away without striking a blow.

The retreat continued unopposed towards Mainz. 'What a mob!' wrote Rilliet. 'Men armed and unarmed, mounted and dismounted, soldiers and employees, sick and wounded. Amazed to see such a multitude, the local inhabitants could not understand why we were abandoning Germany. Alas! how few real soldiers remained in that vast crowd.'

At Mainz, to his astonishment, French customs officials insisted on inspecting the army's baggage, apparently on the Emperor's orders. Opening Rilliet's portmanteau, which resembled a huge sausage, they were put out to find that it contained nothing but soiled and tattered linen.

At 11 a.m. on 3 November the 1st Cuirassiers crossed the Rhine, 'I am practically naked,' Rilliet wrote to his mother. 'Boots torn, trousers ditto, coat not too good. I am going to drape myself in my cloak like the hero of a melodrama.'

Amongst the soldiers who arrived in France, he was glad to recognize the cuirassier trooper who had lost his arm.

IV

By the end of the year the Empire had ceased to exist. Germany was lost, and Wellington was pushing up through the Peninsula; early in 1814 the victors of Leipzig began pouring across the Rhine.

One by one the cavalry leaders were leaving the army. Latour-Maubourg had lost a leg at Leipzig, Walther had died of exhaustion. Murat had returned to Naples, to continue bargaining with the Austrians for his throne; Pajol to Paris to recover from his wounds. The Reserve Cavalry was taken over by General Grouchy.

He found that every horse in his command needed winter shoeing, and that there was no money to pay for it. On 14 January, as he prepared to evacuate Nancy, he asked the Mayor to lend him 15,000 francs, against his own signature and that of Marshal Victor. Not until Grouchy threatened to arrest him and take him away with the cavalry would the Mayor agree.

For two more months Napoleon fought against the inevitable, striking blow after blow at the allied armies advancing on Paris. Under Grouchy and Kellermann, the dragoon regiments that had been recalled from Spain achieved some notable successes. Kellermann fought on with them to the end; but on 7 March Grouchy was badly wounded at Craonne, and took no further part in the campaign.

Nansouty was the next to go. Since Walther's death he had led the cavalry of the Guard, but the sardonic aristocrat was too out-spoken for a Guard command. After the defeat at Laon on 9 March he was replaced by Sébastiani, officially on grounds of ill-health. On his way to Paris the convoy he was travelling with was attacked near the Aisne by Cossacks. Nansouty managed to reach the river bank, but as he urged his horse into the water it was shot under him. The supposedly ailing general swam across to safety, still wearing his heavy cavalry boots.

★   ★   ★

'Marmont,' the Emperor had told his oldest friend after Dresden, 'the game is going wrong.' When Paris fell on 31 March, Marshal Marmont decided that the game was as good as lost.

On the morning of 4 April the Marshal put on civilian clothes and rode away towards the capital, leaving his corps stationed at Essonnes. That evening the divisional generals invited their senior officers to dinner.

Michel Ordener, now commanding the 30th Dragoons, dined with General Bordesoulle. Ordener and his colleagues were tired and anxious to get to their beds, but Bordesoulle was apparently enjoying the occasion and showed no sign of ending it. Finally he seemed to realize that the yawns of his subordinates were intended as a hint. 'Gentlemen,' he told them, 'the Emperor will be here at daybreak with his army, and we are going to form his advance guard. Since we shall be marching for Paris at 3 a.m. there is no point in your going to bed.'

Ordener accepted this explanation.

No-one had the slightest suspicion, and it was the same with the senior officers of the other divisions, whose generals had no doubt told them a similar story. At the prescribed hour we mounted up and set out on the main road to Paris.[18]

The cavalry's march was steady and uneventful, but when Colonel Ordener approached the outskirts of Paris an amazing sight met his eyes.

The Emperor had been betrayed and we, his faithful soldiers, had unwittingly been made accomplices in the act of infamy. On both sides of the road allied troops were drawn up . . . They had their weapons in their hands, and paid us the usual military compliments whilst fanfares were played. At that moment, to heighten the insult, we were told to return their salutes. I went red in the face and shouted, 'If my dragoons draw swords it will be to charge!' Turning to the men, I told them not to put their swords into their hands, so that the enemy would clearly understand that we had had no part in our generals' crime.[19]

The loss of Marmont's corps was the coup de grâce for Napoleon, who abdicated on 11 April.[20] On 2 May King Louis XVIII entered his capital. 'His cherished name has been proclaimed by every mouth,' declared Archbishop Le Coz of Besançon, 'but still more in every heart.'

★   ★   ★

Throughout the month of May, Napoleon's cavalry generals went to the Tuileries to make their submission to the new king. Many of them were aristocrats: and in the eyes of most die-hard Royalists the aristocrats who had fought in the armies of the Republic and the Empire were traitors and turncoats – especially those, like Grouchy and Latour-Maubourg, who had once served in Louis XVI's bodyguard. Nevertheless, they were not unkindly received by Louis XVIII, and with one striking exception they accepted with a good grace the inevitable changes made by the new régime. Edouard de Colbert was appointed to command the lancers of the Royal Guard, and the one-legged Latour-Maubourg was elected to a committee studying the reorganization of the army. Nansouty became a captain-lieutenant in the king's Household Troops; his annual pay, which had amounted to more than 100,000 francs under the Empire[21], was fixed at 25,000.

The exception was Grouchy. Like Latour-Maubourg, Grouchy belonged to one of France's oldest families, and had never had any particular affection for Napoleon. Arriving at the Tuileries he was met by the Duke of Berry, who told him that he would be replacing him as Colonel-General of Chasseurs. General Grouchy subsequently informed the king in writing that, since the post had been conferred upon him on the field at Wagram, it would require a formal judgment to take it away from him. He was ordered to remove himself from Paris and stay at one of his estates until such time as the king might send for him.

*   *   *

Louis Rilliet went home to Geneva, still wearing a tricolour cockade in his hat. His brother officers, who were afraid that he might be lynched by Royalists, had begged him in vain to take it down. 'I was wearing it when I started out,' he told them. 'I'm wearing it going back.' On the way he paid a visit to the cavalry school at Saint Germain, where he found the grounds covered with Russian bivouacs. Leaning against a pillar on the terrace, he gazed sadly up at the window of the room which he had shared with 12 other officer cadets.

'Where were they now? Alas! most of them were lying on those fields of carnage and glory from which no trumpet would ever call them back.'[22]

When he re-engaged in the French army the following July it was as a lieutenant of cavalry in the Maison du Roi. This body also accepted a number of ex-Grenadiers à Cheval, who joined a mounted unit commanded by the Marquis de la Rochejaquelein. The Grenadiers adored their new chief; according to Rilliet they treated him as if he were their king.

Somewhat less popular was the Comte d'Artois, newly appointed honorary colonel of the Carabinier brigade. On 1 November, following a review at Lunéville, the Carabiniers paraded on foot for a distribution of medals in the Grand Riding School; then the officers and men proceeded to a luncheon which had been elaborately laid out on tables nearby. Presiding over this festive occasion, M. le Comte took the opportunity to toast the health of his two regiments; unfortunately a member of his entourage, having drained his glass, hurled it to the ground in the traditional manner.

The Carabiniers immediately followed his example; then drawing their long swords they began laying about them on the tables and smashing everything in sight. Had he been present, for once in his life the Emperor would actually have approved the sight of French heavy cavalrymen using their swords like bludgeons instead of giving point. As bottles, plates and dishes disintegrated, fragments of glass and porcelain were sent flying through the air, and the honorary colonel was lucky to escape injury.

V

Europe was at peace after the long conflict, and the Bourbons had no need of a large standing army. A number of regiments were disbanded and the remainder were reduced in strength. For the conscripts, demobilization was a welcome release, but for most of the veterans it merely compounded the bitterness of defeat. Men who had known nothing but the life of a cavalry soldier said goodbye to their horses and went home to their towns or villages, hoping to get work as grooms and coachmen, carters and blacksmiths, gamekeepers and gendarmes. Many of their officers drifted to Paris, where they played cards and slandered the king in the cafés of the Palais Royal.

'So the drama is ended at last,' Lucien Bonaparte wrote to Marshal Masséna. 'So much glory, marred by so tame an ending. *Bon Dieu,* what memories! What regrets!'

But the drama was not quite over; there was one more act to play.

9

Kellermann

I

When General d'Avenay and his aide de Gonneville passed through
Valladolid in 1809 they were invited to dinner by General François-
Etienne de Kellermann, who was then engaged in holding down several
provinces of Old Castile. For de Gonneville, who had long wanted to
meet the famous cavalry general, the evening proved a great dis-
appointment; he could hardly believe that this admittedly intelligent-
looking little man was the legendary hero of Marengo. Later his dis-
illusionment turned to disgust when he heard the accusations that were
being made against Kellermann in Castile; it was even said that he was
locking up local aristocrats in cells that had been built for the Inquisition
and holding them to ransom.

The stories may well have been true. Kellermann was rightly regarded
as the most rapacious general that even the Napoleonic army produced,
but then he was an unusual case. From the revenues of the First Empire,
Napoleon paid out millions of francs in dotations to his senior officers,
and after a successful campaign even an undistinguished brigade
commander might expect his 10,000 *francs de rente*. Kellermann received no such income, largely because of his undiplomatic utterances
about Marengo.

Napoleon was well aware of Kellermann's contribution to that
celebrated victory. 'That little Kellerman made a fortunate charge to-
day,' he remarked to Bourrienne after the battle. 'We owe him a great
deal. *Voyez à quoi tiennent les affaires!*' Kellermann was not satisfied
with this verdict. 'Would you believe, my friend,' he wrote to Lasalle,
'that Bonaparte has not made me general of division? I who have just
placed the crown upon his head!'[1]

To the end of his life Kellermann believed that Napoleon had
deliberately denigrated his part in the battle; so did Marshal Marmont,
who was one of the last surviving witnesses of Kellermann's charge. 'No

general ever showed a surer eye than did Kellermann in this affair,'
Marmont stated in his memoirs. 'It is absurd and unjust to contest his
glory and the tremendous service that he rendered.'

Napoleon's hostility did nothing to help Kellermann's career, which
was also dogged by ill health and bad luck. His Austerlitz wound kept
him out of the next two campaigns, and while Bessières was leading his
dramatic charges on the Marchfeld Kellermann was in Spain.

Unlike Nansouty's heavy cavalry and Lasalle's hussars, the dragoons
who served in the Peninsula never captured the popular imagination, but
constant fighting and marching had hardened them into the toughest
mounted troops in Europe; under Kellermann's leadership, using
Spanish-made swords of Toledo steel, they charged with a force and
brutality reminiscent of d'Hautpoul's cuirassiers.

In Marmont's opinion Kellermann was the finest tactician in
Napoleon's cavalry. 'During those 25 years of warfare,' he wrote, 'only
three men in the French army really understood how to lead and control
massed cavalry: Kellermann, Montbrun, Lasalle.'

Kellermann had been a general of division when Montbrun was only a
squadron leader: yet in 1812, when Montbrun was given a cavalry corps,
Kellermann was merely offered the command of a division. Officially
because of his recurring neuralgia, he did not take it up.

In 1813 he was appointed to lead the smallest of the five cavalry corps,
which mustered barely 3,000 sabres. At Bautzen he received two more
wounds and had five horses killed under him; a week before Leipzig ill
health put him once more out of action.

When the Bourbons were restored in 1814 Kellermann was made a
Chevalier of St Louis and allowed to remain in the greatly reduced army,
in which he held various inspectorships. It seemed that, at the age of 44,
his active career was over.

Then at the end of February 1815 Napoleon escaped from Elba,
landing in the south of France on 1 March. To intercept him a force was
organized by the Duke of Berry, and Kellermann was given command of
its cavalry. Seemingly anxious to justify the trust that the king had
shown in him, he rode ahead with the advance guard; but at Melun his
men tore off their white cockades, replaced them with tricolour ones,
and refused orders to return to Paris. Kellermann went home to his
estates.

On 19 March King Louis fled from his capital, and shortly after 9
p.m. on the 20th a tricolour flag was hoisted over the Palace of the
Tuileries. For the second time in less than a year, generals of the
French cavalry went to offer their services to a new government, but

Kellermann was not among them. They were received with varying degrees of warmth.

'You are very late,' Napoleon observed to Edouard de Colbert.

'Yes, Sire,' Colbert replied. 'But not so late as Your Majesty. I have been waiting for you these past 12 months.'

One of the many letters of welcome received by the Emperor was from Archbishop Le Coz of Besançon. 'Sire,' it began, 'you really are a prodigious man. . . .'

This opinion was borne out by the speed with which Napoleon organized his last army, which included five corps of infantry, four of cavalry, and the Guard. During his exile on Elba the French cavalry had been cut down to four Guard regiments and 57 regiments of the Line, in which the fifth squadrons had been virtually abolished. It did not greatly matter. In addition to the serving soldiers, Napoleon had thousands of well-trained ex-cavalrymen at his disposal, since the Peninsula veterans had come home to France, as had many prisoners of war released by the allies. They were all recalled to the colours.

Only 16,000 cavalry horses were still in service in March 1815. This number was increased by purchase, by taking half the horses of the mounted gendarmerie, and by reclaiming 5,000 more that had been loaned to farmers to reduce feeding costs; being exceptionally strong and well-trained animals, the 4,000-odd horses provided by the gendarmerie were given to the heavy cavalry regiments. A million francs were put at the disposal of General Bourcier, who was authorized to buy 900 remounts for the heavy cavalry, 787 for the dragoons, 1,084 for the lancers, 2,633 for the chasseurs and 1,152 for the hussars.

The reconstituted Reserve Cavalry was formed into four specialist corps: one of light cavalry, one of dragoons, and two of heavy regiments. In temper, appearance and sheer fighting ability the two heavy cavalry formations recalled the great campaigns of the Empire. 4th Cavalry Corps comprised 24 squadrons of veteran cuirassiers, some of whom had served under d'Hautpoul, Nansouty and Espagne. 3rd Cavalry Corps was even more impressive; two regiments of dragoons, four regiments of cuirassiers, the élite Carabinier brigade, and two batteries of horse artillery.

Very few men in France had the ability or experience required to command these superb units. Nansouty had died in February, and of the remaining handful neither Defrance, Arrighi nor Sébastiani could be spared for a field command.[2] Accordingly General Milhaud was appointed to lead the eight cuirassier regiments of 4th Corps, while the command of the magnificent 3rd Corps was left vacant. No-one was better qualified to fill it than Kellermann, but Napoleon was reluctant to give such an important command to a man who had served in the Duke of Berry's force; thus while the last Napoleonic campaign was being organized in the spring of 1815 the most talented cavalry leader in France remained without employment.

Then at the beginning of June Napoleon made him a peer of France and posted him to the head of 3rd Cavalry Corps. On the 9th, Kellermann arrived at Vervins to take up the finest command he had ever had in his life.

★   ★   ★

Though undeniably impressive in numbers, highly professional and full of spirit, Napoleon's newly-created cavalry force was lacking in discipline. In the line cavalry, the white aiguillettes which men of the regiments that bore the number 1 were entitled to wear caused so much jealousy that Napoleon ordered them to be discontinued. In the 1st Cuirassiers, six officers who had been promoted for encouraging the regiment to join Napoleon were hooted by the rank-and-file at a special parade held in their honour.

'We did just as much as you did,' someone shouted, 'and we've had neither promotion nor reward.'

The men looked with suspicion on those officers who had served under the Bourbons, and only commanders who had incited their troops to defect to Napoleon could be sure of asserting their full authority. For this, the conduct of Bordesoulle and his colleagues at Essonnes the previous year was largely to blame.

In such an atmosphere of distrust there was no question of employing Murat, who had actually taken the field against Eugène de Beauharnais in Italy in 1814. Having been forced to flee his kingdom, Murat took refuge in the south of France, and lost no time in asking Napoleon for command of the Reserve Cavalry. It was given instead to Grouchy, who was made a Marshal.

Many senior generals felt that Grouchy, whose concern for his men was apt to make him over-cautious, was not the ideal man for the French cavalry's highest post, but none could deny that he brought tremendous experience to it.

Unfortunately, he had little chance to apply it. Soon after the campaign began Marshal Grouchy was put in command of two detached army corps, leaving the Reserve Cavalry without a chief at all.

II

The allies planned to invade France with six armies, but at the beginning of June only two of them were in the field. Wellington was in Belgium with a force of British, Dutch and Belgians, as was Blucher with 100,000 Prussians. Since neither of these armies was strong enough to fight without the other, Napoleon intended to destroy them before they could unite. Concentrating with his usual speed, he invaded Belgium on 14 June.

The French army moved forward in three masses: two wings commanded by Ney and Grouchy and a reserve under Napoleon. Kellermann's cavalry corps was attached to Ney, who on 16 June was ordered to march on Brussels with 15,000 men. At 10 a.m. that day Ney's advance guard encountered part of Wellington's army, posted in woods and cornfields about the cross-roads known as Les Quatre Bras. Unaware that the enemy numbered only 7,000, Ney did not attack until 2 p.m.

Meanwhile Napoleon's main body had engaged 80,000 Prussians at Ligny, where a great battle developed. To make it into a decisive victory, Napoleon needed Ney; at 3.15 a staff officer was sent to summon him from Quatre Bras, bearing a dramatic message telling the Marshal that the fate of France was in his hands. Ney was in the toils. His delay in attacking had allowed reinforcements to reach the enemy, which now totalled about 20,000 men. To add to his difficulties a French corps under d'Erlon, on which Ney had been counting for assistance, had been diverted towards Ligny on Napoleon's orders.

Furious at the loss of d'Erlon's corps, and unnerved by Napoleon's reference to the fate of France, Ney sent for Kellermann. As soon as the little general appeared, Ney rode up to him and ordered him to crush the enemy with his cavalry.

Kellermann heard the order with astonishment. Most of his corps was posted in reserve, leaving only two cuirassier regiments available for a charge. Realizing that Ney was over-excited, Kellermann queried the order, pointing out that he had only the 700 troopers of Guiton's brigade under his hand. Ney repeated the order in a brusque and almost insulting tone, ending with the words, '*Partez! Mais partez donc!*'

Riding to the head of Guiton's brigade, Kellermann led it at a fast trot down the Brussels road, finally halting on high ground near the farm of Gemioncourt. For a few moments he breathed his horses. The normal practice for a charge of heavy cavalry was to work up to the gallop by gradual changes of pace; Kellermann, however, was determined not to let his men see what a suicidal task Ney had given them. Forming column

of squadrons, he ordered, '*Pour charger au galop, en avant . . . marche!*'
At this unusual order, Guiton's two regiments launched straight into a
gallop.

East of the road to Quatre Bras stood two squares formed by the 42nd
and 44th Foot. The leading squadrons swerved to avoid them. The
supporting squadrons did the same, but as they galloped past the
British infantry poured musketry into their flank. The cuirassiers were
wearing their cloaks, and at first the Highlanders of the 42nd thought
they were dragoons; then they noticed that Frenchmen who were hit
merely swayed in the saddle and did not fall.[3] 'They're in armour!' an
officer shouted. 'Fire at the horses!'

Transformed into a demon of energy, as he always was on these
occasions, Kellermann rode on towards Quatre Bras. The 69th Foot was
caught in open column; two of its companies were practically destroyed
and the King's colour was captured.[4] The impetus of their charge carried
the cuirassiers almost to the cross-roads; but gradually they began to
realize that they were alone and surrounded by the enemy. The British
musketry had taken a heavy toll. 'Riders in heavy armour fell tumbling
from their horses,' wrote a Highland sergeant. 'The horses reared,
plunged and fell on dismounted riders; steel helmets and cuirasses rang
against unsheathed sabres as they fell to the ground.'[5]

A 15-year-old trumpeter of the 8th Cuirassiers, who had never seen
Scottish uniforms before, mistook the kilted Highlanders for women.
'Their *cantinières* are firing at us!' he told his colonel.

A troop of horse artillery opened up at short range to add to the
slaughter. Falling back towards Gemioncourt the cuirassiers charged
again; but although Ney now sent regiments of lancers to support them
they could make no headway. The horses were blown; the element of
surprise had gone. Despite all Kellermann's attempts to rally them,
Guiton's troopers rode away, leaving 250 dead and wounded behind
them. Kellermann's horse was killed under him; hatless and bruised, he
left the field clinging to the bits of two of his troopers' horses.

That night the Highlanders of Pack's brigade cooked their suppers in
French cuirasses.

'The Count of Valmy led a fine charge,'[6] wrote Marshal Ney in his
report.

★   ★   ★

Beaten at Ligny, Blucher's Prussians retreated northwards, and to keep
in touch with them Wellington was obliged to retire towards Brussels.
He halted his army at the ridge of Mont St Jean, which lies athwart the

Charleroi-Brussels road two miles south of the village of Waterloo. Wellington had been aware of its defensive possibilities for over a year. The sloping ground in front of it formed a fairly steep glacis, but the reverse slope was gentle. The road that ran along its crest was bordered by hedges too thick for cavalry to penetrate, yet not too thick for gun embrasures to be cut in them. Rye in full crop covered the ground, almost to the height of a horse's belly.

On this plateau Wellington disposed his men, confident that he could beat the French with Blucher's help.

On 17 June, under a downpour of drenching rain, Napoleon's army advanced to within sight of Wellington's position. Both armies bovouacked for the night in mud. Next morning the French were late in assembling on the sodden ground, and Napoleon did not give out his attack orders until 11 a.m. Half an hour later the artillery bombardment began and at 1 p.m., under Marshal Ney's direction, the French infantry masses went forward to the assault.

Mounted at the head of 3rd Cavalry Corps, General Kellermann had four hours in which to collect his thoughts. Kellermann had been a soldier for 22 years, 15 of them as a general of division, and he clearly understood the unsatisfactory position in which the French cavalry found itself. With two *corps d'armée* Marshal Grouchy had been detached to deal with the Prussians; with him had gone 45 squadrons, including three hussar regiments of the 1st Cavalry Corps and all the dragoon regiments of the 2nd. Since Grouchy's appointment to command a wing of the army, the Reserve Cavalry had been without a chief; now the ground at Mont St Jean was rapidly turning to mud and the battle was being directed by Marshal Ney, whose orders for the cavalry at Quatre Bras had been those of a madman.

Kellermann's two divisions were posted west of the main Charleroi-Brussels road, with L'Héritier's division on the right. A former colonel of the 10th Cuirassiers, L'Héritier had acquired considerable experience of the heavy cavalry branch. He had a strong incentive to action at Waterloo, since it was a brigade of his division that had been put to flight by the British two days earlier at Quatre Bras.[7]

To L'Héritier's left was Kellermann's second division, commanded by General Roussel d'Harbal.[8] It included the two regiments of Carabiniers commanded by Colonel Blancard, which Kellermann was particularly glad to have at his disposal; according to French cavalry historians, he intended to use them for a dramatic purpose. If the fortunes of the day dictated it, these writers believe, Kellermann had some hopes and every intention of repeating the famous exploit that had turned the tide at Marengo.

The 850 troopers of the Carabinier brigade were the tallest and strongest in the Reserve Cavalry;[9] with Kellermann at their head, and Guard infantry battalions in support, they would certainly have been a force to reckon with.

*   *   *

After four hours' fighting Marshal Ney had failed to dislodge Wellington's army from the heights of Mont St Jean, and Napoleon faced a serious situation. Grouchy had plainly not dealt with the Prussians, whose leading columns could be seen in the distance, advancing to threaten the French right. Staff officers had been dispatched to summon Grouchy, whose two corps were now desperately needed at Waterloo, but as yet there was no sign of him.

Following his usual practice, Marshal Ney was fighting at the head of his men. Shortly after half-past three, having apparently mistaken an unimportant enemy movement for the beginning of a retreat, he sent an aide back to order up a heavy cavalry brigade.

The French heavy cavalry was formed in two separate wings, each supported by cavalry regiments of the Guard. Kellermann's corps, as already noted, was posted west of the Charleroi-Brussels road. Behind Kellermann was Guyot, commanding the Grenadiers à Cheval and the Guard Dragoons. Half a mile to the east of Kellermann was Lefebvre-Desnouettes with the Guard lancers and the Guard Chasseurs, who were drawn up behind the two divisions of Milhaud's cuirassier corps.

Milhaud's divisional commanders, Generals Wattier and Delort, were both veterans of the Peninsula; Delort, in particular, had learned to treat British infantry with respect. His first intimation that something was afoot came shortly before 4 o'clock, when he saw to his astonishment that his leading brigade was moving off in the direction of Mont St Jean. He immediately rode after it and ordered it to halt. General Farine, the brigade commander, explained that he was obeying an order from Marshal Ney, but Delort would have none of this. No brigade would leave his division, he said, except on a direct order from the corps commander, General Milhaud.

It might have been better for the French cavalry if Farine's brigade had been allowed to proceed; as it was, Delort's action had an astonishing and tragic effect on Marshal Ney, who was rapidly losing all judgment and self-control. While Delort was still talking to Farine, Ney himself came riding back, bristling with impatience, to find out why his demand for a heavy cavalry brigade had not been met. According to Delort:

He not only insisted on his original order being carried out, but demanded both divisions [of Milhaud's corps] in the Emperor's name. I hesitated to obey, saying that heavy cavalry ought not to attack heights held by infantry, infantry which had never yet been shaken and which was well placed to defend itself. The Marshal cried, 'Forward, for the sake of France!' I reluctantly obeyed.[10]

Milhaud also obeyed, though he evidently shared Delort's misgivings. It is said that, as his two divisions began their advance, Milhaud rode back to Lefebvre-Desnouettes, shook him by the hand, and told him, 'I am going to charge; support me!' Whatever the truth of this story, as the cuirassier corps moved off the Guard regiments followed on behind.

It was a strange and almost incredible sequence of events. Instead of the six squadrons that Delort had tried to keep back, Marshal Ney now had 38 at his disposal, and 5,000 of the French cavalry's best troopers were riding west across the field to attack uphill against artillery and unbroken infantry.

For Michel Ordener, who commanded the 1st Cuirassiers that day,[11] it was the finest moment of his career, surpassing even the charges at Austerlitz, Eylau, Friedland and Wagram. 'Our four superb lines were practically fresh;[12] they moved simultaneously to cries of *Vive l'Empereur!* . . . Marshal Ney was at our head.'

The horses, however, were not fresh for long; even on the muddy slopes leading to the enemy positions they began to tire. When the packed columns reached the high ground they were blasted by Wellington's artillery, which was posted in front of his infantry and double-shotted with round-shot and canister. Then as the French cavalry approached the gunners crouched under their pieces, or ran back to join the infantry.

As speeds varying from a quick trot to a slow canter, which was all that the horses could manage, the cuirassiers pressed on towards the infantry squares.[13] To a cavalryman on a tired horse, these had a daunting appearance. The men of the front rank were kneeling to receive cavalry, musket butts grounded, bayonets advanced. Unable to break them, Milhaud's squadrons milled about the squares while the standing ranks of infantrymen fired at the horses.

Ney's charge had achieved nothing beyond the capture of the British guns, and even that was temporary. Counter-attacked by cavalry under Lord Uxbridge, the French were pushed back off the heights. The gunners ran back to their pieces, which had not even been spiked, and when Milhaud's men returned to the attack the slaughter was repeated.

For a second time they trotted through an appalling fire of artillery into the deserted batteries, and passed on to repeat their futile gyrations round and round the squares. Unable to pierce the hedges of bayonets, small parties of brave men engaged the red-coated infantry with their pistols . . . The horses, by this time unable to trot, walked round and round the bayonets in helpless swarms till they were shot down.[14]

Ney's first great cavalry stroke had not merely failed; it had actually helped to strengthen Wellington's position. The slopes leading to the plateau had been turned into a quagmire by thousands of hooves – 'poached deep into mud', in Fortescue's expressive phrase – and the ground about the British squares was littered with dead horses. Into this death-trap, Napoleon now chose to send Kellermann's corps and the heavy cavalry of the Guard.

The order was carried by General de Flahaut. If French cavalry traditions may be believed, Kellermann was disposed to query it; but before he could do so General L'Héritier moved off with his division, and Kellermann allowed Roussel d'Harbal's division to follow in its turn. Soon after the movement began, however, the Carabineer brigade was detached from the division on Kellermann's authority and took up position at the halt in a fold of ground. To the brigade commander, Colonel Blancard, Kellermann gave instructions not to move another inch from this position except on his own direct and formal order.

Led by Guyot, the Mounted Grenadiers and Guard Dragoons joined on the end of Kellermann's advance to form a trotting mass of over 5,000 horse.

To reach the slopes Kellermann's cavalry had to pass between the enemy-held strong-points of Hougoumont and La Haye Sainte, and as the regiments closed in to avoid flanking fire intervals and deployment distances disappeared. 'Nearly the whole of the ground between La Haye Sainte and Hougoumont was covered with this splendid array of horsemen,' wrote a British officer.[15] 'Their advance to the attack was made in a manner that showed the highest discipline.'

As the massed squadrons rode up the slopes many of Milhaud's cuirassiers fell in behind them; waiting with his guns on the plateau, Captain Mercer of the Royal Artillery looked down on seemingly endless rows of casques and bearskins.

The spectacle was imposing, and if ever the word sublime was appropriately applied it might surely be so with it. On they came, in compact squadrons, one behind the other, so numerous that those of the rear were still below the brow when the head of the column was but at some 60 or 70 yards from our guns. Their pace was a slow but steady trot . . . They moved in profound silence, and the only sound that could be heard from them amidst the incessant roar of battle was the low thunder-like reverberation of the ground beneath the simultaneous tread of so many horses.[16]

Mercer waited until the leading horsemen were only five or six yards away before he ordered his guns to fire.

The effect was terrible. Nearly the whole leading rank fell at once. The ground, already encumbered with victims of the first struggle, became almost impassable.

Once again the British gunners ran or crawled to safety, and the multitude of horsemen passed on to the chequerboard of infantry squares. From that point onwards, the story becomes confused. French eyewitnesses speak of ten or eleven successive charges taking a terrible toll of the British infantry. 'The charges were made ceaselessly,' claims Colonel Ordener. 'We were almost masters of the plateau, and the English were three parts destroyed. But they seemed rooted in the earth; we should have had to kill them to a man.'

Understandably a very different picture is painted by British participants whose accounts inspired Fortescue's famous description:

There was no thunder of hoofs growing momentarily louder, no wall of dust rushing steadily nearer, no awful emergence of maddened horses and gleaming blades in endless waves from the dust-cloud; no element, in fact, of the terror which cavalry can strike into infantry even in the manoeuvres of peace. Instead of all this there were simply swarms of exasperated men on weary horses, who walked round and round, fetlock-deep in mire, swearing loudly and making desperate thrusts from time to time through the hedge of bayonets, but doing very little harm and offering generally a capital target.[17]

In the midst of this conflict Marshal Ney saw two regiments of French cavalry still halted in the plain below, and recognized them by their copper cuirasses as Blancard's Carabiniers. Galloping back down the slopes, Ney himself led them into action.

With this futile gesture, which served only to establish Ney's authority over Kellermann's, Napoleon's last mounted reserve was thrown away. Whether or not Kellermann could have used his last brigade to any purpose, no-one can say; but in General Delort's opinion an élite cavalry reserve, strongly supported by battalions of Guard infantry, would have stopped the Prussians arriving on the battlefield. Instead of which, at 7 p.m. the foot battalions of the Guard were launched in one last hopeless attempt to break Wellington's line, and there was no longer even a reserve of infantry.

By that time the French cavalry had already broken. From the heights of Mont St Jean the Prussian columns could be seen advancing from the forest of Soignes to threaten the French line of retreat, and even Colonel Ordener realized that the end had come. He wrote:

> Tumult pervaded our ranks. Our cavalrymen's devotion was at an end, and the instinct of self-preservation took over. Our efforts to stop them were useless. Riding back in disorder down the slopes from the plateau, they disappeared under a hail of cannon-shots.[18]

There was nothing left for Kellermann to do but collect what troopers he could and lead them away.

No-one understood better than Kellermann the irony of what had happened at Waterloo. For the first time in a decade, two superb formations of the French heavy cavalry had reached a battlefield in prime condition, untouched by weeks or months of hard marching on inadequate forage, and they had then been thrown away.

Only twice in its existence had Napoleon's cavalry played a decisive role in altering the course of a major battle. At Marengo it had succeeded thanks to Kellermann's initiative and Marmont's case-shot; at Eylau, by the impact of massed squadrons charging over ideal terrain. At Waterloo it had been asked to repeat the miracle, over ground which had robbed it of all its impact and without artillery support.

Even then it might have succeeded, if Ney had handled his infantry properly; for when Ney was leading the last great cavalry attacks up the slopes of Mont St Jean, twelve fresh battalions of Reille's corps were within his call. Had these been ordered to support him, General Kellermann might well have managed to keep the crown for a few months longer on Bonaparte's head.

*   *   *

On 22 June, with the Emperor's final abdication, the Napoleonic era came to an end. As its new Commander-in-Chief, Marshal Macdonald[19] supervised the disbanding of the army, which for the cavalry was especially painful. Many of the horses were turned over to farmers, who found that they could not afford to keep them. They were led into woods and meadows and abandoned. Harness, saddlery and equipment was taken to farms and convents, piled in sheds or outbuildings, and left to rot. 'Regiments with a glorious and distinguished record were lost,' Thomas Aubry complained. 'Many of them had been in existence for centuries.'[20]

In Marshal Murat's opinion, none of this need ever have happened if Napoleon had allowed him to lead the cavalry at Waterloo, but he had better things to do than brood over his brother-in-law's mistakes. In October 1815 he landed with a handful of followers on the coast of Calabria, determined to re-establish himself on the throne of Naples. He was captured almost at once. Five days later he was court-martialled and shot.

Marshal Ney suffered a similar fate. For defecting to Napoleon at the start of the Hundred Days he was tried by the Chamber of Peers, condemned to death, and executed by a French firing-squad. Of the Chamber of Peers, 139 voted for the death penalty, including Kellermann's father.

III

General Kellermann lived another 20 years after Waterloo. His reputation in the cavalry was immense. General of brigade at Marengo, *divisionnaire* at Austerlitz, corps commander at Waterloo, Kellermann was the only senior cavalry general who had been present at all the three great dramas of the Napoleonic wars. Moreover his name evoked that mixture of glory and tragedy which appealed so strongly to French soldiers of the period; glory at Marengo and Alba de Tormès, tragedy at Quatre Bras and Waterloo.

In the soul-searching and recriminations that followed Waterloo, his name was often quoted by Frenchmen who felt that the battle should never have been lost. If Kellermann had been appointed to lead the cavalry, they said, Wellington would surely have been beaten.

Kellermann himself was not much interested in speculation about Waterloo. He was much more interested in explaining his vital contribution to the victory at Marengo, which he claimed had never been fully recognized, and he published two pamphlets critizing what he regarded as General Savary's biased and highly misleading account of the battle.

When his father died in 1820 he inherited the title of Duke of Valmy and a seat in the Chamber of Peers. Divorced from his wife, he continued to live in retirement on his estates at Senlis. He was greatly respected in the locality, partly for his impressive service record and partly for his good works; in addition to erecting a monument to his father on the battlefield at Valmy, he financed the building of a fine church in the neighbourhood of Senlis, complete with graveyard and presbytery. His critics claimed that both monument and church had been paid for with the proceeds of his Spanish extortions.

General Kellermann found their attitude hard to understand. 'What do they suppose I crossed the Pyrenees for?' he asked. 'Change of air?'

10

Memories and Regrets

A handful of Napoleon's cavalry leaders lived on into old age, including Grouchy and the one-legged Latour-Maubourg, who both reached their eighties. Sébastiani died a Marshal of France in 1851, Arrighi in 1853, and despite his 19 wounds General Jacob-François Marulaz survived to 72.

Son of a cavalry NCO, Marulaz joined a hussar regiment five years before the Revolution, hoping no doubt to retire as a sergeant-major. At the age of 23 he was commanding a squadron. Marulaz embodied the spirit that gave Napoleon's cavalry its power on the battlefield: the lust for victory, inherited from the armies of the Revolution, which was turned into an addiction to glory by the greatest mind in Europe. He was the kind of soldier Napoleon liked: 'a good-looking man without refinements, outspoken and tough; an intrepid sabreur and a stubborn disciplinarian, but attractive in his own way.'[1]

For 13 years he commanded the 8th Hussars, and made it one of the best regiments in the French cavalry. 'Superb, Marulaz!' Napoleon is said to have told him after taking the salute at a review. 'Ride them past again!'

In 1806 he was promoted general and led a brigade of d'Hautpoul's cuirassiers, which was not the sort of command that suited him; then at the start of the Polish campaign he was given a light cavalry brigade. At that time he was 37 years old, increasingly troubled by old wounds and rheumatism, and his active career was nearly over; but in the two years that remained of it he proved himself an outstanding leader of light horse. At Aspern-Essling, though still only a general of brigade, he fought at the head of six regiments. When Lasalle was killed at Wagram Marulaz took command of both divisions, and for the rest of the battle the 8th Hussars found themselves once more under their former colonel's orders.

'Hussars of the 8th,' he told them, as they prepared to charge, 'my

145

name is not unknown in your regiment. *Marulaz est avec vous!*'

The wound he received at Wagram having ended his campaigning days, he was promoted general of division and appointed military governor of Besançon. It was not exactly his *métier*. For 16 years he had lived the nomadic life of the light cavalry, whose philosophy had hardly fitted him for routine duties in a provincial town; for when the village children started calling you by your name, French hussars used to say, it was time to bridle up and ride on.

Like his friend Lasalle, Marulaz *divisionnaire* was still a sabreur at heart, used to galvanizing his subordinates with a brusque '*Faites-moi ça, et au galop!*' But if his orders were given with the blunt authority of a senior NCO, the intelligence behind them was as sharp as a Mameluke blade, and when the allies invaded France in 1814 he defended Besançon against seemingly hopeless odds with infinite patience and cunning.

For three months he remained immovable, swearing that he would burn Besançon to the ground rather than let the Austrians in. It was only on 20 April, when he learned of Napoleon's abdication, that he ordered his men to take off their tricolour cockades and put up white ones instead. Even then he refused to allow Austrian columns to pass through the town.

After Waterloo he was replaced by the Marquis de Sorans and settled at Filain, the 17th century château near Besançon that he had bought in 1808. Finding it hard to maintain six children and an estate on his reduced income, he asked to be placed on the reserve of officers, hoping to qualify for the full pension of a general of division. Time passed, and eventually Marulaz turned for advice to the man who had superseded him as governor. The Marquis assured him that his application was in train, but after a further period of silence Marulaz went to Paris and called at the Ministry of War, where he was allowed to see his service record.

Some notable feats of arms had gone to the making of this document, such as the taking of 27 cannon at Golymin and the breaking of three infantry squares at Wagram. Written on his application, in the Marquis de Sorans' handwriting, were the words, 'Unworthy of the favour he asks.'

Marulaz returned to Filain. Shortly afterwards he went to a dinner party in the Prefecture at Vesoul, at which most of the district's dignitaries were present. He took with him his groom Baptiste, who was an ex-hussar, and two sabres wrapped in a piece of serge.

For reasons that were never fully explained, the Marquis de Sorans did not dine with the company that night, but just after 5 p.m. he was seen accompanying General Marulaz and another man to the nearby stables. It was said afterwards that he had been foolish enough to accept a challenge from the general, who had been one of the best blades in the French cavalry; it was also said that the authorities turned a blind eye to the affair, believing that the arrest of a popular hero like Marulaz would have caused more trouble than it was worth.

Six days after the dinner, a local paper announced the sudden death of the Marquis de Sorans, due to his having been kicked in the chest by a horse whilst attending manoeuvres.

★   ★   ★

For the next 15 years Marulaz served as Mayor of Filain. He often enlivened committee meetings with his reminiscences, occasionally unbuttoning his shirt to show the scars on his chest, which had received five bullet wounds at Zurich alone. His colleagues found these talks infinitely more interesting than municipal business, but they sometimes had difficulty in following him; like many other German-speaking soldiers of the First Empire, Marulaz had never completely mastered his adopted tongue.[2] '*Je le tuas*,' he would say, referring to an encounter with some former enemy. '*Non, je le tu-is.*'

After the Revolution of 1830 he was granted his full pension, so that the upkeep of Filain and the education of his children became less of a strain. Two of his sons attended the *lycée* at Besançon, where he was always a welcome visitor. On one occasion, the principal told him that it was the custom for a distinguished guest to request a holiday for the pupils. 'Then give them a month's leave,' Marulaz suggested. The principal said that this was rather too generous, and that one day would be more than enough. 'Well, it was a month's leave in the army,' Marulaz assured him. '*Alors,* permission for one day!'

At Filain he spent much time in his stables, discussing points with his friend Janicot the blacksmith, whom he had co-opted as his veterinary adviser. Every year they went to buy horses at the Horse Fair at Grammont, where they took rooms in the local inn. The fair was held in winter, when the general's wounds were always at their most troublesome. One night, hearing him pacing about his bedroom at the inn, Janicot realized that he was in pain and went in to ask if there was anything he could do to help. 'There's nothing either of us can do,' Marulaz told him. 'It's the Waldeck Dragoons reminding me of our acquaintance.'[3]

In summer-time he liked to sit outside Janicot's smithy, dressed in a long white coat with capacious pockets, from which he produced sweetmeats for the passing children. 'When the distribution was over he would sit down, and for a long time let his memories take their course. Perhaps the sound of the anvil and the whinnying of the horses being shod reminded him of the din of battle, but they did not distract him. Mentally, he was a long way from Filain.'[4]

The few sightseers who passed through that quiet little backwater of France paid no attention to the old man in the white coat sitting in the sunshine. What stories he could have told them!

Despite the summer day-dreaming, there was nothing senile about him. To the end of his life Marulaz kept his lacerated body as fit as possible; at the age of 67 he could still pick up a handerkerchief or a 100-sou piece from the back of a galloping horse. Few people knew that he had a wound in his back which needed cleansing every night.

He died at Filain in the summer of 1842, nearly 60 years after he had first put on the uniform of the Esterhazy Hussars. The autopsy revealed a bullet in his liver that had been lying there since 1799.

His death was briefly reported in the newspapers. 'If he had been a deputy,' wrote a distinguished son of Besançon, 'the Press would have given the event great publicity. But he was merely one of our bravest soldiers, and one of the most honourable men of our old army.'[5]

Perhaps it was understandable. France was at peace, the middle class was prosperous, and the future Marshal Bazaine was still only a captain in the Foreign Legion; Frenchmen had no need, as yet, for harking back to the glories of the First Empire. The Emperor had been dead for over 20 years, and even some of his old cavalrymen had turned against his memory. Thomas Aubry, who had once been so proud to wear the Imperial eagle on his sabretache, was one of them.

Who would have thought that such a soldier, a genius, a man who had given so many proofs of patriotism and obedience to his country's laws, would have ended by betraying the trust of France, the land that had raised him so high and followed him so proudly? Once at the pinnacle, he became mad with ambition, plunging Europe in fire and blood to satisfy his despotic whims. From Lisbon to Moscow, from Rome to the ends of the continent, he turned everything upside down.[6]

For Captain Aubry, the dashing light cavalryman, veteran of Austerlitz and Borodino, the price of glory had proved too high.

How many times have we groaned, we other poor soldiers, at the sack and ruin and devastation of countries whose people were so gentle, so harmless, so happy! How much I could say of all the things that I witnessed, and all the miseries caused by the despotism of one man![7]

General Marulaz would have had no patience with such sentiments; for it was only by turning Europe upside down that the Emperor had been able to give his cavalrymen their chances of glory and promotion. Marulaz was an adventurer, cast in the same mould as d'Hautpoul and Lasalle; for men of that kind warfare was a fine way of life, untrammelled by gloomy reflections about starving peasants, ruined crops and burning villages. For them warfare meant the taste of wine drunk from the bottle, the smell of greased leather and horsesweat, the sound of jingling columns crossing the Rhine and the Danube.

Above all it meant the excitement of the battlefield; light cavalry deploying at the gallop, long lines of trotting cuirassiers: *sabres au clair, casques en tête, crinières au vent*. Cannon-smoke, trumpet calls, thudding hooves and flying artillery: and in the distance, mounted on a superb charger, a mere detail of the conflict yet somehow towering over all, the figure of a man wearing a colonel's undress uniform of the Guard Chasseurs; bare-headed, inscrutable, raising his shabby cocked hat in answer to the swell of cheering and the salute of waving swords.

Notes on the text

Chapter 1 (p 1–pp 31)

1. Quoted in E. Trolard, *Pélérinage aux champs de bataille Français d'Italie. De Rivoli à Marengo et à Solférino,* 1893.
2. A.F.L. Viesse de Marmont, *Mémoires du Duc de Raguse de 1792 à 1841,* 1857.
3. A Frenchman is said to have two countries: France, and the *petit pays* or district in which he grew up.
4. 3rd Dragoons, 14th Dragoons, 7th *bis* Hussars. At this period there were two French hussar regiments using the number 7, hence the designation 7th *bis.*
5. 468 Grenadiers à Cheval and 117 Chasseurs.
6. E.R. Astier de la Vigerie, *Le Lieutenant-Général Comte Defrance,* 1911.
7. Eugène de Beauharnais, *Mémoires et correspondance politique et militaire,* 1858-60.
8. A troop of the 1st Dragoons and two squadrons of the 8th Dragoons.
9. As a protection against sabre thrusts.
10. Joseph Petit, *Marengo, ou Campagne d'Italie par l'Armée de Reserve,* 1801.
11. *Eh, Jean! Comment vas-tu? Te souviens?*
12. i.e. a slight squint.
13. Laure Junot, *Mémoires de Madame la Duchesse d'Abrantès,* 1831-35.
14. The Chasseurs à Cheval drew replacements mainly from the light cavalry regiments of the line. The regiment had also absorbed the Mounted Guides who came back from Egypt after the French army there had surrendered.
15. The Grenadiers à Cheval only accepted men who had served in at least four campaigns. In the Guard Chasseurs the minimum requirement was three campaigns; it could be waived, however, for a man who had been awarded a weapon of honour or a citation for bravery.
16. In Quercy the *frotte,* as it was called, consisted of a piece of bread moistened with walnut oil and sprinkled with salt. French cavalrymen believed that the regular consumption of garlic and pepper helped to prevent stomach upsets and fever.

17. Quoted in J. Ambert, *Cinq epées*, 1884.
18. i.e. worn cross-wise. A cocked hat worn with the points fore-and-aft was '*en colonne*'.

Chapter 2 (pp 32–44)

1. He was advised by a committee consisting of senior cavalry generals and J.-B. Huzard, the agronomist and veterinary expert.
2. A.O. Le Harivel de Gonneville, *Recollections*, 1875.
3. Of the original formation only 50 were of pure Mameluke blood, and by 1814 only 18 of them were left. As manpower wastage occurred, replacements were obtained from French hussar regiments and civilian volunteers. The latter were mainly Parisians – 'turbaned warriors who spoke in the incongruous accent of the Faubourg St Antoine'.
4. Heavy cavalry – two regiments of Carabiniers, 12 regiments of cuirassiers. Medium cavalry – 30 regiments of dragoons. Light cavalry – ten regiments of hussars, 24 regimentts of chasseurs à cheval. Guard cavalry – three regiments.
   The establishment laid down 26 regiments of chasseurs, but the 17th and 18th regiments were not formed until 1811.
5. See Diagram Number 2.
6. The family name was d'Hautpoul-Salette. He preferred the simpler form.
7. There were three types of heavy cavalry boot: the *botte forte,* made entirely of stiff leather; the *botte demi-forte,* which had a soft stem and a stiffened knee-piece; and a soft boot known as the *botte à l'écuyère.*
8. A division of dismounted dragoons was also attached to Murat. At this period, French dragoons were expected to fight on foot if the need arose.
9. J. Chevillet, *Ma vie militaire, 1800-1810,* 1906.
10. The uniform included a fur-trimmed pelisse or jacket and a fur colpack or busby. There were 120 buttons on the pelisse, 90 more on the dolman or tunic, and 54 on the gilet, or vest.
11. After the battle of Eylau in 1807, eight senior NCOs of the Guard Chasseurs were made officers of the Legion; eight more were promoted to be captains in line cavalry regiments. On campaign the Emperor was closely attended by a Guard Chasseur NCO and four troopers. The Guard Chasseurs also furnished a '*peloton d'escorte*' of 3 NCOs, 22 men and a trumpeter. This troop kept its horses saddled and bridled throughout the 48 hours of its tour of duty. The officer who commanded it followed Napoleon wherever he went; no-one but Berthier or Murat could dispute his passage. There was also a squadron known as the '*escadron de service*', provided alternately by the Guard Chasseurs and the Grenadiers à Cheval, which acted as the Emperor's escort.
12. Amand d'Hautpoul, *Souvenirs sur la Revolution, l'Empire et la Restauration,* 1904.

13. 'Close up, cuirassiers! Helmets on heads!'
14. Amand d'Hautpoul, *op. cit.*
15. The prediction proved so accurate that Laville began to wonder if his Marshal might be clairvoyant. After the battle, Bessières explained to him that retreating infantrymen only looked over their shoulders when they were running away from cavalry.
16. General Morland. Eugène de Beauharnais, the Guard Chasseurs' colonel, was not present at Austerlitz.
17. Coignet is one of several eye-witnesses who use this term for the Grenadiers à Cheval. French cavalry historians believe that on a long campaign remounts of various colours must have been used, and that possibly only one squadron would have ridden black horses.
18. This was an exaggeration. The total number of Allied dead, including Austrians, was 15,000.
19. The Empress was not in residence at the time.
20. Thomas Joseph Aubry, *Souvenirs du 12ème Chasseurs, 1799-1815*, 1889.
21. At Colmar, depôt of the 21st Chasseurs, a sub-lieutenant of the regiment had to spend the equivalent of four months pay on a remount in 1806. (T.C. de Brémond d'Ars, *Historique du 21ème régiment de Chasseurs à Cheval*, 1903.
22. Napoleon's Chief of Staff.
23. 16,698 men, 16,976 horses. The cuirassier regiments, however, were stronger than ever. The 1st Cuirassiers, for example, had started out from St. Omer at the beginning of the 1805 campaign with 32 officers, 498 men and 500 horses. The regiment put 388 men into the line at Austerlitz. At the beginning of the 1806 campaign the strength was 510 men, 557 horses.

      Most line cavalry regiments received between 120 and 140 replacement troopers after Austerlitz. Striking exceptions were the 1st and 21st Chasseurs, who received 250 each.

Chapter 3 (pp 45–59)

1. At Saalfeld, on 10 October, a Prussian force was defeated by Marshal Lannes. Prince Louis Ferdinand of Prussia was killed in this action by an NCO of the 10th Hussars.
2. P. de Pelleport, *Souvenirs Militaires*, 1857.
3. Two squadrons of the 5th Hussars and one of the 7th.
4. i.e. hussars wearing green uniforms.
5. The capital of East Prussia.
6. 3rd, 6th, 10th and 11th Dragoons (Division Grouchy).
   17th, 18th, 19th and 27th Dragoons (Division Sahuc).
   2nd and 4th Hussars, 5th Chasseurs (Division Tilly).
   1st, 5th, 10th and 11th Cuirassiers (Division d'Hautpoul).

7. Dahlmann had replaced Morland, the deputy colonel killed at Austerlitz.
8. 3rd Hussars and 10th Chasseurs. Colbert's brigade was normally
   attached to Ney's 6th Corps, and was only temporarily under Murat's
   orders.
9. N-J. Colbert, *Traditions et Souvenirs ou Mémoires touchant la vie du
   Général Auguste de Colbert,* 1866. Colbert was killed in Spain in 1809,
   still at the head of Ney's corps cavalry. For two years after his death the
   3rd Hussars carried black crêpe on the regimental standàrd.
10. Lepic was deputy to General Walther, who had replaced Ordener as
    colonel after Austerlitz.
11. T.J. Aubry, *op. cit.*
12. *ibid.*
13. Victor Dupuy, *Souvenirs militaires 1794-1816,* 1892.
14. Quoted in Frédéric Masson's *Cavaliers de Napoléon,* 1895. Promoted
    Sub-Lieutenant, Chambrotte was transferred to the 1st Cuirassiers and
    died in action two months later.
15. A.O. Le Harivel de Gonneville, *op. cit.* Grand Duke of Berg was Murat's
    Imperial title from 1806 until he became King of Naples in 1808.
16. *ibid.*
17. Quoted in H. d'Espinchal, *Souvenirs Militaires 1792-1814,* 1901.

Chapter 4 (pp 60–73)

1. 5th and 7th Hussars.
2. Quoted in Dr F.G. Hourtoulle's, *Le Général Comte Charles Lasalle* (chez
   l'auteur 1970).
3. A *régiment de marche* consisted of squadrons of various regiments, formed
   into one unit while they were in transit to join their parent regiments.
   As its name implied, a *régiment de marche* existed only whilst it was on
   the march from the depôt in France. A provisional regiment was formed
   during an emergency from whatever units were available. Once the
   emergency had passed it was disbanded.
4. Fourteen years earlier, a Spanish general had fought Dugommier's army
   in Catalonia using a plan that had been drawn up in 1676.
5. Including 30,000 under Junot in Portugal.
6. This girl was her only child by Lasalle; she also had three sons, born
   during her marriage to General Berthier.
7. E.V.E.B. de Castellane-Novejan, *Journal,* 1895-7.
8. Hourtoulle, *op. cit.*
9. F.G. Hourtoulle, *op. cit.*
10. Count, baron and chevalier. Lasalle left the bulk of his estate to his
    daughter.

11. Lasalle's brigade at Medellin comprised the 2nd Hussars, 9th Dragoons, 5th and 10th Chasseurs.
12. Captain A.J.M. de Rocca, *Mémoires sur la Guerre des Français en Espagne,* 1814.
13. P-L. Roederer, *Oeuvres du Comte P-L. Roederer,* 1853-59.

Chapter 5 *(pp 74–89)*

1. The Austrian cavalry employed in the German campaign totalled approximately 22,000 men and consisted of kurassiers, dragoons, chevaulegers (light horse), hussars and uhlans. Kurassier and dragoon regiments had six squadrons each of 133 men, the other regiments eight squadrons each of 149 men. In 1796 the Austrian army had one cavalryman for every four infantrymen; in 1809 the proportion had declined to one for ten.
2. In other words they wore a breast-plate but no back-plate.
3. He was the third son of Leopold II (1747-92) and brother to Franz II (1768-1835), who became Franz I of Austria after the dissolution of the Holy Roman Empire in 1806.
4. The kurassier officer whose experiences in the 1805 campaign have already been mentioned.
5. During a pursuit Bessières frequently lunched in the saddle, but there seems no reason to doubt the story that he was sitting down to a meal on this occasion, which is described by several writers including Thiers. General Thoumas' statement that Bessières was in bed is very hard to believe. Thiers was writing much nearer the event than Thoumas and had either never heard the version quoted by Thoumas or declined to believe it. The story that Bessières was in bed is hardly flattering to him, and as Thiers was not an admirer of the Marshal he certainly would not have tried to suppress it.
6. i.e. '*Allons les écraser comme du fromage de Rocamadour!*' – 'Let's go and crush them like Rocamadour cheese!'
7. L.A. Unger, *Histoire critique des exploits et vicissitudes de la cavalerie pendant les guerres de la Revolution et de l'Empire,* 1848.
8. L.A. Thiers, *Histoire du Consulat et de l'Empire,* 1845-62.
9. When Napoleon re-drew the map of Germany in 1806, Lichtenstein's estates were absorbed in the Confederation of the Rhine. Lichtenstein abdicated in favour of his son, in order to continue serving in the Austrian army.
10. C.A.M. Tardieu de Maleissye-Melun, *Sous les aigles Autrichiennes. Souvenirs du Chevalier de Grueber,* 1909.
11. *ibid.*
12. At Warsaw, after the Russian campaign of 1812.

13. When Bessières was seconded to the Reserve Cavalry at the start of the 1809 campaign, Arrighi took over temporary command of the cavalry of the Guard. He was appointed to lead the 3rd Heavy Cavalry Division three days after Espagne's death.

14. Shaving in the heavy cavalry regiments was regulated according to the season. Cuirassiers were allowed to cut and trim their moustaches between 1 December and 1 March, but for the remaining nine months of the year they had to let them grow.

15. The Archduke Karl was subject to epileptic fits. At a critical stage of the fighting in April he had locked himself in a room of his headquarters for 24 hours.

16. Whose baptism of fire with the Guard cavalry at Austerlitz has already been described.

17. Defrance was delighted to have such an unusual souvenir of the battle, and sent it home to his family. To his lasting regret they had it repaired and restored to its original shape.

18. It was said after the battle that Walther had been ordered to charge by General Macdonald but refused to do so. The Polish Light Horse had been added to the cavalry of the Guard during the 1807 campaign; subsequently equipped with lances, it became the 1st Regiment of Guard Lancers.

19. When muskets were fired over a long period the combustion gases formed a deposit in the barrels and reduced their bore, making them difficult to load. In a battle such as Wagram, infantrymen were sometimes seen urinating into their musket barrels to remove the fouling.

20. The colonel of the 8th Chasseurs mounted his trumpeters on white horses. On the battlefield they took post in the centre of the regiment, making a conspicuous aiming mark for enemy artillery.

    Trumpeter Chevillet never subscribed to the theory that a good soldier should remain motionless under fire; when he saw a round-shot approaching he warned his comrades by calling out *'Gare le brutal!'* and reined his horse to one side. His squadron commander used to respond by sinking as low as possible in the saddle. 'What's the matter, captain?' a junior officer once asked him. 'The young lady only wants to give you a kiss.' 'She's too forward; I don't want to encourage her,' he replied.

21. The same remark was ascribed to General Victor Latour-Maubourg when he lost a leg four years later.

22. Quoted in Captain A. Bué's *Livre d'or des Carabiniers*, 1898. Unlike the cuirassier pattern, the Carabinier helmet had a thick 'caterpillar' crest.

23. i.e. Eugène de Beauharnais, viceroy of Italy, who joined Napoleon just before Wagram.

24. Quoted in G.A. Robinet de Clery's *D'Essling à Wagram. Lasalle*, 1891.

25. His force comprised: 2nd Dragoon Division (3rd, 6th, 10th & 11th Dragoons) Brigade d'Ornano (15th & 25th Dragoons) Brigade Lorcet

(3rd Hussars, 15th Chasseurs).

26. E.F. Sprünglin, *Souvenirs d'Emmanuel Frédéric Sprünglin*, 1904.
27. Quoted in C.A. Thoumas' *Les Grands Cavaliers du Premier Empire*, 1890-1909.

Chapter 6 (pp 90–99)

1. One leader who had formed a small band in 1809 was now regularly paying 12,000 men.
2. There are several different versions of the Guard cavalry's attitude at Fuentes d'Onoro. Marshal Marmont, who was not present, claimed that General Lepic had not only drawn his sword but was biting the blade with frustration.
3. Napoleon's peculiar method of taking snuff consisted of holding it under his nose for a moment without inhaling, then throwing it away. It was said that a boxful of it could be swept up in any room where he had spent quarter of an hour.
4. M.E.G. de Baudus, *Etudes sur Napoléon*, 1841.
5. General Loison, who had recently been wounded. Masséna had upset him by refusing his application for sick leave in France.
6. These regiments were formed from the 30th Chasseurs, six dragoon regiments, (1st, 3rd, 8th, 9th, 10th and 29th) and two regiments of Polish light cavalry. The latter (which became the 7th and 8th Chevaux-légers) retained their Polish-type uniforms.
7. Originally only first-rank troopers of the Chevaux-léger regiments carried lances, which were finally issued to the second-rank troopers at the end of 1811.
8. The blades for the heavy cavalry swords were manufactured at Klingenthal. Half of them were made up into complete swords at Klingenthal; the rest were sent for completion to Versailles.
9. Nevertheless the combination of Klingenthal blades and the brutal cuirassier temperament was an extremely formidable one. 'When you put your sword point in a man's belly,' a cuirassier colonel once told his troopers, 'turn your wrist *en quarte* and tear his guts out.'
10. The Guard cavalry returns show 6,279 troopers. However General Berthezène (who served in the Guard infantry in many campaigns) claimed that the discrepancy between ration strengths and campaign effectives was even greater in the Guard than in the line regiments. He gives the Guard cavalry's effective strength at the start of the 1812 campaign as 5,000: 800 Grenadiers à Cheval; 1,200 Guard Dragoons; 1,200 Chasseurs à Cheval; 1,800 Lancers.

    There were three regiments of Guard lancers in 1812. The 1st was Polish; the 2nd regiment, formerly the Hussars of the Dutch Royal

Guard, had been added to the Imperial Guard cavalry in 1811. These two regiments did not serve under Bessières throughout the 1812 campaign; on the march to Moscow they were attached to Davout's corps, forming a brigade commanded by Edouard de Colbert, Auguste de Colbert's elder brother. The 3rd regiment, composed of Poles and Lithuanians, was raised at Grodno in September 1812. En route to join the Grand Army it was attacked by a Russian force and virtually destroyed.

11. Deputy Minister of War.
12. The strengths of the four corps were as follows:
    1st Corps – 12,077. 2nd Corps – 10,436. 3rd Corps – 9,676. 4th Corps – 7,994.
13. The modern Kaunas.

Chapter 7 (pp 100–112)

1. 'If I had two men like you under my command,' Marshal Davout had told him during the Austerlitz campaign, 'I should have one of them shot.'
2. The French habit of drawing swords at the start of a battle made for stiff wrists and tired sword arms. According to the light cavalry officer Victor Dupuy, it was best to draw sabres just before a charge, since the action raised the men's morale and intimidated the enemy. Also, a mounted man's thighs automatically contracted as he drew his sword, alerting his horse and preparing it for the charge.
3. Colonel Dommanget.
4. Roth von Schreckenstein, *Die Kavallerie in der Schlacht an der Moskwa*, 1858.
5. Having been promoted to general of division, Defrance no longer commanded the Carabinier brigade, but at this time it formed part of his division.
6. Lieutenant Henckens of the 6th Chasseurs.
7. J.L. Henckens, *Lieutenant Henckens*, 1910.
8. Michel Combe, *Mémoires du Colonel Combe*, 1853.
9. After Borodino men in the line regiments said ironically that the French army now possessed a corps which did not fight.
10. Michel Combe, *op. cit.*
11. During the march to Moscow, Napoleon asked a captain of this regiment how many sore-backed horses he had in his squadron. 'None!' he replied. Convinced that he must be lying, Napoleon ordered him to unsaddle his horses and walk them past for inspection. None of them had a sore back.
12. His loyalty was understandable. Habeck had made a great deal of money out of the concession for importing the wines of Bordeaux into East Prussia, which Napoleon had given him after the 1807 campaign.
13. Michel Combe, *op. cit.*

Chapter 8 (pp 113–130)

1. According to Victor Dupuy, General Bourcier knew more about horses than any other officer in the army: 'but his tone was so harsh, and his manner so forbidding, that it was always a relief to escape from his office.' General of division since 1794, Bourcier had been appointed an inspector-general of the French cavalry as early as 1798.

2. The establishment laid down by Napoleon was eight squadrons each of 250 men for both the Chasseurs and Lancers, and five squadrons each of 300 men for the Grenadiers à Cheval. A second decree of 6 March increased the Chasseurs' establishment to ten squadrons, the tenth squadron to be furnished by the Mamelukes.

3. Since Murat had returned to Naples after the Russian campaign, and had not yet rejoined the army, Bessières was temporarily commanding the Reserve Cavalry as well as the cavalry of the Guard. At this stage of the campaign the Reserve Cavalry was still very weak. For example, on 15 April the 2nd Light Cavalry Brigade, which was formed by seven chasseur regiments, mustered only 623 sabres.

   The wastage of cavalry veterans, which continued throughout the 1813 campaign, is well illustrated by the case of the 10th Hussars. On the eve of Lutzen Napoleon gave crosses of the Legion to 25 men of the regiment; at the end of the battle only five of them were left.

4. The debts were liquidated by Napoleon, who also left 300,000 francs to Bessières' son in his will. When the Marshal's Istrian estates reverted to Austria at the fall of the Napoleonic Empire, the Austrian Emperor granted Bessières' widow an annual income of 20,000 francs.

5. See the table of French cavalry organization contained in Lieut. General Baron Ottomar von der Osten-Sacken's *Die Franzosische Armee im Jahre 1813*, 1889. The 13th and 14th regiments of cuirassiers had been formed at the end of 1808 and 1810 respectively.

6. The strengths were as follows:

	1st Corps (Latour-Maubourg)	*2nd Corps* (Sébastiani)	*3rd Corps* (Arrighi)
Squadrons	78	52	27
Guns	36	18	24
Men	16537	10304	6000

	4th Corps (Kellermann)	*5th Corps* (Pajol)
Squadrons	24	20
Guns	12	6
Men	3923	4000

7. C.P.V. Pajol, *Pajol, Général-en-Chef*, 1874.

8. F.J.L. Rilliet, *Journal d'un sous-lieutenant de cuirassiers, 1813*, 1908.

It was not only inexperience that caused injury to so many French cavalry horses; in the Peninsula, where the French cavalry regiments consisted almost entirely of veterans, the British used to say that they could smell their sore-backed horses half a mile away. Victor Dupuy believed that many sore backs were caused by drunken veterans rolling about in the saddle. He claimed that this could have been remedied by making regiments march at the trot instead of the walk, forcing the men to sit upright. In spite of the increased pace, he wrote, the horses would have been better off.

In Rilliet's day the poor condition of young French cavalry horses had been aggravated by the recent adoption of the uncomfortable Dessault bit. Fitted with very long cheek-pieces, in its original form the severity of its action had been lessened by the design of the mouth-piece; the French cavalry, however, adopted a modified and even stronger version, which in the opinion of one riding-master was sheer madness. 'One can imagine,' he wrote some years later, 'what suffering this inflicted on young newly-broken horses of three and a half years, who were already distressed by teething. From the extreme weakness of these young animals to their utter ruin was but a step.' (Quoted in L.A. Picard's *Origines de l'école de cavalerie et de ses traditions équestres*, 1889.)

Although he was such a notoriously bad horsemaster the average French trooper was extremely fond of his horse, which loved him in return. Often on campaign General de Brack saw a tired horse leaning to one side as it walked, so as to keep its drunken or sleeping master in the saddle. When forage was short, de Brack's men would give their last piece of bread to their horses and go hungry themselves.

9. Victor Dupuy, *op. cit.*
10. Rilliet, *op. cit.*
11. Michel Combe, *op. cit.* At Dennewitz in the 1813 campaign, General Defrance's answer to the Cossack menace was to form his cavalry division in square.
12. Rilliet, *op. cit.*
13. Austrians and Russians under Schwarzenberg, Prussians under Blucher, Swedes under the Swedish Crown Prince (the former French Marshal Bernadotte).
14. *Rilliet, op. cit.*
15. French troopers had a low opinion of Hungarian light cavalry sabres, which had a wide blade and a very narrow guard. They tended to turn in the user's hand, which lessened the force of their blows.
16. Rilliet, *op. cit.*
17. Four units of mounted Gardes d'Honneur had been formed in 1813 from young men of good family. They were attached to Guard cavalry regiments.
18. H.E. Lot, *Les Deux Généraux Ordener*, 1910.

19. *ibid.*
20. On 6 April Napoleon tried to abdicate in favour of his son, but the allies would not allow this. The second abdication was unconditional.
21. 54,000 as Guard Cavalry commander, 20,000 as Grand Eagle of the Legion of Honour, 30,000 as *premier écuyer* to the Emperor.
22. F.J.L. Rilliet, *Saint Germain, 1814*, 1908.

Chapter 9 (pp 131–144)

1. Kellermann and Lasalle were both born in Metz and knew each other well. Lasalle had served as aide de camp to Kellermann's father.
2. Arrighi was dispatched on a mission to Corsica; Defrance and Sébastiani were employed in organizing the remount depôts and the National Guard.
3. One eyewitness, however, states that some of the cuirassiers at Quatre Bras were killed by bullets that penetrated their breastplates and passed out through their backplates.
4. It was taken from its dead ensign's hands by Trooper Henry of the 8th Cuirassiers, who was regarded as a bad character in his regiment. He later claimed the 4,000 francs reward which a Paris banker had promised to any French soldier who captured a British colour. In 1909 a British cavalry officer on holiday in France bought the colour at an antique shop in Azay-le-Rideau; his grandson restored it to the Welch Regiment in 1953.
5. James Anton, *Retrospect of a Military Life*, 1841.
6. Kellermann's Imperial title.
7. In addition, he may have been anxious to rid himself of a reputation for lack of initiative that he had acquired in the 1814 campaign. At Mormant, he had allowed a demoralized Russian division to retire under the eyes of his division of dragoons. It was said afterwards that if he had shown more initiative and charged the Russians they would have surrendered.
8. Roussel d'Harbal had entered the French army only five years previously. Up to 1810 he had been in Austrian service, and had fought with the Archduke Karl at Aspern-Essling.
9. Apart from the Grenadiers à Cheval, the Carabiniers had the best physique in the French cavalry. The minimum height for a Carabinier trooper was 5 pieds 6 pouces, or approximately 1 metre 80, against 5 pieds 4 pouces for a cuirassier.
10. L. Stouff, *Le Lieutenant Général Delort 1792-1815*, 1906.
11. His brother Gaston also fought at Waterloo, as a squadron leader in the 7th Cuirassiers.
12. Colonel Ordener is referring to the four lines of the cuirassier corps.
13. The squares, as they are always called, were actually rectangles; the sides

were shorter than the front and rear faces.

14. Hon. J.W. Fortescue, *A History of the British Army*, Vol. X, 1920.
15. General Sir James Kennedy, *Notes on the Battle of Waterloo*, 1865.
16. General Cavalié Mercer, *Journal of the Waterloo Campaign*, 1870.
17. Fortescue, *op. cit.*
18. H.E. Lot, *op. cit.*
19. Prior to Macdonald's appointment, the post had been briefly held by Davout.
20. Aubry, *op. cit.*

Chapter 10 (pp 145–149)

1. Gaston Coindre, *Mon Vieux Besançon*, 1900-12.
2. Born at Leiskamm in the Palatinate, Marulaz did not become a naturalised Frenchman until 1817. Napoleon was always tolerant of his German-speaking cavalrymen's atrocious grammar. 'They *sabre* well in French,' he used to say. ('*Ils sabrent toujours en bon Français.*')
3. When F. Marullaz was collecting material before the First World War for his biography of the general, he actually talked to Janicot, who lived to the age of 97.
4. F. Marullaz, *Le Baron J-F. Marulaz*, 1918.
5. Xavier Marmier, *Lettres sur la Russie, la Finlande et la Pologne*, 1843.
6. Aubry, *op. cit.*
7. *ibid.*

Notes on the diagrams

1. (p. 14) A regiment of four squadrons formed in close column, or *colonne serrée*. The intervals between squadrons of a regiment formed in column varied in size; on the battlefield they might be anything up to twice the width of the squadron's front. In close column, the formation shown here, the interval was twelve metres, measured from the cruppers of horses in the second rank to the heads of the horses in the front rank of the squadron behind.

A regiment formed in close column was easier to control than a regiment formed in open column, but more difficult to deploy.

The number of squadrons in Napoleonic cavalry regiments was changed several times. Usually, though not invariably, regiments of hussars and chasseurs were bigger than those of cuirassiers and dragoons. At one period light cavalry regiments had five squadrons when heavy cavalry regiments had only four. On campaign, however, a regiment which was reduced in strength would be reorganized into a smaller number of squadrons.*

A squadron consisted of two companies, each sub-divided into two troops. The senior company of a line cavalry regiment (i.e. the first two troops) was known as the *compagnie d'élite*. Like grenadier companies in the infantry, it was made up of the toughest and most experienced men in the regiment. In the dragoons and light cavalry, troopers of the *compagnie d'élite* wore a distinctive headdress: bearskins in the dragoons, busbies (colpacks) in the hussars and chasseurs. In the dragoons and chasseurs they also wore epaulettes of red wool. Elite company troopers usually acted as mounted escorts for the brigade and divisional generals.

Charges were generally carried out in the formation shown here, with all the waves in alignment from front to rear. Occasionally charges were made in echelon, that is to say in slightly staggered lines. In echelon, one

---

* By the time it reached a battlefield a cavalry regiment was always reduced below its official establishment, both in men and horses. The establishments were altered several times; in 1805 they were 550 men for a cuirassier regiment, 880 for a dragoon regiment, and 1,075 in the light cavalry. In 1806 the cuirassier establishment was 820 men per regiment; it was increased to 1,040 in 1807.

wing of each wave overlapped one wing of the wave in front, thus protecting it against being outflanked. Bessières sometimes used echelon formation with the Guard cavalry, but it was difficult to keep the dressing straight.

2. (p. 15) This diagram shows how a squadron changed formation from column of troops to line of battle. In this case the squadron forms up in line facing towards its original line of march, with the leading squadrons taking the right of the line. This formation was known as Natural Order (*Ordre Naturel*). In Inverse Order (*Ordre Inverse*) the leading squadrons of the column took post on the left of the line.

The strongest and most intelligent men in each troop were mounted on the best horses and posted in the front rank. As this diagram illustrates, the front-rank men of the four troops became the front rank of the squadron when it formed into line.

The recommended front for a squadron charging in line was not less than 40 files and not more than 48; in other words the squadron was formed in two lines containing a grand total of between 80 and 96 men. The rest of the men in the squadron were formed up in the rear as a reserve.

When a brigade or a division formed line of battle, a space at least 15 paces wide was left between each of its regiments. This distance was measured from the knee of the sergeant on the outermost flank of one regiment to the knee of the nearest sergeant in the next regiment in line.

The most difficult manoeuvre in the French cavalry drill book was the *Passage des Lignes*, designed to be carried out when the leading wave of an attack had lost its impetus and split up into groups. By this manoeuvre the two lines of the following wave formed into column, passed through the intervals of the first wave, and reformed into line to lead a fresh advance.

Sources

MANUSCRIPT

Dossiers of the cavalry leaders mentioned in the text, *Service Historique de l'Armée Française, Chateau de Vincennes*.

PRINTED

i) *Napoleon's Cavalry*

Aubier, L.D.A., *La cavalerie Napoléonienne peut-elle encore servir de modèle?*, 1902.
Brack, A.F.de, *Avant-postes de cavalerie légère*, 1834.
Camon, H., *La manoeuvre Napoléonienne dans le combat de cavalerie*, 1912.
Choppin, H., *Un Inspecteur Général de cavalerie sous le Directoire et le Consulat*, 1898.
Foucart, P.J., *L'armement des cuirassiers en 1811*, 1894.
Masson, F., *Cavaliers de Napoléon*, 1895.
Picard, L.A., *La Cavalerie pendant les guerres de la Révolution et de l'Empire*, 1895.
Roth von Schreckenstein, Baron, *Die Kavallerie in der Schlacht an der Moskwa*, 1858.
Thoumas, C.A., *Les Grands Cavaliers du Premier Empire*, 1890-1909.
Unger, L.A., *Histoire critique des exploits et vicissitudes de la cavalerie pendant les guerres de la Révolution et de l'Empire*, 1848-9; *Ordonnance provisoire sur l'exercice et les manoeuvres de la cavalerie*, 1804.

ii) *French Cavalry: history of specific regiments and branches*

Albert, A., *Manuscrit des Carabiniers*, 1894.
Amonville, M.F.J.R. d', *Les Cuirassiers du Roy: 8ème Cuirassiers 1638-1892*, 1892.
Aubry, T.J., *Souvenirs du 12ème Chasseurs 1799-1815*, 1889.

Bouillé, H. de, *Historique du 13ème régiment de hussards,* 1900.

Bourqueney, M.V.C. de, *Historique du 25ème régiment de dragons,* 1890; *Historique du 12ème régiment de hussards,* 1902.

Bremond d'Ars, T.C. de, *Historique du 21er régiment de chasseurs à cheval, 1792-1814,* 1903.

Bruyère, P., *1635-1885. Historique du 2ème régiment de Dragons,* 1885.

Bué, A., *Livre d'or des Carabiniers,* 1898.

Castéras-Villemartin, J-A-M-P-F. de P. de,: *Historique du 16ème régiment de dragons,* 1892.

Castillon de St. Victor, M.E. de, *Historique du 5ème régiment de hussards,* 1889.

Choppin, H., *Histoire générale des dragons,* 1879; *La Cavalerie Française,* 1893; *Les Hussards. Les Vieux Régiments 1692-1792,* 1899; *Les Origines de la Cavalerie Française,* 1905.

Cuel, F., *Historique du 18ème régiment de dragons,* 1894.

Descaves, P., *Historique du 13ème régiment de chasseurs et des chasseurs à cheval de la Garde,* 1891.

Dupont, M., *Nos Vieux Houzards,* 1933.

Dupuy, R., *Historique du 3ème régiment de hussards,* n.d.; *Historique du 12ème régiment de chasseurs,* 1891; *Historique des régiments de hussards, 1689-1892,* 1893.

Fallou, L., *Nos Hussards 1692-1902,* 1902.

Gay de Vernon, J., *Essai historique sur l'organisation de la cavalerie légère, et principalement sur l'arme des chasseurs à cheval, suivi d'une notice historique sur le 8ème de chasseurs,* 1853; *Historique du 2ème Régiment de Chasseurs à Cheval,* 1865.

Juzancourt, G. de, *Historique du 7ème régiment des cuirassiers 1659-1886,* 1887.

Lamotte, P. de, *Historique du 8ème hussards,* 1891.

Lasuchette, Capt. de, *Historique du 26ème Dragons,* 1894.

Lomier, E., *Histoire des régiments des Gardes d'Honneur, 1813-1814,* 1924.

Lonlay, D. de, *Les Cuirassiers 1672-1886,* 1886.

Louvet, Capt., *Historique du 7ème hussards,* 1889.

Martimprey, A.A. de, *Historique du 9ème régiment des Cuirassiers,* 1888.

Martinet, F.X., *Historique du 9ème régiment de Dragons,* 1888.

Maumené, C., *Histoire du 3ème régiment de cuirassiers,* 1893.

Ogier d'Ivry, H.P.G.M., *Historique du Ier régiment de hussards,* 1901; *Historique du 9ème hussards et des Guides de la Garde,* 1891.

Oré, D.C., *Ier Régiment de chasseurs 1651–1903,* 1903.

Picard, L.A., *Origines de l'Ecole de cavalerie et de ses traditions équestres,* 1889.

Place, R. de, *Historique du 12ème Cuirassiers 1688-1888,* 1889.

Reiffenberg, F.G.E.C.M. de, *Les Régiments de Fer,* 1862.

Rothwiller, A.E., *Histoire du 2ème régiment de Cuirassiers, ancien Royal de Cavalerie 1635-1876,* 1877

Rozat de Mandres, A-J-O, *Histoire du 4ème régiment de Cuirassiers 1643-1897,* 1897.

Susane, L.A.V.V., *Histoire de la Cavalerie Française*, 1874; *Histoire du Ier Régiment de Cuirassiers*, 1889.

iii) *Battles and Battlefields*

Binder von Krieglstein, C., *Aspern und Wagram*, 1906.

Foucart, P.J., *Bautzen, 20-21 Mai 1813*, 1897.

Kellermann, F.-E. de, *Réfutation de M. le duc de Rovigo, ou la vérité sur la bataille de Marengo*, 1828; *Deuxième et dernière replique d'un ami de la vérité à M. le duc de Rovigo*, 1828.

Kennedy, J.S., *Notes on the Battle of Waterloo*, 1865.

Lumbroso, A.E., *Mélanges Marengo*, 1903.

Martin, P., *Causes de la défaite de l'Armée Française à Waterloo*, 1909.

Menge, A., *Die Schlacht von Aspern am 21 und 22 Mai 1809*, 1900.

Perreau, J., *Les Centenaires de 1806 et 1807. Iéna, Eylau, Friedland*, 1908.

Pfalz, A., *Die Marchfeldschlachten von Aspern und Deutsch-Wagram im Jahre 1809*, 1900.

Slovák, A., *Die Schlacht bei Austerlitz*, 1898.

Trolard, E., *Pélérinage aux champs de bataille français d'Italie. De Rivoli à Marengo et à Solferino*, 1893.

Varnhagen, C.A.L.P., *Die Schlacht von Deutsch-Wagram am 5 und 6 Juli 1809*, 1909; *An Account of the Battle fought near Aspern on the Marchfeld*, London, 1809; *La Bataille de Preussisch Eylau gagné par la Grande Armée*, Paris, 1807; *Sammlung der Plane und Nachrichten von den beiden Hauptschlachten von Gross-Aspern und Teutsch-Wagram auf dem Marchfelde bei Wien*, Weimar, 1809.

iv) *Campaigns*

Alombert-Goget, P.C., *La Campagne de 1805 en Allemagne*, 1902.

Balagny, D.E.P., *La Campagne de l'Empereur Napoléon en Espagne 1808–9*, 1902-07.

Becke, A.F., *Napoleon and Waterloo*, 1914.

Bertin, G., *La Campagne de 1812 d'après des témoins oculaires*, 1896; *La Campagne de 1814 d'après des témoins oculaires*, 1897.

Bouvier, F., *Bonaparte en Italie*, 1899.

Brett-James, E.A., *The Hundred Days. Napoleon's last campaign from eyewitness accounts*, Macmillan & Co., 1964.

Buat, E.A.L., *Etude critique d'histoire militaire. 1809. De Ratisbonne à Znaim*, 1909.

Chambray, G. de, *Histoire de l'expédition de Russie*, 1823.

Chandler, D.G., *The Campaigns of Napoleon*, Weidenfeld & Nicolson, 1967.

Charras, J.B.A., *Histoire de la Guerre de 1813 en Allemagne*, 1866; *Histoire de la Campagne de 1815*, 1857.

Chuquet, A., *Human Voices from the Russian campaign of 1812*, 1913; *Lettres de 1812*, 1911; *1812. La Guerre de Russie*, 1912.

Crusy de Marcillac, P.L.A., *Histoire de la guerre entre la France et l'Espagne pendant les années de la Révolution Française, 1793, 1794 et partie de 1795*, 1808.

Cugnac, G.J.M.R. de, *Campagne de l'armée de Résérve en 1800*, 1899-1901; *La Campagne de Marengo*, 1904.

Faber du Faur, C.W. von, *Campagne de Russie, 1812*, 1895.

Fabry, G., *La Campagne de Russie*, 1900.

Fain, A.J.F., *Manuscrit de mil huit cent douze*, 1827; *Manuscrit de mil huit cent treize*, 1824; *Souvenirs de la campagne de France – manuscrit de 1814*, 1914.

Fervel, J.N., *Campagnes de la Revolution dans les Pyrénées Orientales*, 1851-3.

Flores, G., *Estudios militares sobre las campanas de 1793 à 1795 en los Pireneos*, 1854.

Foucart, P.J., *Bautzen : la poursuite jusqu'à l'armistice 22 Mai – 4 Juin 1813*, 1901; *Campagne de Pologne 1806-1807*, 1882; *Campagne de Prusse 1806*, 1887.

Foudras, A., *Campagne de Bonaparte en Italie en l'an VIII de la Republique*, 1800.

Furse, G.A., *Marengo and Hohenlinden*, 1903.

Giguet, P., *Histoire de la campagne d'Italie*, 1853.

Hooper, G., *The Italian Campaigns of General Bonaparte in 1796-7 and 1800*, 1859.

Houssaye, H., *Iéna et la campagne de 1806*, 1912; *1814*, 1889; *1815. Waterloo*, 1906.

Jonquière, C. de la, *L'expédition d'Egypte*, 1899-1907.

Krauss, A., *Der Feldzug von Ulm*, 1912.

Lachouque, H., *Waterloo*, Arms and Armour Press, 1975.

Lemonnier-Delafosse, M.J.B., *Campagnes de 1810 à 1815*, 1850.

M★★★, *Journal d'un Dragon d'Egypte – 14ème Dragons*, 1899.

Mack von Leiberich, K., *Vertheidigung des Ostreichischen Feldzugs von 1805*, 1806.

Martin, P.R., *Histoire des deux campagnes de Saxe en 1813*, 1832.

Maude, F.N., *The Jena Campaign 1806*, 1902; *The Leipzig Campaign*, 1902; *The Ulm Campaign*, 1904.

Mercer, C., *Journal of the Waterloo Campaign*, 1870.

Mikhailovsky-Danilevsky, A.I., *Relation de la campagne de 1805*, 1846.

Oman, C.W.C., *A History of the Peninsular War*, 1902-30.

Petit, J., *Marengo, ou Campagne d'Italie par l'Armée de Résérve*, 1801.

Petre (F.L.): *Napoleon's Conquest of Prussia 1806*, 1907; *Napoleon's Campaign in Poland, 1806-07*, 1901; *Napoleon and the Archduke Charles*, 1909; *Napoleon's Last Campaign in Germany, 1813*, 1912; *Napoleon at Bay, 1814*, 1914.

Piuma, –, *Récit historique de la campagne de Buonaparté en Italie, par un témoin oculaire*, 1808.

Pommereul, F.R.J. de, *Campagne du Général Buonaparte en Italie pendant les années IVe et Ve de la Republique Française*, 1797.

Quinet, E., *Histoire de la Campagne de 1815*, 1862.

Regnault, J., *La Campagne de 1815. Mobilisation et concentration*, 1935.

Saski, C.G.L., *La Campagne de 1809*, 1899-1902.

Ségur, P.P. de, *Histoire de Napoléon et de la Grande Armée pendant l'année 1812*, 1825.

Serieys, A., *Histoire Abrégée de la Campagne de Napoléon-le-Grand en Allemagne et en Italie*, 1806.

Siborne, H.T., *Waterloo Letters*, 1891.

Stutterheim, K. von, *Darstellung des Feldzugs von Jahr 1809 von einem Augenzengen*, 1811.

Thiry, J., *Marengo*, 1949; *La Campagne de France*, 1938; *Waterloo*, 1947.

Valentini, G.M. von, *Versuch eine Geschichte des Feldzugs von 1809 an der Donau*, 1818.

W, *Campagne des Français en Italie en 1800. Par un officier attaché à l'Etat-Major*, 1801.

Welden, L. von, *Der krieg von 1899 zwischen Oesterreich und Frankreich, von Anfang Mai bis zum Friedensschlusse*, 1872.

Wilson, R.T., *Brief remarks on the character and composition of the Russian army and a sketch of the campaigns in Poland in the years 1806 and 1807, 1810; Narrative of events during the invasion of Russia by Napoleon Bonaparte, 1812*, 1860.

Woinovich, E. von, *Das Kriegsjahr 1809 in Einzeldarstellungen*, 1906.

Wood, E., *Cavalry in the Waterloo Campaign*, 1895.

v) *French Army*

Bouchot, H., *L'épopée du costume militaire Français*, 1898.

Détaille, J.B.E., and Richard, J., *Types et Uniformes. L'Armée Française*, 1885.

Fallou, L., *La Garde Impériale*, 1901.

Hapdé, J.B.A., *Les Sépulcres de la Grande Armée ou tableaux des hôpitaux pendant la dernière campagne de Buonaparte*, 1814.

Hauterive, E. d', *L'Armée sous la Révolution 1789-1794*, 1894.

Lachouque, H., *Napoléon et la Garde Impériale*, 1956.

Masson, F., *1792-1809. Aventures de Guerre*, 1895.

Morvan, J., *Le Soldat Impérial*, 1904.

Osten-Sacken und von Rhein, O. von der, *Die Franzosische Armee im Jahre 1813*, 1889.

Richard, J., *En Campagne*, 1885.

Saint Chamant, H.C. de, *Napoléon, ses dernières armées*, 1890.

Saint Hilaire, E.M. de, *Historique anecdotique, politique et militaire de la Garde Impériale,* 1847.

Sauzey, J.C.A.F., *Iconographie du costume militaire de la Révolution et de l'Empire,* 1901.

Titeux, E., *Histoire de la Maison Militaire du Roi de 1814 à 1830,* 1890.

Toussaint, M., *Napoléon Ier et sa Garde,* 1942.

Weygand, M., *Histoire de l'Armée Française,* 1938.

vi) *Polish Army*

Chelminski, V., and Malibran, A., *L'Armée du duché de Varsovie,* 1913.

Chlapowski, D., *Mémoires sur les guerres de Napoléon 1806-13,* 1908.

Rembowski, A., *Sources documentaires concernant l'histoire du régiment des Chevau-Légers de la garde de Napoléon Ier,* 1899

Tyskiewicz, J., *Histoire du 17e Régiment de Cavalerie Polonaise 1812-1815,* 1904.

vii) *Austrian Army*

Angeli, M.E. von, *Erzherzog Carl von Oesterreich als Feldherr und Heeresorganizator,* 1896-7.

Criste, O., *Feldmarschall Johannes Fürst von Lichtenstein,* 1905.

Duller, E., *Erzherzog Carl von Oesterreich,* 1844-7.

Moeckesch, V., *General der Kavallerie M. Freiherr von Melas,* 1900.

Tardieu de Maleissye-Melun, C.A.M., *Sous les aigles Autrichiennes. Souvenirs du Chevalier de Grueber,* 1909.

Teuber, C.O., *Die Oesterreichische Armee von 1700 bis 1867,* 1895-1904.

Thurheim, J.A.G.A.G.M., *Die Reiter Regimenter der K.K. Osterreichischen Armee,* 1862.

Die Nachrichten von dem Krieges-Schauplatzen in Deutschland und Italien, 1809.

Dienst Reglement für die Kaiserliche-Königliche Kavallerie, 1808.

Dienst Reglement für die k.k. Infanterie, 1807.

Erzherzog Karl – Der Feldherr und Seine Armee, 1913.

viii) *Russian Army*

Bennigsen, L.A.G. von, *Mémoires,* 1907-8.

Galitzine, Pr. B., *Souvenirs et impressions d'un officier Russe pendant les campagnes de 1812, 1813 et 1814,* 1849.

Golubov, S.N., and Kuznetsov, F.E., *General Bagration,* 1945.

ix) *British Army*

Anton, J., *Retrospect of a Military Life*, 1841.
Fortescue, J.W., *A History of the British Army, Vol. X*, 1920.
Morris, T., *Recollections of Military Service*, 1845.

x) *Biography, Memoirs and Correspondence*

Ambert, J., *Cinq épées*, 1884; *Les généraux de la Révolution 1792-1804*, 1892.
André, E., *Le Maréchal Exelmans, 1775-1852*, 1898.
Astier de la Vigerie, E.R. d', *Le Lieutenant-Général Comte Defrance*, 1911.
Atteridge, A.H., *Joachim Murat, Marshal of France and King of Naples*, 1911.
Baschet, R., *Le Général Daumesnil*, 1938.
Baudus, M.E.G. de, *Etudes sur Napoléon*, 1841.
Bausset, L.F.J. de, *Private Memoirs of the Court of Napoleon*, 1828.
Beauharnais, E. de, *Mémoires et correspondance politique et militaire*, 1858-60.
Berthezène, P., *Souvenirs militaires par le baron Berthezène, publiés par son fils*, 1855.
Bessières, A., *Le Marèchal Bessières, Duc d' Istrie*, 1952.
Bousson de Mairet, E., *Souvenirs militaires du Baron Desvernois*, 1858.
Bro, L., *Mémoires du Général Bro, 1796-1844*, 1914.
Bruyère, P., *Le Général Bruyère 1772-1813*, 1889.
Casse, P.E.A. du, *Le Général Arrighi de Casanova*, 1866; *Les Trois Maréchaux d'Ornano*, 1862.
Castellane-Novejan, E.V.E.B. de, *Journal*, 1895-97.
Caulaincourt, A.A.L. de, *Souvenirs du Duc de Vicence*, 1837.
Charavay, J., *Les Généraux Morts pour la Patrie, 1792-1871*, 1893.
Chavanon, J., & Saint-Yves, G., *Joachim Murat 1767-1815*, 1905.
Chevillet, J., *Ma vie militaire 1800-1810*, 1906.
Coignet, J.R., *Les Cahiers du Capitaine Coignet*, 1883.
Colbert, N.-J.A., *Traditions et souvenirs ou Mémoires touchant le temps et la vie du Général Auguste Colbert 1793-1809*, 1863-73.
Combe, M., *Mémoires du Colonel Combe sur les campagnes de Russie 1812, de Saxe 1813, de France 1814 et 1815*, 1853.
Curély, J.N., *Le Général Curély. Itinéraire d'un cavalier léger de la Grande Armée 1793-1815*, 1887.
Derrécagaix, V.B., *Les Etats-Majors de Napoléon. Le Lieutenant-Général comte Belliard, chef d'état-major de Murat*, 1908
Drujon de Beaulieu, –, *Souvenirs d'un militaire*, 1831.
Dunn Pattison, R.P., *Napoleon's Marshals*, 1909.
Dupont, M., *Le Général Lasalle*, 1929; *Murat*, 1934.
Dupuy, V., *Souvenirs militaires 1794-1816*, 1892.
Espinchal, H. d', *Souvenirs militaires 1792-1814*, 1901.

Espitalier, A., *Napoléon et le roi Murat 1808-1815*, 1910.

Fain, A.J.F., *Mémoires du Baron Fain*, 1908.

Fauvelet de Bourrienne, L.A., *Mémoire de M. de B..... sur Napoléon, le directoire, le consulat, l'Empire at la restauration*, 1829.

Hautpoul, M.C.F.H.A. d', *Souvenirs sur la Révolution, l'Empire et la Restauration*, 1904.

Henckens, J.L., *Lieutenant Henckens*, 1910.

Hourtoulle, F.G., *Le Général Comte Charles Lasalle*, chez l'auteur, 1970.

Junot, L., *Mémoires de Madame la Duchesse d'Abrantès*, 1831-35.

Koch, J.B.F., *Mémoires de Masséna, rédigés d'après les documents qu'il a laissé*, 1848.

Larrey, D.J., *Mémoires de chirurgie militaire et campagnes de D.J. Larrey*, 1812-17.

Ledru, A., *Montbrun, 1809*, 1913.

Le Harivel de Gonneville, A.O., *Recollections*, 1875.

Lejeune, L.F., *Mémoires du Général Lejeune*, 1895.

Lot, H.E., *Les Deux Généraux Ordener*, 1910.

Macdonald, E.J.J.A., *Souvenirs du Maréchal Macdonald*, 1892.

Macdonell, A.G., *Napoleon and his Marshals*, 1934.

Marbot, J.B.A.M. de, *Mémoires*, 1891.

Marullaz, F., *Le Baron J-F Marulaz*, 1918.

Massé, A., *Journal et correspondance d'un Garde d'Honneur*, 1912.

Mauduit, H. de, *Les derniers jours de la Grande Armée ou Souvenirs, documens et correspondance inédite de Napoléon en 1814 et 1815*, 1847-48.

Méneval, C.F. de, *Mémoires*, 1894.

Merme, J-M., *Histoire militaire de J-M. Merme*, 1852.

Mesmay, J.T. de, *Horace Sébastiani*, 1948.

Napoleon I, *Correspondance de Napoléon I*, 1858–69.

Oman, C.M.A., *Napoleon's Viceroy, Eugène de Beauharnais*, Hodder & Stoughton, 1966.

Pajol, C.P.V., *Pajol, Général-en-Chef*, 1874.

Parquin, D.C., *Souvenirs et campagnes*, 1843.

Pelet, J.J.G., *Mémoires sur la Guerre de 1809*, 1824.

Pelleport, P. de, *Souvenirs Militaires*, 1857.

Perret, E., *Le Maréchal Grouchy*, 1895.

Perrin, C-V., *Mémoires de Claude-Victor Perrin, duc de Bellune*, 1847.

Pineau, P., *Le Général Dugommier*, 1902.

Rabel, A., *Le Maréchal Bessières, Duc d'Istrie*, 1903.

Rapp, J., *Mémoires du Général Rapp*, 1823.

Richardot, J., *Nouveaux Mémoires*, 1848.

Rilliet, F.J.L., *Journal d'un sous-lieutenant de cuirassiers, 1813*, 1908; *Saint Germain, 1814*, 1908; *Souvenirs de 1815*, 1908.

Robinet de Clery, G.A., *D'Essling à Wagram. Lasalle.*, 1891.

Rocca, A.J.M. de, *Mémoires sur la Guerre des Français en Espagne*, 1814.

Roederer, P.-L., *Oeuvres du comte P.-L. Roederer*, 1853-59.

Saint Chamans, A.A.R. de, *Mémoires*, 1890.

Séruzier, Col., *Mémoires militaires du Baron Séruzier, Colonel d'Artillerie légère, 1769-1823. Mis en ordre et rédigés par son ami Le Mière de Corvey*, 1880.

Six, G., *Dictionnaire biographique des généraux et amiraux français de la Revolution et de l'Empire 1792-1814*, 1934.

Sprünglin, E.F., *Souvenirs d'Emmanuel Frédéric Sprünglin*, 1904.

Stouff, L., *Le Lieutenant-Général Delort 1792-1815*, 1906.

Tarlé, A. de, *Murat*, 1914.

Thiébault, D.A.P.F.C.H., *Mémoires*, 1893-95.

Thoumas, C.A., *Le Maréchal Lannes*, 1891.

Viesse de Marmont, A.F.L., *Mémoires du Duc de Raguse de 1792 à 1841*, 1857.

Villemarest, G.M.G. de, *Mémoires de Mademoiselle Avrillion, première femme de chambre de l'Impératrice*, 1833.

Vivien, J.S., *Souvenirs de ma vie militaire 1792-1822*, 1907.

Young, P., *Napoleon's Marshals*, Osprey, 1973.

Zurlinden, E.A.F.T., *Napoléon et ses Maréchaux*, 1910.

xi) *Miscellaneous*

Aldéguier, F. d', *Des principes qui servent de base à l'instruction et à la tactique de la cavalerie*, 1843.

Bismark, F.W. von, *Lectures upon the Tactics of Cavalry*, 1827.

Cadet de Gassicourt, C.L., *Voyage en Autriche en 1809*, 1818.

Cohen, L., *Napoleonic Anecdotes*, 1925.

Coindre, G., *Mon Vieux Besançon*, 1900-12.

Denison, G.T., *A History of Cavalry*, 1877.

Gaume, A., *Recherches sur l'équitation militaire, par un ancien soldat*, 1880.

Jacquinot de Presle, C., *Cours d'art et d'histoire militaires*, 1829.

La Roche-Aymon, A.C.E.P., *Des troupes légères*, 1817.

Marmier, X., *Lettres sur la Russie, la Finlande et la Pologne*, 1843.

Muller, A., *Théorie sur l'escrime à cheval, pour se défendre avec avantage contre toute espèce d'armes blanches*, 1816.

Mussot, P., *Commentaires historiques et élémentaires sur l'équitation de la cavalerie*, 1854.

Nollet-Fabert, J., *La Lorraine Militaire*, 1852-3.

Ordinaire, L., *Deux époques militaires à Besançon et en Franche-Comté, 1674-1814*, 1856.

Roemer, J., *Cavalry – its history, management and uses in war*, 1863.

Sol, E., *Le Vieux Quercy*, 1930.

Thiers, L.A., *Histoire du Consulat et de l'Empire*, 1845-62; *Vignettes et portraits*, 1845.

Thiry, J., *L'Aube du Consulat*, 1948; *Le Coup d'Etat du 18 Brumaire*, 1947.

Vandal, A., *Napoléon et Alexandre Ier*, 1891.
Vidal, P., *Histoire de la Révolution Française dans les Pyrénées Orientales*, 1889.

xii) *Periodicals*

Bulletin de la Société des études du Lot, tome 89 : Hommage à Jean-Baptiste Bessières, maréchal d'Empire, duc d'Istrie, 1768-1813, 1968.
Journal des Sciences Militaires. Le Combat Complet. XI. Rivoli et Marengo. XII. Austerlitz, September, 1898.
Le Moniteur.
Oesterreichische Militar Zeitschrift.
Revue de Cavalerie.

Appendix : Orders of Battle

A   *The cavalry of the Army of Italy at the beginning of General Bona-parte's First Italian Campaign, 1796*

Commander – General Stengel

1st Division (Beaumont)	Men
1st Hussars	600
10th Chasseurs	700
22nd Chasseurs	900
25th Chasseurs	350
5th Dragoons	240
20th Dragoons	300

2nd Division (Kilmaine)	
7th Hussars	400
13th Hussars	250
24th Chasseurs	400
8th Dragoons	368
15th Dragoons	360
Total	4868

B   *The French Cavalry at the Battle of Marengo, 14 June 1800*

1st Brigade (Kellermann)	Men
2nd Cavalry	120
20th Cavalry	300
21st Cavalry	100

2nd Brigade (Champeaux)	
1st Dragoons	450
8th Dragoons	328
9th Dragoons	428

174

3rd Brigade (?   )

6th Dragoons	345
12th Chasseurs	340
5th Cavalry	110

4th Brigade (Rivaud)

21st Chasseurs	359
12th Hussars	300

5th Brigade (Duvignaud)

3rd Cavalry	120
1st Hussars	120

Consular Guard (Bessières)

Mounted Grenadiers & Chasseurs	360

C   *The French Cavalry at the beginning of the Austerlitz Campaign, 1805*

	Men
Attached to 1st Corps	
2nd, 4th & 5th Hussars; 5th Chasseurs (Division Kellermann)	2808
Attached to 2nd Corps	
6th Hussars; 8th Chasseurs; Batavian Dragoons & Hussars	1775
Attached to 3rd Corps	
1st, 2nd & 12th Chasseurs; 7th Hussars	2000
Attached to 4th Corps	
8th Hussars; 11th, 16th & 26th Chasseurs	2119
Attached to 5th Corps	
9th & 10th Hussars; 13th & 21st Chasseurs	1984
Attached to 6th Corps	
1st & 3rd Hussars; 10th & 22nd Chasseurs	2080

Reserve Cavalry (Marshal Joachim Murat)

Division Nansouty:
(Brigades Piston, La Houssaye, St. Germain)

1st & 2nd Carabiniers; 2nd, 3rd, 9th & 12th Cuirassiers	2724

Division d'Hautpoul:
(Brigades St. Sulpice, Fauconnet)

1st, 5th, 10th & 11th Cuirassiers	1987

Division Klein:
(Brigades Fénérolle, Lasalle, Millet)

1st, 2nd, 4th, 14th, 20th & 26th Dragoons	2373

Division Walther:
(Brigades Sébastiani, Roget, Boussard)
3rd, 6th, 10th, 11th, 13th & 22nd Dragoons   2132

Division Beaumont:
(Brigades Boué, Sclalfort, Milhaud)
5th, 8th, 9th, 12th, 16th & 21st Dragoons   2021
(Brigades Laplanche, Sahuc, Verdière)
15th, 17th, 18th, 19th, 25th & 29th Dragoons   2176

Imperial Guard Cavalry (Marshal Bessières)
Mounted Grenadiers, Chasseurs, Mamelukes   1210

D   *The Division Lasalle on 1 July 1807*

		Squadrons	Men
	5th Hussars	3	427
Brigade Pajol	7th Hussars	3	478
	3rd Chasseurs	3	251
	11th Chasseurs	3	483
Brigade Wathier	Bavarian Light Horse	3	260
	Wurttemberg Light Horse	3	388
	1st Hussars	3	525
Brigade Bruyère	13th Chasseurs	3	383
	24th Chasseurs	3	428
	7th Chasseurs	3	436
Brigade Durosnel	20th Chasseurs	3	497
	22nd Chasseurs	3	314
			4870

E   *The Austrian Army at the beginning of the Battle of Aspern-Essling,
     21 May 1809*

   Infantry

	Men
Advance Guard	4029
I Corps	22916
II Corps	20866
IV Corps	20225

VI Corps	13327
Reserve Corps	8776

Total 90139 in 116 battalions

Cavalry			Squadrons
Attached to :-			
Advance Guard	{	Schwarzenberg Uhlans	8
		Stipsics Hussars	8
I Corps		Blankenstein Hussars	8
II Corps		Klenau Chevaulegers	8
IV Corps	{	Carneville Volunteers	1
		Vincent Chevaulegers	8
		Erzherzog Ferdinand Hussars	8
VI Corps	{	Lichtenstein Hussars	8
		Kienmayer Hussars	8

Attached to Reserve Corps :-

Hessen Homburg	Kroyher {	Lichtenstein Kurassiers	6
		Kaiser Kurassiers	6
	Lederer {	Hohenzollern Kurassiers	6
		Kronprinz Ferdinand Kurassiers	6
	Siegenthal {	Erzherzog Franz Kurassiers	6
		Erzherzog Albrecht Kurassiers	6
Kienmayer	Rottermund {	Riesch Dragoons	6
		Erzherzog Johann Dragoons	6
	Klary	Knesevich Dragoons	6
	Provenchères {	Rosenberg Chevaulegers	8
		O'Reilly Chevaulegers	5
	Kérétés {	Neutra Hussars	8
		Primatial Hussars	8

Total cavalry – 148 squadrons, or approximately 15,000 men

F   *The Reserve Cavalry on 1 July 1809*

Commander: Marshal Jean-Baptiste Bessières, Duke of Istria

1st Heavy Cavalry Division (Nansouty)		Squadrons	Men
Brigade Defrance	{ 1st Carabiniers (Laroche)	4	663
	2nd Carabiniers (Blancard)	4	701
Brigade Doumerc	{ 2nd Cuirassiers (Chouard)	4	708
	9th Cuirassiers (Paultre)	4	776
Brigade Berckheim	{ 3rd Cuirassiers (Richter)	4	602
	12th Cuirassiers (Dornez)	4	589
			4039

2nd Heavy Cavalry Division (St. Sulpice)			
Brigade Fitan	{ 1st Cuirassiers (Berkheim)	4	486
	5th Cuirassiers (Quinette)	4	428
Brigade ?	{ 10th Cuirassiers (L'Heritier)	4	592
	11th Cuirassiers (Duclos)	4	488
			1994

3rd Heavy Cavalry Division (Arrighi)			
Brigade Bordesoulle	{ 4th Cuirassiers (Prince Borghese)	4	404
	6th Cuirassiers (d'Haugeranville	4	421
Brigade Raymond	{ 7th Cuirassiers (Dubois)	4	503
	8th Cuirassiers (Grandjean)	4	593
			1921

1st Light Cavalry Division (Lasalle)			
Brigade Bruyère	{ 13th Chasseurs (Demangeot)	4	512
	24th Chasseurs (Ameil)	3	287
Brigade Piré	{ 8th Hussars (Delaborde)	4	610
	16th Chasseurs (Maupoint)	4	434
			1843

2nd Light Cavalry Division (Montbrun)			
Brigade Jacquinot	{ 7th Hussars (Liégard)	3	567
	1st Chasseurs (Méda)	4	325
	2nd Chasseurs (Mathis)	4	327

Brigade de Colbert	9th Hussars (Gauthérin)	3	576
	7th Chasseurs (?)	3	478
	20th Chasseurs (Castex)	3	462

2735

NOTE.   In the 1809 campaign the division of General Marulaz consisted of the following regiments: 3rd, 4th, 19th & 23rd Chasseurs, Hessian Light Horse, Baden Dragoons and Wurttemberg Dragoons. The last-named regiment left the division before the battle of Aspern-Essling, at which the Division Marulaz, though attached to Marshal Masséna, was effectively part of the Reserve Cavalry.

G   *Cavalry of the Imperial Guard 1 July 1809*

	Squadrons	Men
Polish Light Horse (Krazinski)	4	623
Chasseurs à Cheval (Thiry)	4	1024
Dragoons (Letort)	4	995
Grenadiers à Cheval (Walther)	4	994
Gendarmerie d'élite		309

3945

H   *The Cavalry of the Grande Armée at the beginning of the Russian Campaign, June 1812*

Bde – Brigade   Sqn – Squadron

Attached to 1st Corps d'Armée		Men
Bde. Pajol	2nd Chasseurs; 9th Polish lancers	1992
Bde. Bordesoulle	1st & 3rd Chasseurs	1885
Attached to 2nd Corps d'Armée		
Bde. Castex	7th, 23rd & 24th Chasseurs	1242
Bde. Corbineau	20th Chasseurs; 8th Chevaux-légers	751
Attached to 3rd Corps d'Armée		
Bde. Mouriez	28th Chasseurs; 6th Chevaux-légers	937
Bde. ?	11th Hussars; 4th Chasseurs;	
	Wurttemberg cavalry	3477
Attached to 4th Corps d'Armée		
Bde. Ferrière	9th & 19th Chasseurs	1372
Bde. Villata	2nd & 3rd Italian Chasseurs	1451

Bde. Lecchi	Italian Guard Dragoons & Gardes d'Honneur	1429

Attached to 5th Corps d'Armée

Bde. Niemoiewski	13th Hussars; 8th Polish Lancers	1626
Bde. ?	7th & 11th Polish Lancers	1849
Bde. Sulkowski	5th & 14th Chasseurs	1229

Attached to 6th Corps d'Armée

Bde. von Seydewitz	3rd & 6th Bavarian Light Horse	1063
Bde. von Preysing	4th & 5th Bavarian Light Horse	1016

Attached to 7th Corps d'Armée

Bde. von Funck	Saxon Light Horse and Hussars	2186

Attached to 8th Corps d'Armée

Bde. Wolff	Westphalian Gardes du Camp & Light Horse	753
Bde. von Hammerstein	1st & 2nd Westphalian Hussars	1205

Attached to 9th Corps d'Armée

	Lancers of Berg; Baden Hussars; Hessian Light Horse	1333

Attached to 10th Corps d'Armée

Bde. von Humerbein	1st & 2nd Prussian Dragoons; 1st & 2nd Prussian Hussars	2705

Additional cavalry

Austrian cavalry attached to Schwarzenberg's Corps	4000
Danish cavalry attached to the Danish division	1304

Imperial Guard Cavalry (Marshal Bessières)

Grenadiers à Cheval; Chasseurs à Cheval; Guard Dragoons Guard Lancers	5861

Reserve Cavalry (Marshal Joachim Murat, King of Naples)

1st Cavalry Corps (Nansouty)

1st Light Cavalry Division (Bruyère) –

Bde. Jacquinot	7th Hussars	1147
Bde. Roussel d'Harbal	9th Chevaux-légers	769
Bde. Piré	8th Hussars; 16th Chasseurs	2109
Bde. Niewiewski	10th Hussars; 6th Polish lancers; 1st Prussian uhlans	2035

1st Cuirassier Division (St. Germain) –

Bde. Bessières	2nd Cuirassiers	1015
Bde. Bruno	3rd Cuirassiers	1099
Bde. Queunot	9th Cuirassiers; 1 sqn. 1st Chevaux- légers	1124

5th Cuirassier Division (Valence) –

Bde. Reynaud	6th Cuirassiers	950
Bde. Dejean	11th Cuirassiers	730
Bde. De La Grange	12th Cuirassiers; 1 sqn. 5th Chevaux-légers	1214

2nd Cavalry Corps (Montbrun)

2nd Light Cavalry Division (Sébastiani) –

Bde. St. Geniez	11th & 12th Chasseurs	1314
Bde. Burthe	5th & 9th Hussars	1676
Bde. Ornano	1st Polish Chasseurs; 3rd Wurttemberg Chasseurs; 3rd Prussian Hussars	2246

2nd Cuirassier Division (Wathier) –

Bde. Beaumont	5th Cuirassiers	788
Bde. Richter	8th Cuirassiers	754
Bde. Dornez	10th Cuirassiers; 1 sqn. 2nd Chevaux-légers	821

4th Cuirassier Division (Defrance) –

Bde. Chouard	1st Carabiniers	856
Bde. Paultre	2nd Carabiniers	871
Bde. Bouvier des Eclats	1st Cuirassiers; 1 sqn. 4th Chevaux-légers	855

3rd Cavalry Corps (Grouchy)

3rd Light Cavalry Division (Chastel) –		Men
Bde. Gérard	6th & 25th Chasseurs	1253
Bde. Gauthrin	6th Hussars; 8th Chasseurs	1222
Bde. Dommanget	1st & 2nd Bavarian Light Horse	1042

3rd Cuirassier Division (Doumerc) –

Bde. Berckheim	4th Cuirassiers	980
Bde. L'Heritier	7th Cuirassiers	973
Bde. Doullembourg	14th Cuirassiers; 1 sqn. 3rd Chevaux-légers	970

6th Dragoon Division (de la Houssaye) –

Bde. Thiry	7th & 23rd Dragoons	1177
Bde. Seron	28th & 30th Dragoons	1213

4th Cavalry Corps (Latour-Maubourg)

Division Rozniecki –

Bde. Dziemanowski	2nd, 3rd & 4th Polish Lancers	2836
Bde. Turno	12th, 15th & 16th Polish Lancers	2671

Division Lorge –
Bde. Thielman	Saxon Gardes & Kurassiers	1344
Bde. von Lepell	1st & 2nd Westphalian Kurassiers	1272

NOTE. Due to the exceptionally high regimental strengths in 1812, as this table shows, a number of French cavalry brigades were formed from only one regiment, instead of the usual two.

I   *1815*

The Guard Cavalry at Waterloo

	Officers	Men	
Light cavalry (Lefebvre-Desnouettes):			
Lancers	47	833 ⎫	
Chasseurs à Cheval	59	1138 ⎭	14 squadrons
Heavy cavalry (Guyot):			
Grenadiers à Cheval	44	752 ⎫	
Guard Dragoons	51	765 ⎬	13 squadrons
Gendarmes d'élite	4	102 ⎭	

J   *The French Heavy Cavalry at the beginning of the Waterloo Campaign*

RESERVE OF CAVALRY OF THE ARMY OF THE NORTH 4TH CAVALRY CORPS (at 9th June 1815) Lieutenant-General Count Milhaud, officer commanding; Adjutant-Commandant Baron Chasseriau, chief of staff

DIVISIONS	LIEUTENANT GENERALS commanding the divisions and chiefs of staff	Number of Brigades	BRIGADE COMMANDERS	UNITS	UNIT COMMANDERS	Number of Squadrons	PRESENT UNDER ARMS CAVALRY Officers	Men	ARTILLERY Officers	Men	TRAIN Officers	Men
13th division of cavalry	Wathier Saint-Alphonse, lieutenant-general commanding ......, adjutant-commandant, chief of staff	1st	Dubois	1st Cuirassiers	Count Ordener, colonel	4	41	411				
				4th idem	Habert, idem	3	28	278				
		2nd	Baron Travers	7th idem	Richardot, idem	2	21	151				
				12th idem	Thurot, idem	2	22	226				
				1st horse artillery, 5th company					3	75		
				1st train squadron, 8th company							2	79
					Totals	11	112	1066	3	75	2	79
14th idem	Baron Delort, lieutenant-general commanding Legay d'Arcy, adjutant-commandant, chief of staff	1st	Baron Farine	5th Cuirassiers	Gobert, colonel	3	34	380				
				10th idem	Lahuberdière, idem	3	26	309				
		2nd	Baron Vial	6th idem	Martin, idem	4	37	474				
				9th idem	Bigarné, idem	3	32	327				
				3rd horse artillery, 4th company					3	70		
				1st train squadron,							2	89
					Totals	13	129	1490	3	70	2	89
			SUMMARY	13th division of cavalry		11	112	1066	3	75	2	79
				14th idem idem		13	129	1490	3	70	2	89
					Total	24	241	2556	6	145	4	168

Total of 4th Cavalry Corps 3,120

J *The French Heavy Cavalry at the beginning of the Waterloo Campaign*

RESERVE OF CAVALRY OF THE ARMY OF THE NORTH 3RD CAVALRY CORPS (at 1st June 1815)

Lieutenant-General the Count of Valmy, officer commanding; Adjutant-Commandant Tancarville, chief of staff

DIVISIONS	LIEUTENANT GENERALS commanding the divisions and chiefs of staff	Number of Brigades	BRIGADE COMMANDERS	UNITS	UNIT COMMANDERS		Number of Squadrons	PRESENT UNDER ARMS CAVALRY Officers	CAVALRY Men	ARTILLERY Officers	ARTILLERY Men	TRAIN Officers	TRAIN Men
11th division of cavalry	Baron L'Héritier, lieutenant-general commanding; Charles Soubeiran adjutant-commandant, chief of staff	1st	Baron Picquet	2nd Dragoons	Planzeaux,	colonel	4	40	543				
				7th idem	Léopold,	idem	4	41	475				
		2nd	Guiton	8th Cuirassiers	Garavaque,	idem	3	31	421				
				11th idem	Courtier,	idem	2	21	301				
				2nd horse artillery, 3rd company						3	75		
				2nd train squadron, 3rd company								2	81
						Totals	13	133	1743	3	75	2	81
12th idem	Roussell d'Hurbal, lieutenant-general commanding; ...., adjutant-commandant, chief of staff	1st	Baron Blancard	1st Carabiniers	Rogé,	colonel	3	30	403				
				2nd idem	Beugnat,	idem	3	29	380				
		2nd	Baron Donop	2nd Cuirassiers	Grandjean,	idem	2	21	292				
				3rd idem	Lacroix,	idem	4	37	427				
				2nd horse artillery, 2nd company	Lebeau,	captain				3	75		
				2nd train squadron, 4th company	Mauzat,	lieutenant						2	78
						Totals	12	117	1502	3	75	2	78
			SUMMARY	11th division of cavalry			13	133	1743	3	75	2	81
				12th idem idem			12	117	1502	3	75	2	78
						Total	25	250	3245	6	150	4	159

Total of 3rd Cavalry Corps 3,814

Index